The Emperor and the Irishman

The Emperor
and
the Irishman

Napoleon and
Dr Barry O'Meara
on St Helena

by
Dr Hubert O'Connor

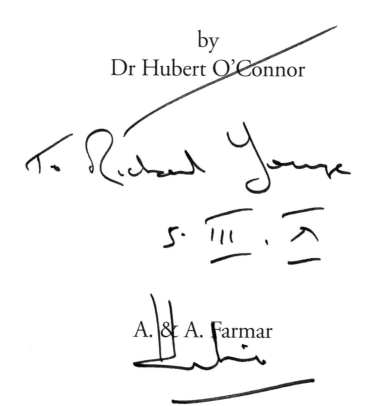

A. & A. Farmar

British Library Cataloguing in Publication Data
A CIP catalogue record for this book is available from the British Library

ISBN-13: 978-1-906353-04-9

First published in 2008
Reprinted with additional pictures 2009
by
A. & A. Farmar Ltd
78 Ranelagh Village, Dublin 6, Ireland
Tel +353-1-496 3625 Fax +353-1-497 0107
Email afarmar@iol.ie

Printed and bound by GraphyCems
Typeset and designed by A. & A. Farmar
Cover designed by Kevin Gurry

Contents

FOR ANNE

PARIS   DUBLIN
6 JUNE 1946   —   13 MAY 2000

NEC FERAT ULLA DIES UT COMMUTEMUR IN AEVO

QUIN TIBI SIM JUVENIS TOQUE PUELLA MIHI

LET NO PASSAGE OF TIME CHANGE OUR AGE AT ALL

I WILL REMAIN YOUR YOUNG LOVER—

YOU MY YOUNG BRIDE

Decimus Magnus Ausonius
AD 310–395
Burdigala (Bordeaux)

Acknowledgements

It is quite impossible to thank all my friends who have encouraged me to write this book. I have given many lectures about Napoleon and Dr O'Meara in many quarters of the globe—including Sydney, London and, most recently, at the University of Lund (Sweden). After every lecture I was urged to write the history of Dr O'Meara. Hence this book.

I must thank my publishers, Tony and Anna Farmar, who were kind, understanding and so tolerant of my written English. (Doctors can't spell—our formal education stops at the age of seventeen, after that it's a whole new language we must learn, hence our bad writing is just a cover-up for bad spelling!)

Tony and Anna have had the unenviable task of reducing the original work of 738 pages down to a readable 280 pages. Thanks to my most tolerant secretaries Liz Reythorn and Maria Freeman, who typed and re-typed many pages without a murmur of complaint. A big thank you to Bruce Bradley SJ and Bob Huddie, who encouraged me back to writing when I had all but given up what I felt was an impossible task. Thanks to John Geary who produced the splendid photographs of Newtown House.

To all these people and many more I am indebted: thank you all.

Hubert O'Connor
September 2008

Introduction

Many years ago, after an enjoyable dinner, an old friend of mine, like myself a doctor, took a tattered, leather-bound volume from my shelves and began to read. The book, a two-volume work I had picked up in a dusty corner of Greene's famous bookshop in Clare Street, on the corner of Merrion Square, was called *Napoleon at St Helena*. My friend was fascinated, and so, intrigued in my turn, I took the book to bed that night and ended up reading till dawn. From that time on, I have pursued the remarkable story of Napoleon's Irish doctor, Barry O'Meara.

The life of a ship's surgeon in the middle of a war can hardly be called hum-drum; but by 1815 the war with Napoleon was definitely over, and like many other British navy officers O'Meara must have been wondering what the future had in store. Then, out of the blue, the chance came up of accompanying the greatest man of the age, the Emperor Napoleon, to the place of his incarceration and to act there as his private surgeon. It was an adventure too good to turn down.

For the next two and a half years O'Meara lived in Napoleon's house on St Helena, visited him virtually daily, sometimes spending long hours in conversation. O'Meara carefully recorded Napoleon's opinions on his generals, his opponents, his women, the Tsars and Emperors he knew, the politics of the Revolution and Napoleon's own political and social ideas. What O'Meara wrote down after those conversations forms one of the liveliest 'table-talk' volumes of western history.

However, the situation he had somewhat impulsively accepted bristled with difficulties. Napoleon very much wanted to get off the island, and saw the semi-official bulletins O'Meara issued on his health and the conditions of his captivity as a way of affecting British public opinion. At the same time, the British were concerned about the possibility of escape (he had, after all, escaped before, from Elba), and these fears were stimulated by wild talk of plots by US-based Bonapartists. The fact that the man whom the British had chosen to be Governor of the island and to supervise Napoleon's captivity, Hudson Lowe, was fidgety, irascible, nervous and out of his depth, did not help.

In between Napoleon and the Governor was O'Meara. He was both a medical man and a navy officer; he therefore owed loyalty to his service and discretion to his patient. Both his patient and the Governor, his military superior, demanded fealty. It was a situation that his upbringing, as an Irish Protestant, intimate with but not entirely trusted by either the colonial British or the native Irish, had prepared him for.

In England, O'Meara's reputation has suffered then and since from the ambiguities of the situation. Where the French saw the Governor as 'perfidious Albion' at work, the English saw a hard-pressed imperial servant maligned by a devious Irishman. This latter point of view was most powerfully put by Walter Forsyth, a barrister, in his 1853 book, which forensically examined every detail then published, pouncing solemnly on every discrepancy. At the same time, from the humourless height of Victorian rectitude, Forsyth took O'Meara's lighthearted Regency robustness as a sign of depravity.

Since then we have learned a great deal more about what happened on St Helena in those fateful six years. More memoirs have been published, including major contributions from such participants in the daily drama as Count Bertrand, Baron Gourgaud, Louis Marchand and Major Gorrequer. And more and more it seems, given the awkward circumstances, Barry O'Meara did an honourable job. Even those prejudiced against O'Meara personally admit that his account is by far the liveliest of the St Helena narratives, and admit furthermore its essential truth. As Aubrey Octave put it: 'As an observer [O'Meara] knew how to use his eyes and to tell what he saw. It is easy to understand the great success of his book when it appeared. Not so comprehensible is the discredit into which it has since been allowed to fall.'

This book, on which I have finally embarked thirty years after that initial dinner, is an attempt to vindicate the reputation of O'Meara, a man from my own country (Ireland), my own city (Dublin), my own university (Trinity) and my own profession (medicine).

This is essentially Barry O'Meara's story. But it also describes Napoleon's final sad years on a distant island. In the course of my research, I have tried to read everything written by or about Barry O'Meara. But regrettable gaps remain in the documentary record and, in places, while striving for the greatest possible accuracy, I have had to bridge the gaps by means of speculative reconstruction. The early 20th-century painter Albert Marquet was famous for his ability to depict atmosphere. In the same spirit, I have tried to paint a personal picture of the Emperor and the Irishman—the great Napoleon himself on St Helena and the Irish doctor who accompanied him there.

Note on sources

The pathos of the great Emperor's last days on St Helena has attracted many writers, critical, romantic and prosaic. In fact the bibliography exclusively relating to the events on St Helena published by the Fondation Napoleon runs to 47 well-filled pages.

The core texts I have used are:

Lucia Elizabeth Abell (*née* Betsy Balcombe) *Recollections of the Emperor Napoleon, during the first three years of his captivity on St Helena: including the time of his residence at her father's house 'The Briars'* (London 1844)

Barry O'Meara *An exposition of some of the transactions that have taken place at St Helena etc.* 2nd ed (London 1819)

Barry O'Meara *Napoleon at St Helena* (London 1888) originally published as *Voice from St Helena* (London 1822).

As well as the published diaries of the various participants, other significant texts include:

Octave Aubrey *St Helena* (Philadelphia 1936)

Arnold Chaplin *A St Helena Who's Who* (London 1909)

George Home *Memoirs of an Aristocrat and Reminiscences of the Emperor Napoleon* (London 1837)

E. T. Lean *The Napoleonists* (London 1970)

Herbert Maxwell (ed.) *The Creevey Papers* (London 1903)

Philip Henry Stanhope *Conversations with the Duke of Wellington* (London 1888).

Of all that has been written about Napoleon, I must mention two works which made a special impression on me and which I found especially helpful in writing my own book: Vincent Cronin's *Napoleon* (London, 1970), and Paul Fregosi's *Dreams of Empire* (London, 1989), the most interesting, factually informative and amusing accounts of the Napoleonic era written to date. I can warmly recommend them both.

Chapter 1: The Irish doctor

For over twenty years, since he first emerged in 1793 as a young artillery officer at a siege in Toulon, Napoleon Bonaparte had been the wonder and the despair of the world. His extraordinary energy had shaken the old countries of Europe to the roots—first France, then Italy, Germany, Spain, Portugal, not to mention Egypt, Russia and Syria—none would be the same after his passing through. By 1814, however, his enemies had been too much for him and he was incarcerated in the Mediterranean island of St Elba, not far from his Corsican birthplace. The diplomats of Europe packed their bags and prepared for a long and enjoyable session of haggling and self-indulgence at the Congress of Vienna. But they had not heard the last of Napoleon.

Aided by devoted adherents, he escaped from Elba in early 1815 and drove north to Paris, gathering more and more enthusiastic supporters as he went. This mesmeric power over the ordinary French people was his strength, not least because it was by far the most populous country in Europe—24 million people against Britain's 10 million and Ireland's 5 million (Germany and Italy were still divided into small states).

Europe quickly declared war against him, and eventually fought him to a stop at Waterloo. What Wellington famously called the 'near-run thing' cost 40,000 French, and perhaps 22,000 Allied soldiers' deaths. Napoleon was soon forced to abdicate a second time.

This time the Allies were taking no chances. The most dangerous man in Europe had vividly shown his power during the hundred days since his escape from Elba, and they, particularly the British, were going to make sure that would not happen again. They identified one of the most remote islands in the world, a tiny victualling post in the middle of the southern Atlantic used by ships travelling to and from India. That was to be Napoleon's new place of exile. Furthermore, the island was going to be policed by as many ships and soldiers as might be necessary to ensure that any escape plans, such as those mooted by Bonapartist refugees in America, should come to nothing.

On board the Bellerophon, *the ship used to transport Napoleon and his entourage away from France, was a young Irish surgeon, Barry O'Meara, who was about to embark on the adventure of a lifetime. We join O'Meara on the first leg of the long voyage from Europe to Napoleon's prison-island, thousands of miles away.*

Late in the afternoon the doctor came on deck for fresh air. The heavy Atlantic swell had made most of the new passengers quite seasick. He had spent many hours in the stifling heat below, tending to those who were ill. It was now a beautifully blue, cloudless evening and there was a moderate fresh breeze. With the measured step of an experienced seaman, he made his way up to the poop deck, where he joined a small group of his fellow officers.

The conversation turned inevitably to the dramatic events of the previous days. Suddenly all those facing the stern stood to attention and removed their caps. The doctor turned and saw the Emperor coming towards them. He was accompanied by marshals and generals but, even though they surrounded him on all sides, there was still the sense of a respectful distance being observed. As one of them recalled later, although obviously a prisoner, 'Napoleon was in fact still an Emperor aboard the *Bellerophon*. The captain, officers and crew soon adopted the etiquette of his suite, showing him exactly the same attention. The captain addressed him either as "Sire" or "Your Majesty".'

After he had climbed up to the deck and nodded to the young officers to be at ease, Napoleon leaned against the rail and for a time gazed down at the clear water and then to the horizon. Eventually, turning back to the group, he noticed the doctor for the first time.

'Are you the *chirurgien major*?' he asked, addressing him in French. In Italian O'Meara confirmed that he was. In Italian also, Napoleon continued: 'What is your native country?' 'Ireland.' 'Where did you study your profession?' 'I studied in Dublin and later in London.' 'And tell me, Doctor, which is the best school of medicine?' 'For anatomy Dublin is best. London is best for medicine.' 'Ah, you only say that because you are Irish!' 'No, no, Sire—bodies are much cheaper to buy in Dublin, so our anatomy and hence our surgery is much better.'

Napoleon smiled at this reply and then changed the subject. 'Where have you seen battle?' the Emperor asked quietly. 'I have fought, Sire, in Sicily, Egypt and. more recently, in the West Indies.' O'Meara told him briefly of some of the more memorable battles in which he had been involved and then, in somewhat greater detail, of the capture of the 74-gun French flagship, the *Rivoli*. 'You appear to have been remarkably fortunate in your sea battles.' 'Yes.' 'The *Rivoli* was a great loss.'

Napoleon wanted to know more about Egypt and the doctor told him of the rescue of a garrison under siege in Alexandria 1807. To his surprise he discovered that Napoleon had watered and fed his horses in the very same stable where he himself had bivouacked at Aboukir.

Napoleon laughed loudly at this, and afterwards 'recognised' O'Meara when he noticed him, and occasionally called on him to interpret or explain English terms. Since one of Napoleon's entourage was ill, O'Meara was frequently in attendance, and Napoleon regularly asked about the patient, and about the malady and the mode of cure.

From these conversations arose a trust between the two men, and eventually an offer that was to set the thirty-two-year-old doctor on a life-changing course.

Newtown House today (John Geary)

The interior of Newtown House today, looking much as it would have in Barry O'Meara's time (John Geary)

Barry O'Meara

Barry Edward O'Meara, third child of Jeremiah and Catherine O'Meara, was born in 1783 in the elegant southern suburb of Dublin, then called Newtown on Strand and now known as Blackrock. He had two elder brothers, Healy and Charles. Some ten years later a sister, Charlotte, was born.

The O'Mearas were comfortably off. Like so many middle-class Protestant Irish, Jeremiah had held a commission in the British army. He had seen service in North America. Later, for 'seizing with his own hands two of the leaders of an armed mob in the North of Ireland, who afterwards suffered the fate they merited' he was granted a pension. Then he met and married a beautiful young woman called Catherine Harpur, whose family, recalled O'Meara, owned 'much land in the counties of Queen's County and King's County'. She herself had a substantial income and as the family grew they could afford a large domestic staff. In addition, she employed her own unmarried sister Heather to act as governess to the children. They got on well with their equally comfortable neighbours in Newtown and could count the young Lord Edward Fitzgerald, cousin of Charles James Fox, who later became Britain's Foreign Secretary, among their many friends.

By 1798, however, when Barry was fifteen, the world was a dangerous place. The British struggle against Napoleon's French army had been long and not very successful; a detachment of French had attempted an invasion of Ireland in 1796, and again three times in 1798; the 1798 Rising caused thousands of Protestants from the south-east to flee to Wales before it was brutally crushed.

In Dublin the medical schools were working hard to fill the great demand for doctors for the army and the navy across the globe. But neither the army nor the navy could afford to maintain the age-old restrictive distinctions between the learned, hands-off physician and the rough and ready surgeon. The services needed men who could combine both surgery and medicine and that is what the Dublin schools provided.

One of those taking advantage of the new curriculum was Barry O'Meara, who began his training at the age of sixteen, attending lectures at the newly-established Royal College of Surgeons and at Trinity. With his easy-going disposition and agreeable personality, he made many friends. He was formally apprenticed (as solicitors and accountants still are) to one of the most successful medical men of the day, the city surgeon William Leake, a founder-member of the Royal College of Surgeons. O'Meara had great respect for Leake, speaking of him as a 'wonderful gentleman, who was able and willing to pass on all his expertise'.

Having qualified in 1804, O'Meara immediately enlisted in the 62nd Regiment of Foot in the capacity of assistant surgeon. In his dark navy-blue uniform, with its red edgings, the young man cut a fine figure in Dublin society. He was elected a member of the fashionable United Services Club. The future looked bright. In early January 1805 the 62nd were ordered to Portsmouth. There was trouble in the West Indies but unfortunately, the flotilla sailed straight into a gale, which soon became a hurricane. The ships turned and, one by one, made their way back to Portsmouth. The regiment were put on half-pay and told to await further orders. When none came, Barry O'Meara asked for permission to continue his medical education and attended various teaching hospitals in London, including St Bartholomew's and Guy's.

Occasionally he was able to return to Dublin and it was during one of these visits that he met an attractive young girl, whose name and subsequent history have disappeared from the records. She became pregnant and it is quite possible that she died during childbirth—an all too common tragedy at that time. The baby boy, whom Barry's relatives named Dennis, survived and was brought up in Newtown by his sister Charlotte, with the assistance of the large domestic staff.

Meanwhile, the 62nd Regiment of Foot was ordered to the Mediterranean.

O'Meara's war

On land Napoleon was uniquely formidable. The Duke of Wellington famously compared his presence on the battlefield as equivalent to 40,000 reserves. His speed, technical mastery and aggression made him the supreme general of his day. By 1805 he had subdued, more or less, the continent and now turned his attention to his last and most formidable enemy—Britain. But a victory by the British navy at the Battle of Trafalgar prevented him from carrying out his long-developed plan to invade. For as long as O'Meara had been a student, the threat of invasion had loomed over Britain and Ireland (Ireland was expected to serve as a soft side-entry to Britain). Martello towers were erected along the exposed British and Irish coasts, and the fervid state of alertness sometimes reached fever pitch. In January 1804, for instance, the *Freeman's Journal* reported that 'an attempt without delay is now hourly expected'; the message was repeated on 17 January, 9 February and 14 February. The Rising of 1798 and the two previous invasion attempts showed that this was no empty threat. There is no doubt that the wave of relief that led to the erecting of Nelson's pillars in Dublin and London was absolutely genuine.

By 1806, Britain had the most powerful navy in the world and was keen to consolidate control of the Mediterranean. However, there were problems everywhere in the region, especially in Egypt and southern Italy. It was for Italy that Barry O'Meara and the 62nd Regiment of Foot were bound.

Returning, perhaps with relief, to land warfare, Napoleon embarked on the re-annexation of Italy. He ordered his troops south to achieve this. Naples having fallen, he prepared to invade southern Italy itself, judging that he should then be able to take Sicily with ease. The prize this would deliver was greater still. As he said, 'he who controls the straits of Messina controls the Mediterranean'.

As the French inched down the peninsula, Major-General Sir John Stuart scored an unexpected victory over the invading French force at Maida in Calabria—a welcome boost to British morale at the time. But his failure to follow up allowed the French to regroup and gradually, over the following year, to conquer the whole of Calabria. His indecision and delay would cost the lives of many of his soldiers. Malaria was rife, and most of the men who became infected subsequently died.

Only the small town of Scylla, with its spectacular castle perched high on a rock overlooking the Straits of Messina, just two miles from Sicily and the British army, resisted the French advance. Having laid siege, the French took Scylla at the end of December 1806 and then began to bombard the castle. Within were over 300 British soldiers and 500 local Calabrians, under the command of Colonel Robertson, of the 35th Regiment of Foot, who was determined to hold out to the last man. The commander of the British forces at Messina, Major-General Sherbrook, reported to the War Office that Scylla would be held, until further resistance became 'an act of imprudence'.

The critical moment soon arrived. Major Robertson sent urgent pleas for food, reinforcements, ammunition and, most of all, medical help. It was in response to the situation in Scylla that Barry O'Meara and the 62nd Regiment had arrived in Messina some weeks before, in early December. They encamped around the outskirts of the town and awaited orders to invade Calabria. But they were very quickly diverted to Egypt.

The situation there had been giving rise to concern in London. There was tribal warfare all over the country and the most powerful tribe was led by Mohammed Ali (actually Albanian by birth), who was hostile to British interests. There was also the danger of another French invasion. An expeditionary force under General Alexander McKenzie Fraser set sail from Messina on 6 March 1807. Fraser's orders were to capture the city of Alexandria, establish British control and show the flag. Preparations had taken a month and the flotilla which sailed comprised 33 ships, with 242 officers, 5,672 soldiers (and 500 horses), and almost 700 women and children on board. The intention was clearly to remain in Egypt for some time.

But, from the start, misfortune dogged the expedition. Fraser was facing a particularly ruthless and powerful enemy in the person of Ali and he was not helped by the fact that his orders were ambiguous. To make matters worse, on the night following the expedition's departure from Messina, a gale blew up which separated 19 of the ships from the rest. Fraser was eventually able to reach Alexandria, with 2,200 men, on the morning of 16 March. He landed his men with considerable difficulty through the pounding surf but was subsequently able to surround and capture the city with ease. It seemed that his mission had been accomplished—all he had to do now was to reinforce his position, 'show the flag' and stay put. But some time later the British Consul in Cairo, Major Missett, advised him that there was widespread starvation in Alexandria. The good news was, however, that in the small town of Rosetta, 40 miles to the east, there was 'abundant food' to be had. Moreover, Rosetta's defences were minimal and the Albanian soldiers there 'just a mere rabble of savages'. Rosetta had not featured in his orders. Fraser was in a quandary. However, as he wrote many years later, 'it was difficult not to yield to Missett's representations so, reluctantly, I gave way'.

Unfortunately, he sent too small a force—just 1,600 men and two canons, under the unfortunate Colonel Meade—to capture Rosetta. Meade reached a small hill overlooking the town on 31 March. The town appeared perfectly still. The gates were opened and, with no precautions, the troops were led through the narrow streets to the centre of Rosetta. Accounts vary on what happened next. Some say that there was no initial opposition of any kind and that British soldiers were actually having lunch in a coffee house when the retreat was suddenly sounded. Shooting began from every window and rooftop. Not withstanding this, the troops managed to retire in good order back to the hills outside the city, carrying their wounded as they went. But the Albanians followed in savage pursuit. They cut off stragglers and any wounded men who were captured were first mutilated and then decapitated. Captured soldiers who could walk were forced to carry the severed head of one of their comrades as a present for the Pasha. Of the 1,600 who had set out, only 460 returned to Alexandria.

Fraser decided that, for the sake of his reputation and wounded British pride, he must make another attempt to take Rosetta. This time he sent 2,500 men and 11 guns. On arrival after three days, the expedition encamped outside the walls, deciding to wait 24 hours before attacking. The next morning they found themselves surrounded by thousands of Mamelukes. There was no choice but to abandon the siege and fight their way back again to Alexandria. Fraser's situation was now desperate. Alexandria was under siege. Food was short. Of the 5000 men with whom he had set out, more than half were killed, wounded, stricken by sickness or in captivity. Those who had survived were dispirited, having had to witness the mutilation and decapitation of their comrades and aware that 400 troops were still being held by the enemy. And he had 380 women in his care. The thought of surrender was too awful to contemplate. He could not abandon Alexandria without making some effort to take back those who had been captured. He decided to attempt negotiation with Mohammed Ali. An officer and two privates marched out of the city with a white flag. But as soon as they reached enemy lines they were shot. Fraser tried again. Again the three soldiers were killed. At this stage he guessed that the Muslim army did not understand the significance of the white flag. This time two Muslims were sent from the city and negotiations were finally able to begin. Mohammed asked quite simply why Fraser was in Egypt and what he wanted.

While the negotiations were taking place, the *Cambridge*, bearing the 62nd Regiment of Foot, arrived at Aboukir harbour. They remained some days and Barry O'Meara bivouacked in horse stables while he treated the many wounded. Two days later they set off for Alexandria, on their way passing the severed heads of fellow-soldiers, impaled on stakes and rotting in the sun. Upsetting as the sight was, it instilled not fear but 'a resolution to fight and win.'

Once the 62nd had reached Alexandria, Fraser's negotiating hand was greatly strengthened. He informed Ali that he would abandon Egypt if all the British prisoners were returned. One of the officers who had been held was released and was able to inform Fraser that his fellow prisoners—as many as 500 in all—had been well treated and that this was owing to the intervention of the French Consul, Monsieur Dournatan. (Fraser later sent heartfelt thanks to the Frenchman for saving so many of his men.) Mohammed Ali agreed to the proposal. All the soldiers who had been captured—even those who had by then been sold into slavery—were returned to Alexandria. Women, children and the wounded boarded the first available vessel. Fraser's now much-reduced expeditionary force was accommodated on a second ship. Last to board, having stayed to the end to ensure that Ali kept his word, were the 62nd Regiment of Foot. Subsequently, Lord Windham's replacement as Secretary for War by Lord Castlereagh led to a change in the policy towards Egypt. The reasoning had been that, to secure Egypt,

Sicily would have to be ignored. But Sicily was England's fortress in the Mediterranean and there could be no question of such an alternative. Egypt must be sacrificed.

The return of the expedition to Messina was met with much rejoicing. But the news from Scylla (sent by semaphore) was not encouraging: Lieutenant Colonel Robertson's situation in the castle was evidently desperate. The senior medical officer in Messina, Dr Greene, sent for his Irish colleague. He had received impressive reports of Dr O'Meara's fortitude under very trying circumstances in Egypt. Would he be willing to help the beleaguered regiment in Scylla? O'Meara immediately promised to row across that night. The Straits of Messina are only two miles wide but the deep whirlpools and strong currents make the journey very dangerous and it was almost daybreak when he arrived at the base of the sheer cliff on which Scylla Castle stands. With great difficulty he managed to gain the summit of the cliff, carrying with him food and a large quantity of medical supplies. In the castle, there were many severely wounded men, some of whom were dying from loss of blood. He did what he could, despite the hopelessness of the situation.

Meanwhile, the French 'bombarded the castle night and day, until it was no more than a pile of rubble'. Robertson decided to abandon Scylla and retreat to Messina. First to go were the wounded. 'At midday the painful journey began', O'Meara recorded. 'Forty-nine stretchers were brought down the narrow stairwell, while French riflemen fired at us from the beach.' With some pride he added: 'All 49 severely wounded men were eventually returned to Messina without loss of life.' (When I visited Messina and Scylla in 1980 the castle was undergoing extensive repairs, and even a fault line in the rock on which it was built was being sealed. What remained, however, was an almost perpendicular line from the sea to the top of the parapet of nearly 200 feet. How Barry O'Meara managed to evacuate his wounded I will never understand.)

A violent thunderstorm delayed the evacuation of the rest but, on 17 February 1807, Captain Troy on the *Electra* was able to put small boats right up against the cliff-face and, within 24 hours, the fortress was abandoned. On returning to Messina, every officer was congratulated personally by Major-General Stuart. Each was awarded an extra bar of soap and advised to keep his hair shorter! But France was now in command of the whole of Italy.

During the long hot Sicilian summer that followed, it was inevitable that arguments and even fighting would break out here and there among some of the troops. Quarrels between soldiers and some of the locals (all of whom carried knives) were regarded as understandable. But fighting among officers could not be tolerated. Major-General Stuart was determined to get rid of duelling, then quite prevalent in Italy. It was at this time that a friend of Barry O'Meara's, Captain Crookshank, became embroiled in a troublesome argument with a fellow officer, a Captain Robertson. Crookshank asked O'Meara to act as his second. O'Meara wrote later: 'I felt myself bound not to withhold my support in a situation of peculiar delicacy. Although the affair was terminated without any injury to either party—a result to which I had the consolation of reflecting I greatly contributed, Stuart insisted that the challenger and his second should be arrested.' Accordingly, in November he was brought to a court-martial at Messina and cashiered from the army.

What to do now? Lack of funds ruled out his return to Ireland, where there was little hope of employment. The court-martial's decision was wounding but it had not destroyed his enthusiasm for service to the forces. He had been in the army for only two-and-a-half years when his career ended but, as he wrote in his memoirs, he knew that 'he got on well with his troops and was popular among his brother officers'. Resourcefully, he decided to try his luck with the navy. Carrying with him letters of introduction from Dr Greene, the most senior officer at Messina, he sailed for Malta.

Although attempts were made much later to smear O'Meara in respect of the reasons he left the army, at the time it was clearly recognised as being hardly more than a technical offence. Furthermore, the service clearly needed skilled medical men. He went to Malta, where, introduced by his old friend Dr Greene he had the good fortune to meet Sir Alexander Ball. O'Meara was appointed assistant surgeon in the Royal Navy. However, before he could become full surgeon to a ship, he would have to do a two-year apprenticeship as an assistant. In August 1809 he joined the *Ventura,* anchored in Valetta Harbour. Early in his career, he served on various ships. He was attached to the flotilla which harassed Murat's army in Messina, at that time attempting to invade Sicily. Murat lost more than 1,200 men in a succession of failed attempts at invasion. When O'Meara came on shore he was greeted enthusiastically by his fellow officers of the 62nd Regiment, as he wrote later in his memoirs when recalling his military career: 'My conduct, while in the army, was not wholly devoid of merit, and . . . my departure from the 62nd was regretted by most of the officers of that regiment—this may be inferred from the very flattering reception I experienced on my return to Sicily.'

His next appointment was to the *Victorious,* under Captain John Talbot, which was sailing in the Mediterranean at that time. At the beginning of 1812 it was ordered to the port of Venice, along with the *Weazel ,* under Captain John Andover. They were instructed to find, engage and, if possible, capture France's newest ship of the line, the 74-gun *Rivoli.*

On the foggy morning of 21 February the *Rivoli* and some smaller vessels were spotted coming out of port and setting a course across the Adriatic for Pola. The *Victorious* followed and, at 4.30 a.m., brought the *Rivoli* into action. As the ships closed on one another, both opened fire. Although a splinter almost blinded Captain Talbot, obliging him to hand over command to Lieutenant Thomas Peake, his deputy carried the battle to a satisfactory conclusion five hours later when the enemy ran aground on a sandbank. This made it easy for the *Victorious* to sail around the stranded *Rivoli* and, once the French vessel's mizzen mast had been lost, the *Victorious* closed in. Fierce hand-to-hand fighting followed but, eventually, the captain of the *Rivoli* was forced to surrender.

At home, much was made of the capture of the newest French battleship, with a complement of 850, by 500 British sailors. The victory had not been secured without a cost: 27 crew-members of the *Victorious* were killed and 99 wounded and the two surgeons on board had to work for hour after hour over the next four days. There were many amputations and more than 200 men from either side had to be treated.

Barry O'Meara's commanding officer, now Sir John Talbot, sent glowing reports of his new surgeon back to the Admiralty, the first time he had been mentioned in dispatches. The good opinion he had won was mirrored in a letter from Dr Greene, who had originally recommended him and who was now the most senior surgeon in the navy. Writing from Malta on 6 May 1812, Greene reported to the Admiralty: 'Mr O'Meara, whom you must recollect in the 62nd Regiment, and who was really—in my opinion—dealt rigidly with, has requested me to introduce him to you once more. I am happy to say that he has not forfeited my good opinion of him. In a most severe action he has proved himself to be a well-informed professional man, and by his good conduct, during nearly three years as an Assistant Surgeon on board the *Victorious,* he has gained the esteem of his captain and officers. Captain Talbot has mentioned him in his public dispatch in very handsome terms.'

O'Meara's name was now entered on the surgical list of the Royal

Barry O'Meara's naval career

Ship	Guns	Date	Captain
Assistant surgeon 1808–9			
Ventura	–	Dec 1808	Thomas Younger
Sabine	18	May 1808	James Donner
Victorious	74	Nov 1809	John Talbot
Senior surgeon 1812–15			
Espiègle	18	Sept 1812	? Taylor
Goliath	56	Nov 1813	Frederick Maitland
Boyne	96	Nov 1814	Frederick Maitland
Bellerophon	74	April 1815	Frederick Maitland

Navy. He was appointed to various ships, seeing action in the Americas and the West Indies. Among other places, he spent a considerable time off the coast of Surinam and the port of Paramaribo. In due course he was fortunate enough to come under the command of an agreeable, softly-spoken Scottish captain, Frederick Maitland, and due perhaps to their common Celtic origin or the fact that Maitland had a young Irish wife, the two men became friendly.

Maitland's high esteem for Barry O'Meara was clearly expressed in a letter of 5 November 1814 to Dr Harness in which he observed that 'during fifteen years of service I have commanded many of his Majesty's ships—I have never had the pleasure of sailing with an officer in his situation who so fully meets my expectations. I am not a judge of his professional abilities—though I have every reason to believe them of the first class and know that to be the opinion of some of the oldest and most respectable surgeons in the navy. I shall only state that during the period of very bad weather which occasioned the *Goliath* to be extremely sickly his attention and tenderness to the men was such as to call forth my warmest approbation and the grateful affection of both officers and men. Were it possible that I should soon obtain another appointment—I know of no man in the service I should wish to have as surgeon so much as Mr O'Meara. As however in the present state of the war, this is not likely, I trust you will do me the favour of giving him an appointment as an encouragement to young men of his description.'

Maitland appears to have been more successful in his intervention on the young doctor's behalf than he had expected and was able to persuade the Admiralty to allow Barry O'Meara to follow him on to two further vessels. The second of these was an old but still impressive 74-gun man-of-war, the *Bellerophon*.

Chapter 2: The fateful decision

Following his defeat at Waterloo Napoleon retreated to Paris, and for a moment there contemplated continuing. But it was clear that the French had little heart for further fighting. He abdicated on 21 June, and left Paris, first for his palace at Malmaison and then for the south, escaping just ahead of the vengeful Prussian army. On 3 July 1815, Napoleon arrived at Rochefort to a tumultuous welcome. Meanwhile, on that same day, Blücher and his troops entered Paris, proclaiming, in the intoxication of victory, that he wanted Napoleon 'hunted down like a dog, and hanged from the nearest tree'.

Realising that those who had welcomed his arrival in Rochefort so profusely might now be in danger, Napoleon decided to move to the island of Aix, hoping to formulate some plan of action there. His position, as an abdicated monarch, was full of formal and legal difficulties for the occupying powers. He enquired about the French frigates in the bay—the *Saale,* and the *Méduse* (which was destined to find sad notoriety off the coast of Senégal some six months later, as depicted in the famous painting by Géricault). In addition, two fast American merchant ships, the *Pike* and the *Ludlow,* lay off La Rochelle. All were prepared to sail the Emperor to the New World. His brother Joseph even offered to take his place, letting Napoleon escape, hidden in an empty wine barrel. Grateful as he was for the generosity of this offer, the indignity of the exercise was such that he could not consider it.

The *Bellerophon*, under Captain Frederick Maitland, with Surgeon O'Meara on board, was alerted to the possibility of Napoleon's slipping away, and was given the order to make all dispatch for La Rochelle. It was to block 'all roads into the ports of La Rochelle and Rochefort'. On 20 June 1815, the *Bellerophon* arrived on the coast and dropped anchor off the Isle d'Aix. Here the *Bellerophon,* with three smaller ships, the *Myrmidon,* the *Daphne* and the *Slaney,* cruised all the three channels off La Rochelle, between the islands of Ré, Oléron and Aix. There was no escape.

On 10 July two of Napoleon's closest aides stepped on board the *Bellerophon* and handed Captain Maitland a letter declaring that Napoleon had chosen the United States as his retreat. The object of the visit was to procure the passports which he claimed had been promised. In reality this was something of a diplomatic try-on, a probe by Napoleon as to the British intentions, as passports had not been promised, and it was not likely that they would be provided.

So Napoleon began pondering another possibility. Among his entourage (now swollen to 64 people, including women and children) was Count Emanuel de Las Cases, who had lived in London for many years and spoke English fluently. During the Reign of Terror, the diminutive aristocrat had escaped from France by hiding in a boat sailing to London from Amsterdam. To ease his penury he found work teaching French to the children of a noble household and, in the process, as he explained, he had formed 'a most agreeable impression of England and the British way of life'. Napoleon himself had a favourable view of England's tolerant society and was attracted by the English sense of justice and fair play. Prisoners of war were not ill-treated. England had given refuge to the Huguenots and to the Corsican leader Pascal Paoli. And so his thoughts turned to that country, which had been a haven for other refugees from France during the Reign of Terror. He had given Castlereagh (currently Foreign Secretary) safe passage from Paris in the past—perhaps the favour could now be returned.

He summoned Las Cases. Their discussion carried long into the warm afternoon. At one point a swallow flew into the room. Napoleon's private secretary, General Gourgaud, eventually managed to catch the bird, declaring its appearance an omen: 'Let us see which way he flies— west to America or north to England. There lies our destination!' He walked to the window and released the swallow which immediately flew north. Napoleon's mind was made up: he would surrender to England and Las Cases would commence negotiations with Captain Maitland of the *Bellerophon* to that effect. On 13 July he himself wrote to the Regent:

Your Royal Highness,

A victim of the factions which distract my country and of the enmity of the greatest powers of Europe, I have terminated my political career, and I come like Themosticles, to throw myself upon the hospitality of the British people. I put myself under the protection of their laws, which I claim from your Royal Highness, as the most powerful, the most constant, and the most generous of my enemies.

Napoleon

When General Gourgaud read the letter, tears came to his eyes. When the Prince of Wales eventually received it, he called it 'a capital letter' (it was not often that George IV, as he became, was referred to in such flattering terms) and then passed it to Castlereagh. It was Napoleon's proposal to live somewhere between London and Oxford, in a warm house with a good library in which he would be able to write his memoirs. He would adopt the name of Colonel Muiron, a brave general who had fallen in battle by his side.

Sadly, even if the British leaders had been prepared to set aside the feelings generated by twenty years of war, this dream took no account of the growing political conflict in England, aggravated by the collapse of markets at the end of the war. It was impossible to believe that so powerful and active a figure—not yet forty-six years old—could have prevented himself from becoming involved.

Las Cases sailed over to the *Bellerophon* and told Captain Maitland of Napoleon's wishes. He handed over Napoleon's letter and asked if safe passage to England could be guaranteed. Maitland responded as obligingly as he could. Although unable to anticipate his government's wishes, he assured Las Cases that England would be magnanimous in victory and said he could guarantee the safe passage requested. Fortified by these assurances, Las Cases sailed back to Aix.

Napoleon gathered his friends around him and explained the position. Of all his enemies, the British appeared the most tolerant and generous and surrender to England was the most reasonable option. Las Cases was sent to the *Bellerophon* once more. His final note to Maitland read: 'Before dawn the Emperor will present himself at the gangway of the *Bellerophon* either to be given safe passage to America or to be conveyed to England.'

This resolved Maitland's ambiguous position in respect of Napoleon's status. There would be no question of escape if Napoleon was once on board. He wanted to do everything he could to help but he felt an urgency to get Napoleon on board as soon as possible. Rumours quickly spread through the *Bellerophon* that Napoleon would be boarding the next morning. The ship had to be made spick and span for his arrival and the excitement among the crew was palpable. A young ship's rating, George Home, described the atmosphere in his memoirs: 'The evening of the 14th was calm and delightful as we lay at anchor, awaiting the great event of the morrow. All was expectation and excitement. The first lieutenant was engaged seeing all the belaying pins get an extra polish, and that every rope was coiled down with more than usual care, while every hush from the shore, or speck on the water, was listened to and watched with intense anxiety, lest our prey should escape us.'

On the following day, 'I had the middle watch, and just as I was relieved about half-past four in the morning of the 15th, and a lovely morning it was, we saw a man-of-war brig get under way from Aix Roads, and stand out towards us, bearing a flag of truce.' The brig made little headway against the current. At 6 a.m. the lookout announced the arrival of a large ship, the *Superb*, bearing Sir Henry Hotham. Captain Maitland gave immediate orders to lower the barge and help the brig towards the *Bellerophon*. 'A general's group of marines was ordered aft on the quarter-deck, and the boatswain stood, whistle in hand, ready to do the honours of the side. . . . the captain, evidently in much anxiety, kept trudging backwards and forwards between the gangway and his own cabin.' First to board the *Bellerophon* was Savary, Minister of Police, followed by Marshal Bertrand, who bowed and stood to one side. (General Comte Henri de Bertrand, was one of Napoleon's most loyal and trusted friends and stayed with him to the end.) The whistle blew loud and long. The marines snapped to attention. Then came Napoleon dressed in a grey greatcoat buttoned up to the chin, a cocked hat and Hussar boots but no sword. Maitland stepped forward, removed his cap, bowed, and welcomed Napoleon aboard. Napoleon replied briefly that 'he had placed himself under the protection of the British nation'. Captain Maitland nodded and turned to conduct the Emperor to his cabin. 'As he passed through the officers assembled on the quarter-deck,' wrote Home, 'he repeatedly bowed slightly to us, and smiled. What an ineffable beauty there was in that smile, his teeth were finely set, and as white as ivory . . . I marked his fine robust figure as he followed Captain Maitland into the cabin, and, boy as I was, I said to myself, "Now have I a tale for futurity". . . .

'We were engaged during the forenoon of the 15th bringing on board the suite and luggage of the Emperor . . . About 10 o'clock Napoleon appeared on deck "surrounded by his faithful few".' The sun shone bright on the fallen Emperor accompanied by a great many officers in rich colourful uniform. At noon Admiral Hotham came on board and was introduced to Napoleon on the quarter-deck. Sir Henry immediately uncovered and remained so throughout the conversation.

From that moment onwards, every officer removed his cap when approached by Napoleon on deck. This was a signal everyone on board desired. The Emperor should be treated with all the respect due to a crowned head of state. Captain Maitland slung his cot in the ward-room, and gave up his cabin to the Emperor. Flags were folded up and placed on deck as sofas for the ladies to rest on during the day. Port nettings were erected to prevent children from falling overboard.

Next morning the Emperor, accompanied by Captain Maitland, was invited on board the *Superb* to breakfast with Sir Henry. Before leaving the *Bellerophon* a whole body of marines were drawn up to receive him as he came from his cabin. He returned their military salute. Suddenly he stopped and approached the captain of the marines. He asked the men to be put through a few drill exercises, which they did enthusiasti-cally without a flaw. Then Napoleon took hold of a musket, removed the bayonet and carried out some drill exercises himself, much to the astonishment and admiration of the marines.

Napoleon was treated like royalty on board the *Superb*. The ship's company were dressed in blue jackets and white duck trousers and he was piped on board where he stayed for two hours. On his return from the *Superb* the *Bellerophon* immediately weighed anchor and made for the open sea. The journey to Torbay took six days. Despite the excellent weather (the sun shone the whole way) the sea swell made all the French quite seasick and the doctors on board were kept busy for the duration of the journey.

George Home describes his own never-to-be-forgotten meeting with Napoleon early one morning as the ship was sailing past Ushant, the last tip of France the Emperor would ever see: 'I had come on deck at four in the morning to take the morning watch, and the washing of the decks had just begun, when, to my astonishment, I saw the Emperor come out of his cabin at that early hour and make for the poop-ladder.' As the deck was wet, Home approached, removed his hat and offered his arm, which Napoleon took at once. Having gained the poop deck he sat down on one of the cannons and smiled thanks for the attention. He pointed towards land and said, 'Ushant, Cape Ushant'. Home re-plied 'Yes, Sire,' and withdrew. 'He then took out a pocket glass and applied it to his eye, looking eagerly at the land. In this position, he remained from five in the morning to nearly mid-day, without paying any attention to what was passing around him, or speaking to one of his suite, who had been standing behind for several hours. . . . his emotion was visible, he hung upon the land until it looked only a speck in the distance and then, turning, stepped from the gunslide into the arms of faithful Bertrand who stood ready to receive his fallen master. He uttered not a word as he tottered down the poop ladder, his head hung heavily forward, so as to render his countenance scarcely visible, and in this way he was conducted to his cabin.'

The mood changed the next day, and Home recounts that there was much gaiety on board. The ladies walked the deck and, the children running around, all wanted to touch the Emperor or take his hand, which he seemed to enjoy. He had a gold snuffbox in his hand which he appeared to use quite often. In order to lighten the tedium of a sea passage, one of the lieutenants decided to produce a Shakespearean play for the passengers. What the play was, no one remembers, but Napoleon did attend, and instructed Barry O'Meara and Countess Bertrand (whose father, General Arthur Dillon, before he was guillotined, had been an Irish officer in the French army) to stand by and translate for him. Napoleon appeared to enjoy the performance but thought that the ladies in the play (who were in fact young sailors) were 'a little Dutch built for fine ladies'. The *Bellerophon* reached Torbay on 24 July.

England

It was a cloudless, blue, calm summer morning in the south of England. As usual, a number of small boats came out and slowly rowed around the great ship, seeing if there was anything to buy or sell. Suddenly a small bottle was thrown overboard. It stayed afloat. It obviously contained a message. Two young boys eventually recovered the small bottle—it had contained eau de cologne. Inside was a hastily scribbled note, which read: 'Napoleon on board'.

They turned, and made for land as quickly as possible, with this extraordinary news. Within hours the *Bellerophon* was surrounded by hundreds of boats of all sizes, packed with people, especially young women, hungry for sight of the great celebrity. When he did come on deck there was a tumultuous cheer, Napoleon waved back, but immediately went below deck.

At 7 a.m. the first lieutenant was put on shore with dispatches for the most senior Admiral, Lord Keith. Young Home was the midshipman of the party. Once he landed 'he was taken prisoner by some twenty young ladies, marched off to a fine house in the little town, regaled with tea and clouted cream, and bored with five thousand questions about Napoleon, the ridiculousness of which I have often laughed at since. "What like was he—was he really a man? Were his hands and clothes all

Napoleon and his entourage approaching the Bellerophon

over blood when he came on board? Was his voice like thunder? Etc. etc. etc.'"

When the first lieutenant returned, he brought greetings, and a letter from Admiral Keith for Napoleon, thanking him for ensuring his wounded nephew received medical attention the day before Waterloo. More and more boats surrounded the great ship. Bands in several boats played French airs, hoping to attract the attention of the Emperor. 'The ladies looked gay as butterflies.' There were now over a thousand boats tightly packed around the ship. But now Captain Maitland began to find his situation somewhat disagreeable. The crowd had become too numerous. There was also the possibility that in the crush someone might get hurt, or worse, might use the crowd as cover to an attempt to rescue Napoleon. Therefore, on 4 August, they weighed anchor and moved further out to sea.

The politicians discuss Napoleon's fate

During the eleven days Napoleon and his entourage waited at Torbay, there was nothing but confusion on shore. The government was now forced to make up its mind about Napoleon. It was a legally and practically unprecedented situation. When the jurists of the country were consulted they were unhelpful. Some thought he should be sent to France to be tried for treason; others went so far as to condemn him outright as '*hostis humani generis*'—an enemy of humankind. Should he be treated as a guest of the British people, like so many exiles before and since, or was he a prisoner of war—though given the ending of the war, what did that mean? He certainly had liberal friends in England—notably Lord and Lady Holland, and even the younger brother of the Prince of Wales, the Duke of Sussex. There were also, of course, many more people whom the war propaganda of twenty years had embittered. (And in nurseries up and down the country, as Betsy Balcombe recalled in her memoirs of her time on St Helena, Napoleon featured as 'a huge ogre or giant, with one flaming red eye in the middle of his forehead, and long teeth protruding from his mouth with which he tore to pieces and devoured naughty little girls, especially those who did not know their lessons.') It now fell to the British Cabinet to settle the fate of the defeated leader, determine his status and decide upon measures to be taken. There was no question of other countries being consulted.

The Cabinet was also stung by a letter recently published in the influential paper, *The Morning Chronicle*, by the brilliant Capell Lofft, a landlord and radical reformer who had some years before been thrown off the Suffolk magistracy for interfering in a case of a young girl about to be hanged for petty theft. Capell Lofft's arguments were a direct attack on the Government. It certainly gave the Cabinet cause for anxiety. Letters poured into *The Morning Chronicle* in support of Napoleon.

A firm decision was imperative! A small select committee gathered around the Prime Minister Lord Liverpool. They were not a large-minded group, as their social policy was later to show. Furthermore, they were still afraid of Napoleon, and fear is not conducive to generosity. For many of them their entire political careers would have been spent in the fight against his France; Lord Liverpool himself had been Foreign Secretary at the time of the abortive Peace of Amiens in 1802. Lord Eldon, the Lord Chancellor (described as 'a tedious but sound judge, a poor speaker, a lively hater of Roman Catholics and a victim of parsimony'), proposed 'keeping him under restraint in some remote region, where he should be treated with all indulgence'. The crowds at present surrounding the *Bellerophon* underlined how unlikely it was that Napoleon would have been able to find a quiet resting place in Britain. So he was to be sequestered from the world. To prevent enthusiasts attempting to free Napoleon by writs of *habeus corpus* or actions for false imprisonment

Eldon suggested sweeping away the legal ambiguities with an Act of Parliament.

The Cabinet eventually agreed on deportation—but where? The Azores—too near! St Helena was then suggested. Wellington had once called to the island briefly on his return from India. He remembered it as 'pretty and healthy'; he failed, however, to recall that it had been denuded of trees by goats, and that the mountains were covered in mist for nine months of the year. (He also did not tell of his brush with death there. The Duke had never learned to swim. The boat carrying him ashore at St Helena capsized in surf. He was saved by a young midshipman—who later in life opened a pub in Cornwall. He was known to all as 'the man who saved the man who saved England'!)

St Helena was decided upon 'because in such a place and at such a distance all political intrigues would be harmless'. Responsibility for taking Napoleon there was given to Admiral Sir George Cockburn, a tall imposing figure of a man who had recently been knighted. In the meantime, Captain Maitland on the *Bellerophon* had been informed of the government's decision. Perhaps, it was suggested, it would be prudent and diplomatic if he could warn Napoleon before it was officially announced. On the following day Lord Keith, the head of the Admiralty and Sir Henry Bunbury, under-Secretary of State for War, came aboard. When they entered the small cabin Napoleon did not stand.

In broken, 'schoolboy French', Lord Keith introduced himself and Sir Henry. He then produced a piece of paper and read out the decision of his Majesty's Government. Napoleon did not quite understand, so he asked Sir Henry to translate it for him. Bunbury translated slowly: 'That it would be best, for the political stability of Europe, that Napoleon should be incarcerated on the island of St Helena, because in such a place, and at such a distance, all political intrigues would be impossible.'

Though no doubt shocked and surprised, Napoleon accepted his fate with stoic realism. He felt, however, that some sort of protest should be made. 'I have thrown myself into your hands seeking justice and protection. In all our wars we treated our prisoners fairly and with compassion—and you dare to treat me thus!' replied Napoleon. There was nothing the British officers could say. They were acutely embarrassed, especially Keith. The previous evening he had informed the Government that it was with the greatest reluctance that he would tell Napoleon of their decision. He found the whole situation most distressing, so distasteful in fact that he wished to have nothing more to do with this whole sad affair. His opinion was that 'Napoleon had surrendered in good faith and should be treated as a prisoner of war.'

However, a decision had been made. A letter of protest was written by Napoleon to the government protesting against the legal and human infringements. Two more were to follow, arguing the illegality of the decision. His followers were equally shocked by the remote spot to which they were to go. For a short while Countess Bertrand became hysterical and threatened to throw herself overboard. 'Let her do it if she wants to!' was Napoleon's cold-water response.

When poor Dr Mangault, Napoleon's physician, was informed of their destination, he became acutely ill. The six-day journey to England had quite overwhelmed him. He was so dehydrated be could hardly walk. A 70-day journey to the south Atlantic would certainly kill him. He explained his condition in detail to Napoleon, saying that he would not survive such a long sea journey and begged to be excused from this his last mission. Napoleon understood at once, and ordered him back to France, as soon as possible.

Now the Emperor needed a physician. He remembered the Irish doctor of the *Bellerophon*, who spoke Italian and some French. Bertrand was delegated to approach Captain Maitland and ask if Mr O'Meara would consider the post of personal surgeon to the Emperor. Maitland passed this information on to the Admiralty. Lord Keith interviewed Barry O'Meara and asked him to consider the request. O'Meara was intrigued, fascinated, and flattered. He admired, he even liked the fallen Emperor. It would be a challenge—a great adventure.

Lord Keith then raised the security advantages of having a British officer in the enemy camp, so to speak. Despite his military background, and his long service with the army and navy, immediately O'Meara refused to act as a spy. 'I will only go as his surgeon,' he exclaimed. Obviously, if he had word that Napoleon planned to escape he would inform the authorities—but nothing else. This was agreed upon.

Looking to the future, O'Meara also stipulated that he should not forfeit his rank as a naval surgeon, that he should not lose his pension, and that he could leave St Helena at any time he wished. All three requests were agreed to. O'Meara now sent his letter of acceptance to the Admiralty. The letter is typical of him—he writes as he thinks, one sentence running into another, without full stops.

The Admiralty decided that Admiral Cockburn would take over the responsibility not only for taking Napoleon to the island, but for setting him up when there. Cockburn was a formidable and efficient sailor, who did not suffer fools gladly. He had fought in the North American campaign, and in 1812 had personally been responsible for the burning down of the White House in Washington.

The *Bellerophon* was regarded as too old and too slow for the long journey. (In fact this was her last voyage. By 1817 she had been dismasted and fitted out as a prison hulk holding 400 men—like Magwitch in *Great Expectations*. Later, she was used as a boys' prison for 320 lads under fourteen.) To replace *Bellerophon* they needed a fast reliable ship. They settled for the 74-gun *Northumberland,* now in dry dock undergoing repairs. A most reluctant crew were recalled (they had just been on shore leave). On 6 August the *Northumberland* dropped anchor alongside the *Bellerophon.*

The following day Napoleon had his last interview with Captain Maitland. He forgave the Scottish captain who, he believed, had been an unwitting accomplice in the behaviour of the British government. He bade farewell to the officers and crew of the ship and thanked them for their hospitality. Lastly, he bade farewell to the French officers who were not going to accompany him.

On board the *Northumberland,* Napoleon greeted the captain with: 'Here I am, Captain. I place myself under your care.' Napoleon went to the quarter-deck where he spoke with some of the more senior officers on board, though, by Admiralty instruction he was not accorded the same respect on the *Northumberland* as on the *Bellerophon.* Around them hundreds of small rowboats each hoped to get a last glimpse of the Emperor. A large cutter brutally circled the ship in order to keep the small craft away. Tempting fate, one of the small boats was sunk, and several people drowned. Two young women (who could not swim), however, were kept afloat by the billowing effect of air trapped beneath their silk skirts. They were brought on board the *Northumberland,* where they were resuscitated, and given fresh sailor clothes. Once they had recovered, they were returned to shore, in the same cutter that had sunk their rowboat.

On 8 August, two frigates and several brigs joined the *Northumberland.* Food, water and essential supplies were loaded. The 53rd Regiment of Foot (2nd Battalion) under the command of Lieutenant Colonel John Mansel came on board. Altogether there were 1,080 souls aboard the ship. Napoleon had his own cabin and the use of a private sitting room, which Admiral Cockburn very rarely used. Special cabins were erected for the French families only; all other passengers, be they male or female, had to share cabins. Once everybody had settled in and there was enough food and water to see them as far as Madeira, the ship hauled up its heavy anchor—they were on their way.

Chapter 3: Journal of a voyage

The voyage to St Helena was to take Admiral Cockburn's convoy two and a half months. The following account is based on Napoleon's Last Voyages, *the combined diaries of John Glover, Secretary to the Admiral on board the* Northumberland, *and Admiral Sir Thomas Usher, Captain of the* Undaunted. *(Incidentally, in the original document Glover records the* Northumberland *as east of the meridian. It should have been recorded as west. This was due to the 'local magnetic anomaly'. The ship was following the 'magnetic north' and not the 'true north'. St Helena lies 6° west and not 6° east of the central meridian. For the sake of clarity I have corrected this error. Interpolations by me are in italic.)*

Sir George Cockburn was responsible for the whole flotilla which had to sail together. The Northumberland *depended on other ships for food and water en route. 'Our first (and only) port of call would be Madeira. Here we would all gather for fresh water and fruit.' The conditions on his ship were quite cramped. Cockburn was a strict disciplinarian—he had to be. At sea he was a stickler for law and order. His demeanour and height demanded respect. Initially the Admiral disliked Napoleon. This quickly changed to admiration and eventually friendship. He decided to treat the Emperor, not as a prisoner of war, but rather as a guest aboard his ship. He would offer his arm to Napoleon while they were walking on the swaying deck.*

Wednesday 9 August 1815 Plymouth

That evening, the heavy anchors were hauled on board. The flotilla sailed, with the tide, into a stiff north-westerly wind down the Channel.

The first meal on board was at 6 o'clock in the evening. Napoleon sat at the head of the table and was in good spirits. On his right side sat Sir George Cockburn and on his left Countess Bertrand. All were amazed at Napoleon's spirits.

Dr Wharton describes the dinner that evening: 'At six o'clock dinner was announced. When we all sat down, Napoleon appeared in good spirits. Bonaparte ate from every dish at the table. He preferred rich dishes to plain food and touched no vegetables. He drank claret, out of a tumbler, keeping the bottle before him. He spoke throughout the

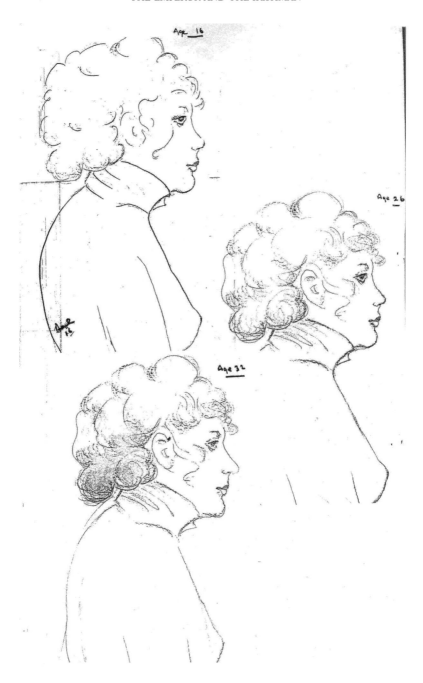

Three ages of Josephine, Napoleon's first wife—top aged sixteen, centre aged twenty-six, bottom aged thirty-two (author's drawing)

whole dinner, discussing the Russian campaign, the burning of Moscow and the early frost (which he admitted was the cause of his defeat). "The natives, not the French, burnt Moscow," he explained.'

Napoleon drank his coffee quickly, got up from the table and walked out onto the deck, leaving the British officers to finish their wine. Napoleon had set a precedent. Cockburn issued orders that the cloth should be removed when Napoleon stood. Meanwhile he and his officers would remain at table and have their port. Even in defeat, at this humiliating moment, he still behaved like an Emperor.

Napoleon walked the deck for approximately an hour. Later that evening he invited Admiral Cockburn, Captain Ross, and Mr Glover to join him for a game of cards. They played vingt-et-un until 11 o'clock, when they all retired to bed.

Thursday 10 August 1815 49°N 4°W

The weather moderate with a considerable swell.

Following an hour's walk on deck, Napoleon retired to his cabin at 4 p.m. He played chess until dinner time. Throughout dinner he discussed France's relationship with America. 'Mr Madison was too late in declaring war,' he said. 'He never made any request for help from France,' but 'I would have readily lent any number of ships Mr Madison might have wished for.'

Following dinner, he drank his coffee quickly, got up from the table, and walked the deck. (When he walked, it was usually on the arm of Sir George Cockburn or Dr O'Meara.) After this he played cards until bed time.

Sunday 13 August 1815 45°N 8°W

The weather had improved. The sea was calm. There was a moderate wind. At dinner everybody ate heartily. Napoleon spoke throughout the meal with the evening's guest, Rev. George Russell, the ship's chaplain. Napoleon constantly questioned the poor Reverend about the Protestant religion.

Do they have music? Did they have Extreme Unction? Whether they prayed for the dead? How many sacraments they had? How long before a clergyman could be ordained? Do they believe in transubstantiation?' And so it went on and on all evening. The poor Rev. Russell was quite exhausted at the end of dinner.

Again Napoleon walked the deck with some of his followers until dark. On his return he played vingt-et-un until bed time. As it was

Marie-Louise of Austria (author's drawing)

Sunday neither Sir George Cockburn nor Captain Ross joined the party.

Tuesday 15 August 1815 43°N 10°W

At the dinner that evening Admiral Cockburn was informed that it was Napoleon's birthday. He ordered everyone to stop eating. He demanded the best wine on board ship. He then ordered all his officers to charge their glasses, and drink to Napoleon's health. The Emperor appeared in very good form and was delighted with their kind wishes. Napoleon was forty-six years old.

Wednesday 16 August 1815 42°N 10°W

At dinner the conversation returned to Josephine and Napoleon's divorce. He explained to the Admiral that he needed an heir. 'Josephine was sterile'—he therefore had to search Europe for a fertile, preferably young and titled wife. There were princesses all over Europe waiting for a husband. This long list was eventually reduced to three potential wives: Princess Augusta in England, Princess Anne in Russia and Princess Marie

Louise in Austria. He was advised that the English mission was not a viable proposition. Princess Anne in Moscow was a possibility. Some years beforehand he had promised Tsar Alexander that he might consider marrying his younger sister, thus uniting France with Russia. He even went so far as to promise the young Tsar that he would build a Greek Orthodox chapel in the Tuileries for her. Unfortunately, Princess Anne's mother was against the union. She did not like Napoleon. 'Princess Anne was far too young—she had not yet reached puberty and would not be fertile for another few years,' she firmly emphasised.

The best choice was Marie Louise of Austria. She was eighteen, tall, blonde, beautiful and belonged to the noblest line in Europe. She was the eldest daughter of the last Holy Roman Emperor, and brought up from the very day of her birth to be a princess. It would help in making a non-aggression pact with Austria. 'An alliance with the Hapsburg dynasty, rather than the Romanovs, appealed to me. I decided on Marie Louise and sent a proposal to Francis I of Austria—who acceded without hesitation to everything. I was highly pleased with the arrangement,' said Napoleon, admitting also that he had never seen Marie Louise, 'until she arrived in France as my wife.'

Thursday 17 August 1815 41°N 11°W

During dinner, Napoleon and the Admiral compared the French and British armies. In the French army, promotion was by merit alone, not by inheritance.

'I was a general at the age of twenty-four. I had conquered Italy at the age of twenty-five. I had risen from nothing, to be Sovereign of France at the age of thirty. It was my misfortune that I was not killed at Moscow.'

Friday 18 August 1815 48°N 11°W

The discussion concerned his time at Elba. 'Caroline, my sister, paid me a visit; she had just returned from Vienna and informed me about my son. She had asked Marie Louise: "Why have you not joined your husband at Elba?" Her reply was: "My father would not allow me to do so."'

Later during their conversation the Admiral enquired as to which were the bravest soldiers—Napoleon thought the Russians and Poles were the best soldiers in Europe. He ended by stating how important it was that Poland be preserved 'to act as a barrier between Russian and Europe'.

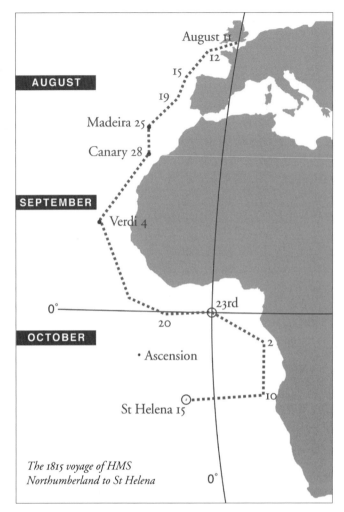

AUGUST

August 11
12
15
19
Madeira 25
Canary 28

SEPTEMBER

Verdi 4

0°
20

OCTOBER

23rd

2

• Ascension

10

St Helena 15

*The 1815 voyage of HMS
Northumberland to St Helena* 0°

Saturday 19 August 1815 39°N 11°W

There was light air and good weather. All was quiet on board and
everyone was in good humour. The discussion around dinner concerned Napoleon's conquest of Egypt. He gave an amusing account
of being admitted as a Muslim, when in Egypt. He said that the
sheikhs and other chiefs had many consultations on the subject but
at last they admitted him, and his followers, among their faithful.

They were given special permission to drink wine—provided that
on opening every bottle, they would determine to do some good action
that day. He also discussed the assassination of Kléber. *(When Napoleon
left Egypt in 1799 he left Kléber in command of his forces there. In 1800*

Kléber was knifed to death by a Syrian student.)

'He was an excellent man and a good solder, but he did not understand the people of Egypt. If Kléber had not been murdered I am convinced that Egypt would have remained in French hands.'

Sunday 20 August 1815 37°N 12°W

Good weather but much swell.

Napoleon did not walk the deck before dinner. Not one of the guests attended Divine Service.

Wednesday 23 August 1815 34°N 13°W

Arrived at Madeira. The weather was hot and unpleasant. There was heavy swell, so Napoleon, rather 'out of sorts', kept to his cabin.

Thursday 24 August 1815 30°N 17°W

Remained 'lying to' off Funchal. The British Consul, a Mr Veitch, came on board, with a crate of wine for the Emperor. Mr Veitch dined on board and later walked the deck with Napoleon for the rest of the evening. There were no card games.

Friday 25 August 1815 30°N 13°W

There was a violent storm in the evening caused by the sirocco. Captain Ross put out to sea to avoid being dashed against the volcanic rocks. The mizzen mast, which had been broken during the storm, was repaired.

Sunday 27 August 1815 25°N 20°W

When the tempest died down they returned to port and took on more fresh water and much-needed provisions. The supplies ship would be in constant attendance for the whole journey. Should the *Northumberland* outstrip the supplies ship, sails would have to be shortened in order to keep in touch. Due to the heavy swell, there was much difficulty in loading the ship with supplies today.

During the afternoon the harbour master (*an Irishman*) came on board with a crate of excellent Madeira wine for Napoleon. He did not see Napoleon—unfortunately the Emperor had retired to bed earlier than usual.

Monday 28 August 1815 25°N 20°W

Napoleon out of sorts. The hot weather did not allow good sleep. He also could not read in bed, as Admiral Cockburn would not allow lights to be burned in any of the sleeping cabins at night.

Tuesday 29 August 1815 24°N 20°W

Slow progress—sea calm. Napoleon took very little exercise. He appeared lethargic and somewhat depressed. He just leaned on the gunwale and stared out to sea for a considerable length of time. It was quite obvious that the Emperor was becoming very bored.

Friday 1 September 1815 17°N 25°W

Rough seas, but reasonable progress. The weather continued bad. Heavy seas confined everyone to their cabins. Even Napoleon refused to go out for fresh air. The *Northumberland* could not make the Verdi islands for much-needed water.

Monday 4 September 1815 17°N 25°W

At dinner they discussed the Syrian campaign and the Siege of Acre. Despite Kléber's great victory at Mount Tarbour (*2,000 French had a resounding victory against a Muslim army of 15,000*), Napoleon again described his problems with plague and his retreat from Acre: 'I had to accept that without arms or ammunition the siege of Acre would be a failure. I decided to abandon the siege and return to Egypt.'

Friday 8 September 1815 11°N 22°W

Napoleon was in very good spirits and after dinner, walked the deck in a downpour of rain. The Admiral advised him not to go out, but he replied, 'It would not hurt me any more than the sailors working on deck.' He was joined by a grudging Bertrand and Las Cases, who returned 'soaked to the skin' after an hour walking.

At dinner Napoleon, in conversation with the Admiral, discussed many of the leading characters in England. He said he had the greatest respect for the late Lord Cornwallis, Charles Fox, and Captain Usher *(the captain of the ship who took him to Elba)*, the latter for whom he had the utmost affection. He was not so generous with his compliments when discussing the Royal Family or the Prince of Wales.

Saturday 9 September 1815 9°N 18°W

This morning a mulatto sailor became drunk. He was sentenced to 20 lashes. Still drunk, he was tied to the rack and given 20 strokes, while the ship's crew stood in silence on the deck.

Bertrand was quite appalled by this brutal punishment. 'It was ugly, embarrassing and humiliating. This sort of behaviour would not be tolerated in the French navy—there would be instant mutiny,' he declared.

Monday 11 September 1815 8°N 1 8°W

The mulatto became drunk again. Rather than face any further punishment he jumped overboard. Admiral Cockburn immediately ordered all sails to be dropped. Row boats were launched. The search carried on until well after dark. Flares were lit to try and attract his attention if he were still alive. His name was shouted across the silent still waters. The poor man had disappeared. There was a sombre atmosphere on board all night.

Thursday 14 September 1815 7°N 17°W

Light winds slowed progress. Again they discussed Russia. Napoleon told them that he was invited by Emperor Paul of Russia into an alliance in order to humble Great Britain. In return 'Paul would act against England's interest in India—unfortunately King Paul was assassinated.'

Played at whist all evening.

Tuesday 19 September 1815 3°N 11°W

In the Gulf of Guinea the weather was good and seas were calm. Admiral Cockburn decided to send one of his supply ships to the nearest island for fresh water and fruit. Napoleon discussed his invasion plans for Ireland. He said that he 'had arranged everything with that country and if only he was able to land his troops he had every reason to suppose they would have succeeded in possessing themselves of the whole island of Ireland.'

He went on to explain that 'he kept up a constant communication with the disaffected parties, which he said was by no means confined to the Roman Catholics. They also had a large proportion of Protestants in their ranks. He acquiesced in everything they wished for, leaving all arrangements respecting the country, religion etc. entirely to themselves. His only object was to gain an advantage point in separating Ireland from England. Those who came to him from Ireland generally came and returned through London, by which means he obtained much information respecting both countries.'

Friday 22 September 1815 1°N 5°W

There was not a breath of wind. The *Northumberland* was becalmed. The sea was like glass. Bottles and refuse thrown overboard were still floating about the ship for many days.

Saturday 23 September 1815 0°S 0°W/E

Slowly the great ship drifted over the equator at noon. They were 0° latitude and 0° longitude. The sun cast no shadow. The ship's log records this remarkable event as follows: 'Today the ship crossed the line just before noon. It an occurrence worthy of remark, that this day we passed 0° of latitude and 0° of longitude and the sun the zero of its declination.'

This striking coincidence did not escape the notice of the sailors, who certainly credited it to Napoleon's presence.

To distract attention Sir George decided to start 'crossing the line' festivities earlier than planned. The oldest sailor on board dressed up in a long white beard and crown. The youngest (who had not previously crossed the equator) were covered in red paint and porridge. Later they were dumped in a large tub of cold water. There was an air of happiness and celebration on deck.

Napoleon, who had remained in his cabin for most of the day, wished to give a present to the sailors. He suggested one gold coin for each of 200 lowest ranking service men on board ship. This offer was refused. Cockburn was not going to allow any attempt to confuse the seamen's allegiance. He was polite in his refusal, and informed Napoleon that he could make a donation of 10 gold coins to the sailors' fund. He brought the festivities to an abrupt end and asked for full sail.

Monday 25 September 1815 0°S 3°W

At dinner that evening Napoleon asked Admiral Cockburn why he took such an unusual route to the island. Surely, he asked, it was 'better to sail towards Brazil, and following the trade winds they then could reach St Helena perhaps 20 days earlier.' The Admiral's reply was not recorded. However, it was obvious to all that he wanted to avoid the popular shipping lanes.

Wednesday 27 September 1815 2.4° S 0.20°W

The weather was cool and pleasant. Napoleon was in good health He was not very communicative. He did not play vingt-et-un, instead he played chess. Much of his time, he said, was spent in trying to learn English.

At dinner he asked Admiral Cockburn if he knew anything about St Helena. Apparently the Admiral knew quite a lot.

Thursday 28 September 1815 4°S 3°W

Again Napoleon in very good spirits. During his long walk with the Admiral they discussed French seamen. 'The French navy was so little employed that their new officers were unaccustomed to command in difficult circumstances. On my return from Egypt I had to instruct

Admiral Sir George Cockburn commanded the flotilla that took Napoleon to St Helena and remained in command until April 1816 when Sir Hudson Lowe took over.

Admiral Ganteaume where to sail, in order to avoid capture by the British navy—whose ships were constantly criss-crossing the Mediterranean Sea. During my voyage to Alexandria, I had a discussion with Admiral Bruix—the same Admiral explained in minute detail the disadvantages a fleet must labour under if attacked at anchor. Yet, some weeks later the good Admiral proved his point when attacked by Nelson. The French were at anchor. He not alone lost his whole fleet but his own life.'

The French navy, he explained, 'spent too much time trying to form "a line" before battle started.'

Following this long conversation, there was no time for vingt-et-un.

Sunday 1 October 1815 5°S 6°W

The fine weather continued. Napoleon listened to *The Life of Nelson*, read to him by General Bertrand.

Tuesday 3 October 1815 6°S 6°W

During his walk with the Admiral Napoleon enquired as to the time of their arrival at St Helena. He was told approximately 16 October. That night at dinner they discussed one of his greatest victories—the Battle at Wagram.

'It was my greatest army ever—180,000 men and over 1,000 cannons. General Clausel was the most able military general in France—but I believe you English think that Lord Wellington was the best,' he said with a smile.

Wednesday 4 October 1815 8°S 7°W

There is a fine fresh breeze. Everyone is comfortable and in good form except Madame Bertrand who has spent a considerable time below deck. The children are remarkably healthy and much improved by the voyage. We make good progress.

Saturday 7 October 1815 8°S 8°W

It was noted that the troop ship was delaying the flotilla. Therefore the Admiral, determined not to be further delayed, gave 'full sail' and declared to all, that they should make landfall within a week.

Sunday 8 October 1815 9°S 8°W

At dinner Napoleon described his early life and in particular the battle at Toulon. After the battle at Lodi he felt strong enough to be able to interfere with the French Government. Jealousy at home made the Government appoint him as commander of an army to lead the invasion of England. When he declared that 'this was impossible' they proposed an invasion of Egypt. This was a challenge he readily accepted. On his return from Egypt he found that there was no party strong enough to oppose him.

Saturday 14 October 1815 10°S 5°W

At long last the south-east trade winds and good weather arrived. Good progress, and on the morning of the 14th the Admiral declared, 'We should see land at 6 p.m. that evening'. True to his word, at 6 p.m., the island of St Helena became visible. The French were astonished at the accuracy of his forecast. The sails were dropped. The ship 'lay to' for the night. The *Icarus* was ordered to the island to inform the Governor that they would anchor at Jamestown harbour the following day.

Chapter 4: Early days on St Helena

In his memoirs Barry O'Meara recalls the shock the travellers received at the first sight of their new home. 'We arrived at St Helena,' he wrote, 'on the 15th of October. Nothing can be more desolate than the appearance of the exterior of the island.' William Forsyth (the lawyer who was to attack O'Meara's account of his time with Napoleon but who never actually visited the island) combined travellers' tales and described it thus: 'Its appearance from the sea is gloomy and forbidding. Masses of volcanic rock with sharp and jagged peaks tower up around the coast and form an iron girdle which seems to bar all access to the interior. And the few points where a landing can be effected were then bristling with cannon, so as to render the aspect still more formidable. The whole island bears evidence of having been formed by the tremendous agency of fire, but so gigantic are the strata of which it is composed, and so disproportionate to its size that some have thought it the relic and wreck of a submerged continent. Its seared and barren sides without foliage or verdure, present an appearance of dreary desolation.'

One of the most isolated places in the world—St Helena. This photograph was taken more than a mile distant from the island. The sea at this point is two miles deep, the cliffs are 200 feet high.

St Helena, one of the most isolated places in the world, is not an island paradise. A gaunt bare rock more than 1,200 miles from the nearest land mass, its appearance, as Betsy Balcombe put it in her memoir of her stay there, 'is certainly but little calculated to make one fall in love with it.' The island is about 10½ miles long, 6¾ miles wide and 28 miles in circumference (rather smaller than Lough Neagh). It was discovered by the Portuguese in 1502 and it was they who introduced the goats that rapidly destroyed the inland woods and most of the unique indigenous plant life, making the island even bleaker. Other unknown sailors accidentally introduced the rats which were such a feature of island life. St Helena was captured by the British in the 17th century and leased by Charles II to the East India Company, which used it as a staging and victualling post on the long journeys to and from India before the Suez Canal was built. The wind blows constantly and steadily from the south-east.

Like so many tropical stations, it was, as Barry O'Meara discovered, a very unhealthy place. Dysentery, inflammation of the bowels, liver problems, fevers all took their toll. (It was later discovered that the poor water supply was a major cause of these ailments.) The island, as O'Meara put it, was 'so unfavourable to longevity that very few persons pass their 45th year.' When British propagandists declared that St Helena was 'positively and decidedly healthy', O'Meara indignantly recorded that 'during my residence at Longwood there was not a single individual of Napoleon's suite (with the exception of Count Bertrand) who had not been seriously and most of them dangerously ill; either with fever, dysentery, inflammation of the bowels or liver. All of Count Bertrand's and General Montholon's children had been dangerously ill; and three deaths occurred at Longwood from inflammation of the bowels, and dysentery in as many weeks.' The island's good reputation, so blithely affirmed by Wellington, derived, O'Meara believed, from the fact that few Europeans (at least until Napoleon arrived) spent a considerable time on the island, and they would have found any landfall a pleasant change after the cramped, damp and uncomfortable conditions on board an East Indiaman.

In April 2005 I visited St Helena. We sailed from Cape Town on a 38,000-ton ship which even at a steady 18 knots took seven days to reach the island (in Napoleon's time a 74-gun ship such as the *Northumberland* would have been lucky to average 6 knots on such a voyage.) The island, lost and isolated in the vast southern Atlantic loomed big-

Mr Henry Porteous' lodging house, where Napoleon spent his first night on St Helena

ger than I had imagined.

For the most part it is made of tall volcanic mountains composed of black magma whose peaks have been bleached white by the sun. From the sea the most visible aspect are the looming cliffs of volcanic rock, some reaching as much as 200 feet above the sea. There are only two or three little places where a landing can be made—making St Helena an ideal prison island.

We dropped anchor a thousand metres from shore and were ferried to land by lifeboat. Jamestown is still the only town on the island, jammed between two steep mountains on the warmer side of the island facing a natural harbour. There are about 400 houses. Some one-fifth of the 5,000 population lives in Jamestown, the rest in small farms scattered across the island.

Some of the interior is fertile, and there are numerous small farms filled with cows and sheep; other parts are no more than bare rock.

The present population is a delightful mixture of races—English, Chinese, Indian and African. They speak a kind of sing-song English, and are remarkably happy, helpful and pleasant. They appeared delighted to see us, but oddly uninterested in Napoleon. The house where he stayed his first night on the island is perversely called Wellington House, and only the efforts by the French have preserved Longwood and Napoleon's tomb for posterity. Nonetheless, I was reluctant to leave this island of happiness.

In 1815 the government took the island over from the East India Company to house its illustrious prisoner—and to forestall any Bonapartist rescue attempts they simultaneously took over St Helena's immediate neighbours, the Ascension Islands, half a dozen rocks a mere 600 miles away, and Tristan da Cunha. At this time the population on St Helena was some 3,000 souls most of whom lived in the one town, Jamestown, which sits uncomfortably in the cleft of a wedge on the leeward side of the island, facing a deep sheltered bay. The town consisted of a small street across the beach, the marina, and another, about 300 yards long, at right angles to it.

In October 1815 the townspeople were, of course, in a considerable state of excitement, having heard a day or two before of their guest. (They were so isolated that the news of his coming among them was the first that they had heard of his escape from Elba.)

The Governor General, Colonel Wilks, came on board the *Northumberland* soon after it moored. He was introduced to Napoleon. There was, he explained, some difficulty finding accommodation for the French, so everyone had to remain on the ship for the next 24 hours. The normal and reasonably private accommodation for distinguished guests was Castle House, but it was too near the sea.

Eventually, accommodation was found in a boarding house on the main street owned by Mr Henry Porteous. To prevent 'many prying eyes on his arrival', Napoleon requested that they delay their disembarkation until the evening time.

The gig carrying Napoleon and Count Bertrand arrived at Jamestown harbour after sunset. By this time most of the crowds that had been anxiously waiting for a glimpse of the great man had dispersed, but rumour quickly circulated that Napoleon and his entourage were in Porteous'. A crowd gathered outside, hoping he might show his face at the door or even the window. The house was clean and neat, but small and completely lacking in privacy. O'Meara recalls: 'Counts Bertrand and Montholon (who, with their ladies, Count Las Cases and his son, General Gourgaud and myself) were also accommodated in the house.' Napoleon was unable to go out or even walk from his bedroom without being seen.

'At a very early hour on the morning of the 18th Napoleon, accompanied by the Admiral and Las Cases, proceeded to Longwood, a coun-

Longwood as it appeared in 1816

try seat of the Lieutenant-Governor's which had been chosen as the place most proper for his future residence.' This house, for Napoleon and his entire retinue, was situated high in the mountain about four miles from Jamestown. Although Napoleon was keen to get away from the prying eyes of the townspeople, as Barry O'Meara put it, Longwood's appearance was 'sombre and unpromising'. It was no better than a lightly-built country cottage, with five rooms, intended for use only a few months a year. It was totally inadequate for the Emperor and his suite which was eventually to amount to over forty persons. O'Meara learned later that the locals were astonished at the choice, regarding the situation as bleak and exposed. The house had never before been lived in for more than a few months a year. Local rumour assumed that a winter residence would also be provided.

The location was evidently chosen more for security reasons than any thought of the personal comfort of the inhabitants. Longwood was perched on a high plateau at an altitude of 1,800 feet, and crucially on the windward side of the island. For the three hottest months of the year the cool was attractive. For the remaining nine months the house was regularly surrounded by a thick damp mist and subjected to a piercing cold southern wind. It often rained for days on end—unrelentingly. There was no water, and no shade—the few trees were bent horizontal by the constant wind. The nearby 1,500-acre estate of gumwood trees was depressingly called Deadwood.

The state of the house made it clear that a considerable amount of work would be necessary to make Longwood habitable. On the way up Napoleon had noticed a beautiful little house in a quiet valley about a mile and a half from Jamestown. Called 'The Briars' it belonged to a Mr William Balcombe, a purveyor for the East India Company. The house was surrounded by trees, a green lawn and a well-kept garden. To the side, on the elevated plateau, stood a small pavilion consisting of one good room on the ground floor and two attic rooms above. It looked beautiful and peaceful, just what Napoleon wanted. Admiral Cockburn and the party accordingly went to The Briars, and the Emperor expressed his desire to remain there.

In her *Recollections* Betsy Balcombe takes up the story: 'My family at the time of the Emperor's arrival consisted of my father, my mother, my elder sister, myself and my two brothers, who were quite children. My father had offered Sir George Cockburn apartments at the cottage, and he immediately assured us of his willingness to resign them to General Bonaparte as the situation seemed to please him so much. Napoleon determined on not going down to the town again, and wished his rooms to be got ready for him immediately.' Betsy, who was possibly fifteen at the time, was quickly smitten by the great man, the celebrity of the world landed in their garden, and there is no doubt that Napoleon was happy to encourage her. Her *Recollections*, written many years later, after an unfortunate marriage, is the diary of a teenage girl who falls in love with a very powerful man.

Napoleon's camp-bed was put up without delay and to keep him company, Count Las Cases and his fourteen-year-old son occupied the two garrets overhead. A marquee was attached to the front of the building and fitted up as a dining-room. Here Napoleon spent the first two months of his island captivity in total relaxation, the first such episode since his abdication. The house was private as it was surrounded by trees; there was a high waterfall to the back. The garden was warm, secluded, and filled with various fruits such as peaches, lemons, grapes, figs, oranges and mangoes. Napoleon spent his time reading and dictating his memoirs to Las Cases.

In the evening he invited himself into the family to play cards, eat or perhaps just to enjoy the family life. Of the two teenage girls, Jane, the eldest, was quite reserved and somewhat afraid of Napoleon. Betsy was tall for her years, blonde, and was jealously described by Madame Bertrand as 'a fully-grown woman with the mind of a teenage girl'. Both girls spoke French. Betsy in particular had an excellent singing voice and played the guitar quite well. During the months of his stay at The Briars, she tried to teach the Emperor English, and also dancing, the guitar and tried even to make him sing—the latter with very little success as Napoleon was tone deaf! However, the Emperor enjoyed all her efforts immensely.

Once arrangements were completed the Admiral and the rest returned to Jamestown. (Dr O'Meara would come up to The Briars each morning.) Some chairs were brought out on the lawn and seating himself, Napoleon asked Betsy to sit beside him. In her *Recollections* she describes his appearance: 'I was able to inspect his face more carefully. He had a remarkable profile, straight nose, strong jaw, olive skin and fine brown silky hair, just like a child's. He had perfectly white straight teeth and when he smiled it was like the sun coming from behind a cloud.' He enquired if she knew the capitals of Europe, France, Italy, and Russia? 'Petersburg now,' she replied, 'Moscow formerly.' 'On my saying this,' she remembered, 'he turned abruptly round and fixing his piercing eyes full on my face, he demanded sternly: "*Qui l'a brûlé?*" Betsy hesitated—she was afraid to answer. He repeated the question more forcefully. She stammered "I do not know, Sir." "*Oui, oui,*" he replied, laughing violently. "*Vous savez très bien, c'est moi qui l'a brûlé!*' On seeing him laugh I gained a little courage and said, "I believe, Sir, the Russians burned it to get rid of the French."'

That evening Napoleon came into the house and as neither Mr nor Mrs Balcombe spoke French he addressed himself to Betsy. He asked her if she played music—adding that he supposed she was too young to play herself. Rather piqued, she replied that not alone could she play but she could also sing, which she did. When she finished, Napoleon said that it was the prettiest English air that he had ever heard. Betsy replied rather brusquely that it was Scottish. He then asked her to sing 'Vivre Henri Quatre'. She said she did not know it, so Napoleon stood up and sang, but 'as with his subsequent attempts at singing I never could discover what tune he was executing.' Despite this, so passed Napoleon's first pleasant evening with the happy Balcombe family.

There followed a curious moment of calm in the Emperor's life. It was, after all, barely a year since he had escaped from his previous island prison, Elba, reasserted himself as ruler of France and plunged once

The pavilion at The Briars, where Napoleon spent his first two months on the island.

again into warfare against the massed armies of Europe. Now he was to spend two months as the guest of an English country gentleman, with as his principal companion a hoydenish fifteen-year-old girl. Betsy Balcombe had a wild streak which evidently appealed to the Emperor. Napoleon allowed her a fool's privilege of entry to his presence, and encouraged her chatter about local doings (she and her sister had learned French from a servant). Most of his day was spent working on his memoirs with Las Cases or Bertrand, Montholon or Gourgaud. Visitors called, but Napoleon did not leave the grounds.

According to Betsy, the Emperor's habits during his stay were simple and regular. He got up at 8 a.m. and had nothing more than coffee for breakfast. He lunched at 1 and dined at 9 p.m. in the evening. He retired to bed at about 11 p.m. Betsy recalls constantly meeting him: 'His manner was so unaffected, kind and amiable that in a few days I felt perfectly at ease in his company and looked upon him more as a companion of my own age rather than a mighty warrior!'

Napoleon lived very simply and cared little or nothing about what he ate. When finished he abruptly pushed his chair away from the table and quit the dining-room, 'apparently glad it was over!' Betsy records in her memoirs many trifling incidents—such as getting Napoleon to pretend he was a monster. Napoleon enjoyed romping, physical games; he

had, she reports, a 'boyish love of mirth and glee, not unmixed sometimes with a tinge of malice'. She records her indignation at his shame-
less cheating at cards. He regularly teased her about marrying young
Las Cases, who was then only fourteen. Betsy was furious at Napoleon
treating her as a child (especially as she wished to attend a ball some
weeks later which she feared her father might not allow). The Emperor,
noting her annoyance, held both her hands behind her back and ordered the young lad to kiss her, which, being a gallant Frenchman, he
did. Once Betsy was free she hit him as hard as she could across the
face.

On another occasion Napoleon showed her his 'costly and elegant
sword'. Impulsively she decided to take revenge for some earlier slight,
and 'drew the blade out quickly from the scabbard and began to flour-
ish it over his head, making passes at him, the Emperor retreating until
at last I had him fairly pinned up in the corner. I kept telling him all the
time that he had better say his prayers for I was going to kill him. My
sister and Las Cases ran in and begged me to instantly desist, but I only
laughed and maintained my post—until my arm dropped from sheer
exhaustion.'

Napoleon then caught her ear (which had been pierced only the day
before) and pinched it, giving rise to great pain. He then pulled her
nose heartily in good fun. His good humour never left him during the
whole scene. On another occasion, coming at the end of a single file
descending a narrow garden stairway, she deliberately crashed into the
person in front of her so that they tumbled like dominoes and, to the
horror of Las Cases, even knocked Napoleon. Sometimes indeed she
went too far—on one occasion her father punished her rudeness to
Napoleon by locking her in the cellar. The dark and gloom were bad
enough, but the worst were the famous St Helena rats 'who leaped about
me on all sides. I was half-dead with horror and should most certainly
have been devoured alive by the vermin had I not in despair seized a
bottle of wine and dashed it among my assailants.' The contest continued, at the expense of Mr Balcombe's cellar, until both she and the rats
were overcome by alcohol.

Meanwhile Admiral Cockburn and his seamen were bustling about
getting Longwood ready. Their brisk activity caused no little surprise
among the local tradesmen who were unused to such a pace of work. As
O'Meara put it, 'the Admiral was frequently seen to arrive at Longwood
shortly after sunrise, stimulating by his presence the St Helena work-

men who, in general lazy and indolent, beheld with astonishment the dispatch and activity of the sailors.' By early December (high summer in those latitudes) Longwood was ready for some of Napoleon's party. So, greatly to the besotted Betsy's dismay, Napoleon, Count and Countess Montholon and the Las Cases moved into what was to be the Emperor's last home. O'Meara lived in a tent at Longwood until his room was ready.

Longwood

The building chosen to be Napoleon's residence was originally a barn erected to store the oats, barley and wheat that attempts were being made to grow nearby. These failing, in 1797 the Governor General had it converted into a makeshift 'holiday home' for use a couple of months a year. It had been built on a high desolate plateau on the coldest and wettest part of the island. During the hottest months of the year, January, February and March, it afforded some relief from the equatorial heat of Jamestown. For three months the climate was almost Mediterranean. However, for the remaining months of the year the house was shrouded in mist and fog. It would rain constantly for many days. From April until the end of the year the cold southern wind would increase, and once this hit the high cliffs and mountains of St Helena it would be swept up into the atmosphere creating clouds, mist, fog and constant heavy rain.

Despite its proximity to the equator (16° south) the plateau often became extremely cold. Once the sun went down the temperature could fall by over 10°C. The evening air would turn into a claustrophobic wet mist, blocking out everything, the sun, the moon, the stars. Unlike around The Briars, the vegetation was sparse. Apart from a few eucalyptus trees, few plants could thrive on this inhospitable plain. Only rough grass, which was quite inedible for animals, and a peculiar gumwood tree could survive here. The sap from these ugly looking trees provided nourishment for millions of large blue flies. For the consumption of the British public, this bleak environment was presented as a wooden palace, 'the gardens teeming with flowers'; and a fanciful drawing was released of 'Longwood House, from the flower garden', embellished with parterres, trees and shrubs.

During the hot summer months the relentless sun would beat down on the cardboard roof painted with thick coats of tar. The burning tropical heat would melt the tar; this would, in turn drip down. More problematic were the rats. It was they, so it was said, that had caused the failure of the crops, and now they were everywhere. As O'Meara wrote, 'the rats are so numerous at Longwood, and so fearless that they often assemble even in daytime to feed when the kitchen offal is thrown out *(in their feeding frenzy they often devoured one another)* . . . the floors at Longwood were so perforated with their holes as to resemble sieves. Napoleon's own dining-room was particularly infested with them; one of these obnoxious animals sprung out of his hat when he was going to put it on after dinner.'

The rooms were separated by a wooden double panelling, just sufficiently wide to allow the passage of these large black rats. To eliminate the pest, rat-hunting became a favourite sport. At dusk the servants would uncover the holes and wait until the rats crept out looking for food. On a signal they would charge in with dogs and cats, close up the holes and start to slaughter the vermin. The rats would turn on their attackers, biting some of the servants quite viciously.

When the rains came there was the additional problem of leaking roofs, when water came in everywhere. O'Meara recorded: 'This is partly caused by the bad construction of the roofs which are in a great measure formed of boards and brown paper, smeared over with a composition of pitch and tar which when melted by the rays of the sun runs off and leaves open a number of chinks through which the rain finds an easy admission.' In the rainy season 'the French officers and their ladies have been repeatedly compelled by the rain to get up several times in the night to shift their own and their children's beds'. Madame Montholon had great difficulty in keeping her children, sleeping in their cots, dry at night, and making sure there were no rats asleep with them. Daily repairs, plugging up holes with cloth or wood were very often insufficient to keep the place dry. O'Meara's own room was frequently inundated, but, as an old seadog, he was more used to such inconveniences.

Life in Longwood

Napoleon's household at Longwood consisted of around forty persons. The principal attendants were Count Montholon and his wife and three children, General Gourgaud, and Count de Las Cases and his young son. Count Bertrand, with his wife and children, lived in a separate house about a mile away. There were also numerous servants, headed by Louis Marchand, Napoleon's valet, and including three stable hands. Barry O'Meara also had a room in the house, as did Captain Poppleton, the orderly officer, under whose immediate care Napoleon was.

In the claustrophobic atmosphere the aristocrats did not, unfortunately, see eye to eye: Montholon and Gourgaud indeed were so much at loggerheads that Napoleon had to forbid them to fight a duel. In his memoirs Gourgaud refers to Las Cases as 'a Jesuit' who was only on the island to get what he could out of the situation. In addition, Montholon blamed Las Cases for mishandling the situation immediately after Napoleon's abdication that had led them to their present plight. Many writers, including myself, believe that Napoleon had an affair with Madame Montholon, and perhaps others, and certainly Longwood residents conducted affairs with women of the island. It should be remembered that all the actors in this drama were comparatively young. Napoleon himself was forty-six, Bertrand forty-two, Gourgaud and Montholon thirty-two; Las Cases was the old man of the party at forty-nine. Barry O'Meara was now thirty-three.

The conditions set by Admiral Cockburn in which England's great prisoner was kept were elaborately strict. No one could risk a repetition of his escape from Elba only eighteen months before. It was estimated that the total cost of keeping Napoleon on St Helena was £91,000 a year (almost the same as the £65,000 paid to the Prince of Wales plus the £35,000 a year paid to his estranged wife.) More than half of this went in sustaining the naval surveillance, including the islands of Tristan da Cunha and Ascension.

On the island a central space was allotted to Napoleon within which he could ride or walk without being accompanied by a British officer. Within this space were camps of the 53rd and 66th regiments which supplied the troops for the guards at the entrance to Longwood and around the perimeter. At night these guards closed in to create a tight cordon, and Napoleon was not allowed to leave the building. Visitors required permission firstly from the Governor and then from Count Bertrand.

Further sentries were placed on all the paths leading to the sea, and around the island two warships patrolled constantly. No foreign vessels, unless in severe distress, were allowed into Jamestown harbour, and all the island's fishing boats were numbered and checked in every night by a naval officer. The strict controls insisted on by the authorities affected the people of the island also. On one memorable occasion a large party, including Betsy Balcombe and her family, went on a picnic on a remote side of the island. Unfortunately, the journey and the festivities took so

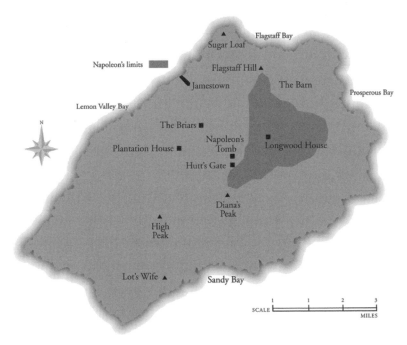

St Helena in 1815

long that they were still out when the great gun on Ladder Hill, James-town, announced the curfew. Now nobody could move about the is-land without authority; since the Balcombes did not know the pass-word, when they were accosted by a sentry they had to spend the night in a guard room—'a wretched night' as Betsy Balcombe remembered, 'eaten up by fleas, mosquitoes and all sorts of horrible things'. The tight control kept over the island was illustrated by Betsy Balcombe's story of a young midshipman rowing guard around the island. Apparently his voice giving the password could not be heard over the roar of the surf. Not hearing the countersign, the guards instantly opened fire on the boat, though fortunately without injury.

The rats and rain of Longwood did not appear to upset Napoleon much. What worried him was boredom. Despite the appalling state of the house he decided to turn it into as near as possible an Imperial Palace. He established a protocol, which would be maintained until the very end. Every one of his staff knew their place. He would be addressed as *'Votre Majesté'*. People would stand and remove their hats when he entered a room. They would remain standing until the Emperor sat down. No one could sit until directed to do so. No one was expected to speak unless spoken to. The four aristocratic officers, who were in attendance upon him, only spoke in muted whispers. As their memoirs reveal, they were in constant jealous competition with one another in trying to please Napoleon.

Once they had settled in Napoleon gave everyone a specific daily task. Boredom accompanied by bad food and cold weather would be disastrous. They all realised that they were in for a long stay. Napoleon insisted that everybody must be occupied, especially those nearest to him—Bertrand, Montholon, Las Cases and his secretary Gourgaud. To each, he gave the task of writing part of his military history. This would keep them at arm's length from one another.

Longwood would be kept as clean and as tidy as possible. The food—what there was of it—would be prepared properly, and every evening they would dress for dinner.

The first few months at Longwood were quite pleasant. The new visitors were fortunate with the weather. Occasional flowers appeared and the view was perfect. The sun at mid-day was unbearably hot despite the altitude and the cold trade winds from the south-east. When Napoleon was feeling well, a lively conversation would take place over dinner, usually about the day's events. Often the meal would take place quickly and in silence. Dinner was always served by candlelight as there was only one small window in the dining-room. The servants, dressed in livery, stood on either side of the Emperor, ready to serve him the next course immediately. Napoleon always ate quickly. Following dinner, he would seek out a play or have some pages from a novel read aloud. He usually retired to his room at ten or eleven and went to bed soon afterwards.

Social life on St Helena

Despite its isolation in the vast expanse of the southern Atlantic Ocean, Jamestown was, to the dismay of Napoleon's gaolers, in constant contact with the outside world. There was an active social life and with the influx of British soldiers the island took on the appearance of an English colony in India.

The islanders were delighted with the addition of over two thousand Europeans. Among these were, of course, the officers and men sent to guard Napoleon, and also three Commissioners sent by the Allies to oversee the conditions on the island: Baron von Sturmer and his wife on behalf of Austria, Count Balmain on behalf of Russia and the Mar-

The author standing in front of Longwood as it is today. Note the French flag.

quis de Montchenu on behalf of France. Long before the arrival of the *Northumberland,* Jamestown had been quite a busy port. Every week two or three large vessels, sailing either north or south, would drop anchor at Jamestown, pay an agreed fee. and take on fresh water and food. Visitors were many. While Napoleon was in residence, as Barry O'Meara put it, 'officers and respectable passengers from China and India came in numbers to Longwood to request a presentation to the fallen chief; in which expectation they were rarely disappointed.'

Monotony was relieved by many activities such as cocktail parties, evening balls, private theatricals, dinner parties, shooting parties and most important of all the bi-annual race meeting at Deadwood. This race meeting, organised by Captain Henry Rous (a future director of the English Turf Club) was the social event of the year. Eight horses would run in each race.

Napoleon settled into a routine. As Barry O'Meara recorded, he rose at seven and wrote or dictated until breakfast which was generally served in his room between nine and ten. After breakfast he worked again on his memoirs, and at two or three received such visitors as had been directed to present themselves. Between four and five, when the weather permitted he rode out on horseback, accompanied by his suite, and then dictated or read until eight when dinner was announced.

When bored or when he had finished with his dictation, he would ask Barry O'Meara to translate some English newspapers or perhaps a novel that he could not understand. This inevitably led to long conversations on the subject matter which O'Meara had translated. They would discuss for hours problems of medicine, philosophy, religion and war. In the course of these discussions Napoleon would occasionally exercise his curiously physical way of showing affection, by gently slapping O'Meara's face, or pinching his earlobe.

So far, Napoleon had adapted well to the island. He took plenty of exercise and made sure he ate properly. He was waiting. He had hoped for a change of heart in the British government or even a change of government, which might allow him to return to England. He knew that there was a small but well-connected group of Bonapartists urging his return. His treatment on St Helena, in differently exaggerated stories, had certainly become something of a *cause célèbre* in England, but in the prevailing conservative mood it was, in truth, unlikely that he would be allowed back to Europe.

For the moment all was well. The weather was agreeable and apparently the French were settling in. People came to visit Napoleon each day. Barry O'Meara was often invited to join Napoleon and his companions at dinner. His conversation apparently livened up their evening meal, which sometimes had been eaten in total silence. They all appeared to appreciate his company. On 15 April 1816 O'Meara was again invited to join the French for their formal evening dinner. Before the coffee was served Napoleon turned to him and said, 'Dr O'Meara, you must write your diary.' 'That is very generous of you, your Excellency—but why should I write such a diary?' Napoleon replied, 'because, my good friend—it will make you a fortune! Promise me, however—you will not publish your work until I am dead.' O'Meara replied: 'I am flattered and greatly honoured, your Excellency. Yes, I will do so. I will even start this evening, and yes, I promise I will not publish this work until you are dead.' 'Good, good', replied Napoleon, 'now for coffee.'

That night O'Meara returned to his room. By guttering candlelight he dipped his quill pen into a black inkpot and wrote the first page of his massive diary. This work would extend to over 1,800 pages of tightly written, almost illegible script. He would record all the events of each day, as he saw it, for the next three years. He would also remain true to his word and not publish until the death of Napoleon in 1821.

Although Napoleon retained his sense of outrage that the British had, as he thought, so illegitimately captured and imprisoned him, life on the island was tolerable. But on 15 April 1816 a new Governor Gen-

Approaching St Helena in 2005: the looming cliffs of volcanic rock reach as much as 200 feet above the sea.
'Nothing,' wrote Barry O'Meara, 'could be more desolate than the appearance of the island.'

St Helena harbour in 2005—as in Napoleon's day, ships drop anchor a thousand metres from shore and visitors are ferried to land by lifeboat.

Jamestown is still the only town on the island, jammed between two steep mountains on the warmer side of the island. There are about 400 houses.

eral, Sir Hudson Lowe, came to replace Sir George Cockburn. The *Phaeton*, with Sir Hudson and his family and staff, actually arrived the previous evening. As it was Sunday, Lowe decided to delay his landing. He wished to have a large welcoming committee for his arrival. Life on the island was about to change forever

Sir Hudson Lowe

The new Governor-General was to remain in office as long as his distinguished prisoner was alive. Sir Hudson Lowe was a small, thin, rather nervous individual. He was born in Ireland, in Galway, four months before Napoleon in Corsica, and three months after Wellington, in Dublin. His father was a Scottish surgeon in the British army, who had fought with distinction in the Seven-Year War. Posted to Ireland, the surgeon there met a young Irish girl, whom he eventually married. In 1769 she gave birth to a small, puny, redheaded boy, whom they christened Hudson. Within three months of the delivery Dr Lowe was sent to the West Indies. Mrs Lowe became pregnant again, but sadly, both she and her new-born daughter died in childbirth.

The young boy, Hudson, was destined to follow his father around the world, grabbing here and there what little education he could. At the age of twelve he became an ensign in the Devon militia, and at the age of nineteen he was commissioned into the army. His army career was not marked by great military achievement. He appears to have been constantly on the move, more a bureaucrat than a fighter. In Gibraltar he was reprimanded by the great General O'Hara. Given leave of absence, he was allowed to travel in southern Europe in order to improve his·Italian and French. Once back in the army he was sent to Corsica, to Ajaccio. However, despite the legend, he did not live in 'Casa Bonaparte'—that distinction is given to an Irishman, Lieutenant Ford, who wrote: 'I was treated very kindly and entertained by three young girls running around barefooted. Madame Letizia was kind, but always gave me the impression I was not there.'

Hudson Lowe was transferred to various islands in the Mediterranean, ending up in Minorca. This island had many Corsican immigrants—most had been forced into service. Hudson Lowe selected 500 of these immigrants, and formed a small battalion, called the Corsican Rangers. This group was sent to Egypt with Abercrombie. There is no record of the Rangers having taken part in any of the action at Alexandria. Lowe always appeared to be on the periphery of battles. One evening he advised a sentry not to shoot an approaching stranger who turned out to be Sir Sidney Smith. Much has been made of this; Captain Lowe has been 'acknowledged' as having saved the life of the heroic Admiral who for once appeared to have been on dry land. In 1803, Sir Sidney Smith placed Captain Lowe and his Corsican Rangers in command of the small island of Capri. He had cannon and 1400 men. When General Lemarque attacked the island, Hudson Lowe surrendered. As with so much of the career of this awkward man, this action became controversial. The official story is that the French attacked the island with over 3,000 men, and that with the poor quality of his Maltese auxiliaries and a lack of sea support Lowe had no choice. Others, including notably the historian of the Peninsular Wars, Sir William Napier, took a tougher view; Napier reported that 'Hudson Lowe first became known in history—by losing in a few days a post that could have been defended for just as many years!' All the soldiers were made prisoners of war. General Lemarque dropped Hudson Lowe back on the warm sands of Sicily—to explain his disastrous defence of Capri.

Over the next few years Lowe was sent to various islands in the Ionian Sea. He eventually returned to England and, with Sir Alexander Home, was sent to Sweden in order to persuade Count Prince Bernadotte to fight against Napoleon.

Just before the Battle of Waterloo in 1815 he was in Brussels and fell foul of the Duke of Wellington. As the Iron Duke later told the old parliamentary gossip Thomas Creevey, 'I found him Quarter-Master-General of the army here and I presently found the damned fellow would instruct me in the equipment of the army, always producing the Prussians to me as model; so I was obliged to tell him I had commanded a much larger army in the field than any Prussian general and that I was not to learn from their service how to equip an army. I thought this would have stopped him, but shortly afterwards the damned fellow was at me again about the equipment etc. of the Prussians; so I was obliged to write home and complain of him and the Government were kind enough to take him away from me.' Sir William de Lancey replaced him and was killed during battle. Returning to Belgium, Hudson Lowe proposed that a monument should be constructed at Mont St Jean. Later that year, when living in Marseille, he was informed that he had been appointed Governor-General of St Helena with specific instructions in respect to Napoleon.

When asked about Hudson Lowe's appointment, Wellington replied

Sir Hudson Lowe—a typical French portrayal, accentuating 'perfidious Albion'

that it was 'a very bad choice; he was a man wanting in education and judgement. He was a stupid man, who knew nothing of the world . . . and he was suspicious and jealous . . . I always thought that Lowe was the most unfit person to be charged with the care of Bonaparte's person.' (We have seen that Wellington claimed intimate knowledge of St Helena as a result of calling in on his way from India. 'I looked at every part,' he told Creevey, 'on my return from the East Indies. There are only three or four places by which a prisoner could escape, and they could be guarded by a mere handful of men.') Another senior officer said that Lowe 'is troublesome and unreasonable beyond endurance. He is stupid, suspicious, and occasionally jealous. He appears to succeed in quarrelling with everyone.'

On his appointment, Hudson Lowe rushed back to London. His detailed instructions from Lord Bathurst, the Government Minister in charge of the colonies, stressed that he was to make every effort to ensure that Napoleon should not escape from the island. On the other hand, subject to security, he was also asked to try and make life as agreeable as possible for the new inhabitants of St Helena. Achieving a sensible balance between these two objectives was to prove impossible for the prosaic military bureaucrat.

Before Hudson Lowe's departure to St Helena he was invited to Holland House, the epicentre of British Bonapartism. News of Napoleon's deportation to the Southern Atlantic they found quite shattering. Lady Holland skilfully organised no fewer than eight excellent dinner parties for Sir Hudson. She invited close family friends, Captain Maitland and even the dull Post Master General, Lord Ossulston (whose main claim to fame was that he had been at the famous meeting in the Star and Garter where the rules of cricket were established).

Lady Holland found Sir Hudson Lowe 'humourless, reserved, and occasionally abrupt'. On each occasion she was unable to win over the stern autocratic Lowe. At their final dinner she enquired if Sir Hudson had ever seen Napoleon. 'Yes,' was the reply, 'at the battle of Bautzen in 1813.' (Las Cases reports that Napoleon learned of this and augured well from the coincidence: 'We have then probably exchanged a few cannonballs together, and that is always in my eyes a noble relation to stand in.')

Lady Holland asked if she could communicate with Napoleon or even Madame Bertrand. The reply was that 'all letters must go through the Governor-General's house on the island. These are my instructions, Madam.' While in London, Hudson Lowe took the opportunity to visit Mrs Susan Johnston—the sister of Sir William de Lancey, his successor as Quarter-Master-General who had been killed at Waterloo. This was Mrs Johnston's second bereavement in just one year. Some days following the first interview Lowe returned with a proposal of marriage. The startled Mrs Johnston said 'she would consider it'. She was a widow. She had two teenage daughters to support. If she accepted the proposal she would have a title, wealth and most importantly, position. It was not too difficult to make up her mind. Within a week they wed, and at the end of February 1816 she, now Lady Lowe, sailed with her family to St Helena.

The frigate *Phaeton* arrived at Jamestown in mid-April. The journey from England had taken 75 days. On board were Lieutenant-General Sir Hudson Lowe, KCB, GCMG, his wife and step-daughter Charlotte Johnston; his staff, including Sir Thomas Reade and Colonel Lyster of the militia, Mr Baxter, Inspector of Hospitals, and others, especially Major Gorrequer, Lowe's private secretary, whose racy diaries of life inside the Governor's residence, *Plantation House,* were subsequently decoded and published. These men were to form the critical support group to Lowe in his struggles with Longwood. He moved immediately into Plantation House, and made plans to see Napoleon as soon as possible.

Barry O'Meara describes how 'a little before nine a.m. Sir Hudson Lowe arrived in the midst of a pelting storm of wind and rain, accompanied by Sir George Cockburn and followed by his numerous staff. As the hour fixed upon was rather unseasonable, and one at which Napoleon had never received any persons, intimation was given to the Governor that Napoleon was indisposed and could not receive any visitors that morning.'

Hudson Lowe was disconcerted. He did not know quite what to do. 'After pacing up and down before the windows of the drawing-room for a few minutes,' he accepted defeat and arranged an appointment for two the following day. When the group appeared again the following day, a minor farce ensued. Hudson Lowe and Admiral Cockburn were shown into an antechamber. Two men, Santini *(a Corsican usher who eventually became the guardian of Napoleon's tomb at Les Invalides)* and Noverraz *(third valet at Longwood)*, stood guard on either side of the door leading to Napoleon's room. The visitors were invited to sit while Count Bertrand announced their arrival to the Emperor. After a considerable wait, the door opened, and the Governor was called for. Hudson Lowe moved quickly into Napoleon's room, leaving the Admiral behind. When Sir George presented himself he was refused entry by Noverraz. 'Only one,' he said.

The door was closed. Napoleon was leaning with his elbow on the mantelpiece. Lowe, standing erect, removed his helmet and declared: 'I am Lieutenant-General Sir Hudson Lowe. I am the new Governor of the island.' Napoleon did not move but said, rather flatteringly, 'I hear you speak both Italian and French?' 'I am quite fluent in both,' replied Lowe. 'Very well then,' replied Napoleon, 'we will speak in Italian—you may sit down.'

The conversation came to nothing. Napoleon started first by declaring the illegality of his detention on the island. He also complained about the sanitation and the dreadful state of Longwood. 'Surely there must be a better house on the island where the weather is more agreeable?' Lowe answered that his orders, which came directly from the Government and Lord Bathurst, must be obeyed to the letter. After twenty minutes or so of futile conversation, Napoleon realised that there was no point to the meeting. He firmly informed the Governor that 'he could go'—and dismissed him.

This was the first act in a long conflict from which neither side emerges with credit. At the same time as he described Lowe as 'a damned fool', Wellington, in his commonsensical way, described it thus. 'Bonaparte is so damned intractable a fellow there is no knowing how to deal with him. To be sure, as to the means employed to keep him there never was anything so damned absurd.' Lowe and the British Government's greatest fear was that Napoleon would escape. To prevent this possibility Lowe insisted that three ships should constantly sail around St Helena. Cannons were mounted on every vantage-point. Sentries were posted on every road. He ensured that the elaborate system of flags and military signals devised by the government and sent to his predecessor Governor Wilks be utilised so that the Governor's residence, Plantation House, could be informed immediately of any unexpected event. A blue flag (he had nightmares about this colour) would indicate that 'General Bonaparte is missing'.

Dispatches from London made Lowe even more nervous. The responsibility was far too much for him. He was constantly made conscious of wild schemes being devised by Bonapartists, notably those with a

General Lallemman in Texas (Napoleon's brother Joseph was living in Philadelphia at this time). If Napoleon disappeared, his career would end in failure. As a result, a series of increasingly petty and restrictive measures were taken with a view to isolating the French. Typical of these rules was one forbidding the local shopkeepers from selling them goods on credit; then the officers of the 53rd, who were in the habit of visiting Madame Bertrand in her house at Hutt's Gate were officially discouraged, and the guards were told to report to the Governor the names of those who did visit. Those who did visit were expected to provide the Governor with detailed reports of the conversation. Barry O'Meara reported 'a sensation of unwillingness to approach the exiles' among the ordinary people of the island, no doubt officially stimulated, that was very different from the cheerful and hearty welcome previously experienced before Sir Hudson Lowe arrived.

Chapter 5: Barry O'Meara's diary

After six months on St Helena, encouraged, as we have seen, by Napoleon, Barry O'Meara began to keep a daily record of his doings and conversations with his great patient. This chapter consists of extracts and summaries from those diaries (which in the original constitute over 1800 pages). Where necessary, I have added comments in italics.

The diary is in the well-known European genre of 'table-talk' of the great, which stretches from Luther and Voltaire to Dr Johnson. It constitutes a major source for Napoleon's attitudes and ideas, and there is no reason to suspect that O'Meara was not an accurate recorder of what he understood. Napoleon's position is more nuanced; he is reluctant to admit mistakes, for instance in the invasion of Spain or Russia, or at Waterloo; occasionally he uses the presence of an eager hearer to work off scores, particularly against those still politically prominent in France such as Talleyrand or Chateaubriand; a constant theme is the character of the English, of whom O'Meara, an Irishman, is taken as representative; at other times the true voice of the Revolution comes through, or the statesman with a striking view of the plasticity of world affairs.

Despite many rivals this remains the most vivid and exciting account of Napoleon's captivity; the insider's view of the contest between Napoleon and his chief jailer is, of course, a major theme. As with everything to do with Napoleon, it has proved controversial, particularly in its depiction of Hudson Lowe and the British officials on the island.

The great 19th-century Scottish writer Thomas Carlyle spoke for many, however, when he declared that 'O'Meara's work has greatly increased my respect for Napoleon'. He was entranced by the spectacle of 'this great man in his dreary prison house, captive, sick, despised, forsaken, yet rising above it all by the stern force of his own unconquerable spirit.'

The diary starts a few days after the arrival on 14 April of the Phaeton, *bearing Sir Hudson Lowe, his staff and party, and the awkward first visit of the new Governor.*

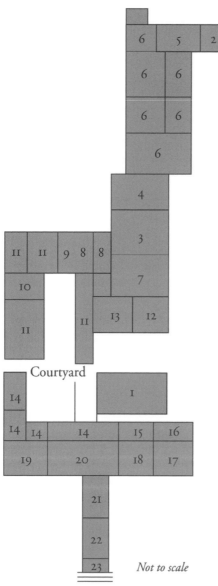

1 Servants' room
2 O'Meara's room
3 Dining-room used by
O'Meara & officers
4 Gourgaud
5 O'Meara's room
6 Montholon family
7 Duty officers
8 Las Cases
9 Pharmacy
10 Silverware
11 Servants
12 Linen room
13 Kitchen
14 Staff quarters
15 Valet
16 Bathroom
17 The Emperor's bedroom
18 The study
19 Library
20 Dining-room
21 Sitting-room
22 Billiard-room
23 Veranda

A ground-plan of the rooms as Longwood

18 April 1816

I brought some newspapers to Napoleon. When he asked 'who had lent them?', I replied, 'from Admiral Cockburn'. He then said, 'I believe he was rather ill treated the day when he came with the new Governor. What does he say about it?' I replied 'The Admiral considered it an insult offered to him, and certainly felt greatly offended by it.' Napoleon, remembering certain indignities offered to him when he was first on the *Northumberland*, replied, 'I shall never see him with pleasure, but he did not announce himself as being desirous of seeing me.'

During our discussion, a letter from Sir Hudson Lowe arrived demanding that all the domestics who worked in Longwood and who were willing to stay, must sign a form stating so. Once signed, they would be compelled to remain on the island during the lifetime of Bonaparte. This, however, did not deter anyone of them from signing the paper.

19 April 1816

The weather has been extremely bad for some days. Napoleon was a little depressed. 'In this *isola maladetta*, there is neither sun nor moon to be seen, just constant rain and fog,' he complained. Later he commented on some absurd falsehoods in the newspapers respecting him. 'Was it possible,' he asked, 'that the English could be so foolishly credulous as to believe all the stuff published about him?'

21 April 1816

Colonel and Miss Laura Wilks came up to Longwood and had a long interview with Napoleon. He was greatly pleased with Miss Wilks (a highly accomplished and elegant young lady) and gallantly told her 'she exceeded the description, which had been given of her to him'. (*Wilks was the East India Company's Governor from June 1813 to April 1816 when he was replaced by Hudson Lowe. Towards the end of his life Wellington said that it had been a mistake removing Wilks who was 'a very intelligent, well-read man and knew everything that had been passing in Europe and Napoleon had become attached to him.'*)

24 April 1816

The weather still gloomy. Napoleon at first out of spirits but gradually became enlivened. We discussed Admiral Cockburn, who he professed to esteem as a man of talent in his profession. 'But he is rough, overbearing, vain, choleric, and capricious; never consulting anybody; jealous of his authority; caring little for the manner in which he exercises it and sometimes violent without dignity.'

Napoleon asked me if I took fees for attending sick people on the island. I replied in the negative, which seemed to surprise him. 'In your country, particularly, every man has his trade; the member of Parliament takes money for his vote, the ministers for their places, the lawyers for their opinions.'

26 April 1816

Napoleon asked me if every ship in the Royal Navy was supplied with a chronometer; to which I replied in the negative. He commented that a vessel might miss the island without one. 'How shameful it is,' he added, 'for your Government to put three to four hundred people on a ship destined for this place without a chronometer, running the risk of ship and cargo together with the lives of so many *poveri diavolo* for the sake of saving three or four hundred francs for a watch,' he said.

3 May 1816

The weather has been extremely wet and foggy with high winds for several days, during which Napoleon did not stir out of doors. This made the Governor very anxious to verify Napoleon's presence. He finally, after some difficulty, succeeded in obtaining an interview with Napoleon in his bedchamber which lasted about a quarter of an hour.

4 May 1816

Sir Hudson Lowe went to see Count Bertrand, with whom he had an hour's conversation which did not appear to be of a nature very pleasing to him. He left Hutt's Gate on his horse, beating the animal furiously and 'muttering'—evidently out of humour.

5 May 1816

Napoleon sent Marchand *(his valet)* for me about nine o'clock. After a few questions of no importance, he asked: 'I want to know from you precisely and truly as a man of honour in what situation you conceive yourself to be? Do you have orders to report every trifling occurrence or illness or what I say to the Governor?'

I replied: 'As your surgeon, to attend you and your suite, I have orders to report if you are seriously ill, in order to get advice from other physicians.'

'First obtaining my consent,' he demanded. I reassured him I would not report without his permission; I was placed about him as a surgeon and by no means as a spy. 'No,' he continued, 'Do not suppose I take you as a spy—on the contrary, I have never found any fault with you. I have a friendship for you, and an esteem for your character.'

Napoleon then said that 'during my recent mental depression the Governor proposed that an officer should enter my chamber to see me if I did not stir out. Any person,' he continued with much emotion, 'who endeavours to force his way into my apartment shall be a corpse the moment he enters. If he ever eats bread or meat again, I am not Napoleon.'

I tried to reassure Napoleon that the English ministry would never be capable of what he supposed.

Following this long conversation Napoleon then complained of an attack of gout. I suggested that he drink lots of water, and perhaps a bit more exercise might help. 'What can I do in this execrable island, where you cannot ride a mile without being wet through—even the English complain, though used to humidity?'

(As Hudson Lowe began to make his weight felt, the sensitivities of O'Meara's ambiguous position, as both Napoleon's confidential surgeon resident in Longwood and an officer of the Royal Navy, began to become obvious. There was also the matter of his regular letters to a friend in London. When these started, his friend, who happened to be an Admiralty official, had doubted the propriety of his receiving such sensitive letters. He consulted his superior who consulted his Minister who told the Cabinet. They were happy to have another source of information on St Helena, so O'Meara was encouraged—though neither Napoleon nor Sir Hudson Lowe knew of these letters.)

6 May 1816

Conversation with Napoleon on the same subject as yesterday. I submitted that it was impossible for me to meet the Governor and not be able to report anything. I reminded him that I have been often used as a means of communication between Longwood and Plantation House.

'I do not mean to bind you to silence,' he said, 'or to prevent you from repeating any *bavardage* you may hear me say. I only want to prevent you from allowing yourself to be cajoled and made a spy of.

'During the short interview I had with the Governor the other day one of the first things he proposed was to send you away and take his own surgeon in your place. This he proposed twice, and twice I firmly refused the offer. I never saw such a horrid countenance. He sat directly opposite me on my couch, between us was a small table with a cup of coffee. His face looked so awful that I thought his evil eye had poisoned it. When he left I ordered Marchand to throw it out the window.'

(The Governor's lack of enthusiasm for O'Meara must have been a factor in Napoleon's continuing confidence in his surgeon. It is fascinating to see how Napoleon's dislike for Lowe brings out the traditional Corsican in him.)

14 May 1816

Napoleon had a bad cold. 'I have promised to see a number of people today. Though indisposed I shall do so. By the way, I have an invitation from Plantation House to see Lady Moira. To send such an invitation knowing that I must go in charge of a guard if I wished to avail myself of it was an insult.' *(Lady Moira, visiting the island on her way to England, was the wife of the Governor-General of Bengal, famous for his support of the Prince of Wales in the Regency debates.)*

16 May 1816

Hudson Lowe had an interview with Napoleon for about half an hour which did not appear satisfactory. Saw Napoleon walking in the garden in a very thoughtful manner. 'Here has been this *viso di boja a tormenti,*' he said 'Tell him I never want to see him again, and that I wish that he might not come again to annoy me with his hateful presence. Let him never again come near me, unless it is with orders to despatch me. He will then find my breast ready for the blow.'

17 May 1816

Napoleon in very good spirits. Demanded to know what the news was. I informed him that the ladies he had received a few days before were highly delighted with his manners, especially since they had expected something very different. 'Ah!' he said, laughing, 'I suppose that they imagined I was some ferocious horned animal.'

19 May 1816

Napoleon in very good humour. Told him that the late Governor of Java *(a British colony at the time)*, Mr Raffles, and his staff had arrived, on their way to England, and were desirous of paying their respects to him. 'What kind of man is the Governor?' asked Napoleon.

I replied that 'He is *un bravissimo uomo* and possessed of great learning and talents.' 'Very well then,' said he, 'I shall see them when I have dressed'.

He then observed how unnecessary and vexatious it was that he should have to tell Poppleton *(the British orderly officer resident in Longwood)* that he wanted to ride out. 'I have been forced here con-

Charles Tristan Comte de Montholon (1783–1853)

trary to the law of nations and I will never recognise their right to detain me. My asking an officer to accompany me would be a tacit acknowledgement of it. It is necessary for my health that I should ride seven or eight leagues daily, but I will not do so with an officer on guard over me.'

(Tacitly recognising the unsuitability of Longwood, the British had agreed to erect a new, prefabricated, house nearby. The official British newspapers took this as yet another sign of their Government's generosity.)

'This "palace" they are building for me,' said he, laughing, 'is so much money thrown into the sea. I would rather they sent me four hundred volumes of books. In the first place it will take some years to build it and before that time I shall be no more. All must be done by the labour of those poor soldiers and sailors. And yet,' he said, '*They* treat me with every respect, and even appear to feel for me.'

Following this we had some discussion about the Spanish campaign. Napoleon complimented *(Sir John)* Moore, 'a brave soldier, an excellent officer, and a man of talent. He was in command of the Reserve in Egypt, where he behaved very well and displayed talent! He died gloriously,—he died like a soldier.'

The conversation turned upon French naval officers. 'Villeneuve,' *(the French admiral at Trafalgar)* said he, 'was a brave man, though possessed of no talent.

'Captain Barre, whom you captured on the *Rivoli,* was a brave and good officer. When in Egypt I asked him to take soundings of the channel into the Bay of Aboukir. He reported to me that there was sufficient water on one part of the channel for the 80-gun ships. Admiral Brueys disagreed and hesitated. In the meantime Nelson came in and destroyed Brueys and our fleet.'

28 May 1816

Napoleon *(who, like most Frenchmen, had a fixed idea that the English drank to excess)* asked me if I had not a large party to dinner yesterday. 'How many of you were drunk?' 'Bah! What, none?'

I told him that the Queen of Portugal was dead. 'The Queen,' he said, 'has been mad for a long time, also the daughters were all ugly.' *(Until invaded in 1807 by a Franco-Spanish force, Portugal was a notable hold-out against Napoleon's continental blockade. Queen Maria may have suffered from porphyria, like George III.)*

29 May 1816

Napoleon playing ninepins with his generals in his garden. I told him that a Bill had been brought into Parliament to enable ministers to detain him in St Helena and to provide the necessary money. 'Did it meet with any opposition, from Brougham or Burdett for instance?' he enquired. 'I believe that Mr Brougham said something.'

7 June 1816

Breakfasted with Napoleon in the garden. Had a long medical argument with him. *His* practice when ill was to eat nothing, drink plenty of barley water and no wine, then have a good ride for seven to eight leagues to promote perspiration.

We also discussed marriage. Napoleon said 'marriage ought to be a civil contract. They both should go to a magistrate and enter into an engagement before witnesses. If they wished it they might go to the church afterwards and get a priest to repeat the ceremony.'

15 June 1816

Napoleon at breakfast in his bath. *(His personal medical theory prompted him to take frequent very hot baths.)* 'Have you seen Miladi Lowe?' he asked. 'I have been told that she is a graceful and a fine woman.' I replied that I had heard so. 'It is a pity,' said he, 'that she can't bestow a portion of her wit and grace on her husband.'

Then the conversation turned to the manner of living in France and England. 'Which eats the most,' said he, 'the Frenchman or the Englishman?' I said, 'I think the Frenchman, who though they nominally make but two meals a day really have four.' Napoleon said he only ate two meals a day. 'Your cookery is more healthy than ours. Your soup, however, is terrible—nothing but bread, salt and pepper. You drink an enormous quantity of wine.'

17 June 1816

Told Napoleon that the *Newcastle* frigate was in sight. At breakfast some of the absurd falsehoods in the *Quarterly Review* respecting his conduct while at The Briars were repeated to him. '*Cela amusera le public*' he replied. A guest observed that all Europe was anxious to know his opinion of Lord Wellington as a general. To this he made no reply, and the question was not repeated.

(The 'conduct at Briars' referred to his light-hearted romps with Betsy Balcombe and her sister, censoriously described by Count Montholon in letters and thence leaked to the general press. Perhaps conscious of this, Barry O'Meara rarely refers to Napoleon's 'little friend', as he calls her.)

Three Commissioners *(sent by the Allies to oversee Napoleon's captivity)* arrived in the *Newcastle*: Count Balmain for Russia, Baron Sturmer for Austria, accompanied by his wife, and the Marquis de Montchenu for France.

18 June 1816

Napoleon asked me, 'What sort of man is the French Commissioner?' 'He is an old émigré, extremely fond of talking, but his looks are not against him. When I was standing with a group of officers opposite the Admiral's house, the Marquis came out and said to me in French, "If you or any of you speak French, for the love of God make it known to me, for I do not speak a word of English. I have arrived here to finish my days among these rocks," he said pointing to the hills surrounding him, "and I can't speak a word of the language!"'

Napoleon laughed very heartily at this, and repeated '*bavard, imbecile*' several times. 'What a folly it is to send these Commissioners out here. Without charge or responsibility they will have nothing to do but to walk the streets and gossip.'

Rear-Admiral Sir Pulteney Malcolm was in charge of naval operations on St Helena from June 1816 to June 1817. He and his wife got on well with Napoleon.

20 June 1816

Admiral Sir Pulteney Malcolm and some other officers came and were presented to Napoleon. *(The Admiral was responsible for the naval stations of St Helena and the Cape.)*

21 June 1816

Saw Napoleon walking in the garden and went down to met him with a book I had procured for him. He said he had seen the new Admiral. 'Ah, there is a man with a conscience, really pleasing, intelligent, frank and sincere. There is the face of an Englishman. I am sure he is a good man. He carries his head erect and speaks openly and boldly, what he thinks, without being afraid to look at you in the face.' Some conversation now passed relative to the protest made by Lord Holland to the Bill for his detention.

Napoleon asked about the reduction of the English army and said it was absurd for the English Government to try to establish the nation as a great military power without having the population sufficient to vie with even the second-rate continental powers, while they neglected the navy.

23 June 1816

Several cases of books were brought out in the *Newcastle*. Found the Emperor in his bedchamber surrounded by heaps of books; his countenance was smiling and he was in perfect good humour. He had been occupied in reading nearly all the night. 'What pleasure I have enjoyed! I can read forty pages in French in the time it would take me to read two in English'. *(Although we know Napoleon was a voracious reader, history and science were his preference. Literary authors are very rarely mentioned in O'Meara's diaries.)*

24 June 1816

Saw Napoleon in the garden. Told him that seven more cases of books had been sent up and also hunting guns on the percussion principle for his use. 'It is useless to send me guns,' replied he, 'when I am confined to a place where there is no game!'

(One might have expected Napoleon, as an artillery man, to have shown more interest in the new percussion technology, which was to replace the flintlock in the French army in the late 1820s.)

Sir Hudson Lowe told me that 'he had offered to Bonaparte to forward any letters or statements he wished to England, and not only would he do so, but he would have them printed in the newspapers, in French and in English.'

28 June 1816

A proclamation issued by Sir Hudson Lowe declaring that any person holding any correspondence with Napoleon Bonaparte, his followers or attendants, receiving or delivering to him or them letters or communications, without express authorisation from the Governor, was guilty of an infraction of the Act of Parliament and would be prosecuted with all the vigour of the law. Anyone who received a communication from him or them, or made money available whereby his escape might be furthered, would be considered aiding and assisting the same.

1 July 1816

Count Bertrand received a letter from Sir Hudson Lowe forbidding any communication written or verbal with the inhabitants except such as known to him though the orderly officer.

Since the arrival of his books, the Emperor has been daily occupied in reading and collecting dates and other materials for the history of his life. The state of the weather also, with strong winds continually blowing over the bleak and exposed condition of Longwood have contributed much to keep him indoors and disgust him with his present residence.

4 July 1816

Sir Pulteney and Lady Malcolm had an interview of nearly two hours with Napoleon. He entered deeply into a description of the battle of Waterloo, naval tactics etc.

The meat was so detestable that Captain Poppleton felt obliged to send it back and write a complaint to the Governor

8 July 1816

Servants from Longwood bringing provisions to Count Bertrand in Hutt's Gate were forbidden to enter the courtyard, and had to pass the viands over the wall. The sentries allowed no conversation.

When my servant bought some medicines for Bertrand's servant, around one of the *bottes* there was a label in my handwriting containing directions. This was written in French, and the sentinel, not being able to understand it, thought it his duty not to suffer it to enter and it was accordingly torn off. This increased rigour is no doubt caused by the recent court-martial of a soldier who had allowed a black into the courtyard to get a drink of water.

(On 8 July the French Government passed on information to London that an American called Carpentier was equipping a fast ship in the Hudson River with a view to allowing Napoleon to escape. Later that month conspiratorial messages were passed by a banking firm in Milan to the British government, including the information that 'Your Government is deceived. Napoleon has already gained over a person at St Helena.')

9 July 1816

A letter of complaint was sent to Sir Hudson Lowe. The officers of the *Newcastle* said that an ice-making machine had been sent by Lady Holland for Napoleon's use but this has not yet made its appearance.

10 July 1816

There was a shortage of wine, fowls and other articles. Wrote to Sir Thomas Reade *(Deputy Adjutant-General)* for more provisions. Captain Poppleton went into town to lay the matter before Sir Hudson Lowe.

11 July 1816

Sir Hudson Lowe asked me in what part of the island would General Bonaparte wish to have his new house built? I replied, 'He would like The Briars.' Sir Hudson said this would never do, that it was too near the town. He then asked if he would prefer any part of the island to Longwood? I said, 'Most certainly he would prefer to live on the other side of the island.' *(Sheltered from the constant south-easterly trade winds.)*

After this he went to Longwood where he had a long conversation with General Montholon chiefly about altering, enlarging and improving Longwood House.

12 July 1816

Napoleon rather out of spirits. I informed him that the Governor had been at Longwood yesterday and had plans for building a new house on another part of the island. Napoleon replied: 'I hate this Longwood. Let him put me on the Plantation House side of the island, if he really wishes to do anything for me. But what is the use of his proposing things and doing nothing? I do not wish him to do anything to this house or this dismal place. Let him build a house on the other side of the island, where there is shade, verdure and water and where I may be sheltered from this *vento agro*.'

13 July 1816

Went to town and communicated Napoleon's reply to Sir Hudson Lowe, who did not seem to like it, and said he could not be so easily watched there.

16 July 1816

'It appears,' said Napoleon, 'that your Ministers have sent out a great many articles of dress for us and this Governor selects what he pleases and sends them up in a contemptuous manner as if he were sending alms to a set of beggars.

'I am astonished that he allows you or Poppleton to remain near me. He would willingly watch me himself always were it in his power. Do you have galley-slaves in England?' I replied, 'No, but we did have convicts forced to work in Portsmouth and elsewhere.' 'He should be in charge of them,' said the Emperor, 'that is exactly the office suited to him.'

17 July 1816

Napoleon called me into the garden, and told me that the Governor had again increased the restrictions on both himself and his staff.

He then spoke about the new house: 'I am of the opinion that as soon as the affairs of France are settled, and things quiet, the English Government will allow me to return to Europe and finish my days in England. I do not believe that they are foolish enough to be at the expense of eight millions of francs per year to keep me here, when I am no longer to be feared; therefore I am not very anxious about the house'. *(Napoleon retained this hope almost to the end. He thought that if he could keep the awful conditions of St Helena in the public mind, a new British ministry might relent. Did he, though, really believe that they would or could establish him incognito in a manor house between Oxford and London, as he so often claimed?)*

18 July 1816
A billiard table was brought up to Longwood.

19 July 1816
The drawing-room in Longwood was discovered to be on fire at about five o'clock this morning. It was extinguished in half an hour by great exertions by Captain Poppleton and the guards, aided by the household.

22 July 1816
Dined in the camp with the 53rd Regiment, for the occasion of the anniversary of the Battle of Salamanca. *(1812: Wellington's first major success in Europe; the 53rd fought with the Sixth Division under Major General Clinton.)*

24 July 1816
The Admiral sent a lieutenant and a party of seamen to pitch a tent, as no shade was provided by the trees at Longwood.

25 July 1816
Told Napoleon that the *Griffin* had arrived from England with news of the condemnation of General Bertrand to death, though absent. Napoleon appeared for a moment lost in astonishment, but recollected that such a sentence could not be carried out without a further trial. He expressed, however, much regret at it on account of the effect which it might possibly produce upon Madame Bertrand *(who was pregnant)*.

28 July 1816
Informed by Cipriani *(the maître d'hôtel)* that in the beginning of 1815 he had learned in Leghorn that it was the determination of the Congress of Vienna to send the Emperor to St Helena. This contrib-

uted to determine Napoleon to escape from Elba and attempt the recovery of his throne.

2 August 1816

No vegetables except potatoes have been sent up for three days.

5 August 1816

Sir Hudson Lowe came to Longwood, and, calling me outside in a mysterious manner, asked if I thought that 'General Bonaparte' would take it well, if he invited him to a ball in Plantation House, on the occasion of the Prince Regent's birthday. I replied that in all the circumstances he would look on it as an insult, especially if he were addressed as General Bonaparte.

(This is the first entry that raises a theme—how Napoleon was to be addressed—that was to remain a major cause of contention. In the 1814 Treaty of Paris Napoleon and his family had been specifically permitted to retain their titles; although of course the escape from Elba had changed things.)

10 August 1816

Sir Hudson Lowe came up while Napoleon was at breakfast in the tent, in order to see him, but did not succeed.

12 August 1816

Grand field day in camp in honour of the Prince Regent. Napoleon asked if I had been invited to dine with the Governor. I replied, 'No, but I was asked to the ball in the evening.'

14 August 1816

'That *sbirros* Siciliano,' said Napoleon, 'has been here. *Mi ripugna l'anima il vererlo.* He appears always in a passion with somebody, or uneasy, or as if something is tormenting his conscience and he was anxious to run away from himself.'

15 August 1816

Anniversary of Napoleon's birthday. Breakfasted in the tent with the ladies and all his suite. In the evening the second class of domestics, including the English, had a grand supper and dance. To the astonishment of the French not an Englishman got drunk.

16 August 1816

Sir Hudson Lowe again came up and had a long conversation with General Montholon and myself, principally about reducing the expenses of the establishment. One of Leslie's pneumatic machines for making ice was sent up to Longwood this day. Napoleon asked several question about the process and was evidently acquainted with the principles of air pumps. He spoke highly of the science of chemistry and how he had always encouraged it.

A cupful of water was then frozen in his presence in about fifteen minutes. Napoleon observed to me what a gratification that would have been in Egypt.

(*Betsy Balcombe remembered how 'after making a cup of ice Napoleon insisted upon my putting a large piece into my mouth and laughed to see the contortions it induced from the excessive cold. It was the first ice that had ever been seen at St Helena and a young island lady Miss de F—, who was with us, would not believe that the solid mass in her hand was really frozen water until it melted and streamed down her fingers.'*)

18 August 1816

Sir Hudson Lowe with Sir Pulteney Malcolm, Sir Thomas Reade and Major Gorrequer arrived at Longwood while Napoleon was walking the garden with Counts Bertrand, Montholon, Las Cases and his son. His Excellency *(as O'Meara often referred to Lowe)* sent to ask for an interview with Napoleon, which was granted. Captain Poppleton and I stood to one side as the small group walked to the end of the garden where an animated conversation took place. Napoleon appeared to be the principal speaker and appeared at times considerably agitated. Sir Hudson's manner also appeared hurried and greatly agitated. After about half an hour Sir Hudson Lowe turned abruptly and withdrew without saluting Napoleon. The Admiral bowed and departed. While Sir Hudson was passing me he said, 'General Bonaparte has been very abusive to me!' He then mounted his horse and galloped away. It was quite evident to all the interview had been very unpleasant.

19 August 1816

Saw Napoleon in his dressing-room. He was in very good humour, asked how Gourgaud was and when I said I had given him some medicine, he said, 'medicines are only fit for old people. He would have done better to have dieted himself for a few days.'

He then said: 'The Governor came here yesterday to annoy me. He saw me walking in the garden, so I could not refuse to see him. He wished to reduce the expenses of running Longwood. He told me he had made visits to me on two or three occasions previously but, appar-

Napoleon spent much of his time on the island dictating his memoirs—here with Count Las Cases and his son.

ently I was in my bath. I replied: "No, Sir, I was not in my bath, but, I ordered one on purpose, to avoid seeing you!"

'He said that I did not know him, and that if I did I would change my opinion. "Know you, Sir," I answered, "how could I know you? People make themselves known by their actions; by their commanding in battle. You have never commanded any but a band of vagabond Corsican deserters. I know the name of every English General who had distinguished himself in battle, but I have never heard of you. You have never commanded or been accustomed to men of honour!"

'He then said he had not sought this employment and that he was only doing his duty and acting according to orders. I replied, "so does the hangman."

'I said "You, Sir, have power over my body, but none over my soul. That soul is as proud, fierce and determined, at the present moment as when it commanded Europe!"' *(It is difficult to imagine how Napoleon could have been more offensive or to have struck a note of melodrama more irritating to the English sensibility.)*

Gave the Emperor Sarrazin's *Account of the Campaign in Spain. (Sarrazin, a brigadier-general in the French army, deserted to the English in 1810.)* 'Sarrazin,' explained Napoleon, 'was a traitor—a man without truth, honour, or probity. When I returned from Elba he wrote to me offering his services, to betray to me all the secrets and plans of the English. It was my intention to have him tried as a traitor but I was so much occupied that it escaped my memory.'

22 August 1816

Sir Hudson Lowe sent for me and discussed his recent conversation with Napoleon. He denied that he told the Emperor that he had offered to resign his post. He asked me to tell Napoleon that he would only resign his position if the Government disapproved of his conduct. I was then asked to repeat my entire conversation with Napoleon—I refused, saying it would only be disagreeable to him. Lowe insisted, so I repeated some parts. Sir Hudson said that though he had not commanded an army against Napoleon he had probably done him more mischief by his advice and information during the conferences at Châtillon than if he had. *(The Châtillon conference of February and March 1814 was a last-minute attempt to find common ground between Napoleon and the Allies; it was overshadowed, however, by military success, first of Napoleon and then of the Allies. By 30 March Paris was in Allied hands.)*

Sir Hudson then walked about for a short time biting his nails. He suddenly stopped and asked if Madame Bertrand had repeated to strangers any of the conversation? 'She had better not, lest it may render her and her husband's situation much more unpleasant than at present.'

He walked about the garden repeating again some of the observations until he had worked himself into quite a passion and said: 'Tell General Bonaparte that he had better take care of what he does, as if he continues his present conduct, I shall be obliged to increase the restrictions already in force.' *(This characterisation of Sir Hudson 'working himself into a passion' was regarded in England as a typical Irish exaggeration, intended to blacken his name. Not until the diary of Lowe's secretary, Major Gorrequer, was deciphered and published in the 1960s did this account receive corroboration.)*

Observing that Napoleon had been the cause of the loss of the lives of millions of men and might be again if he got loose, he concluded by saying, 'I consider Ali Pasha to be a much more respectable scoundrel than Bonaparte.' *(This was not a compliment. Byron described Ali Pasha, ruler of Greece and European Turkey, as 'a remorseless tyrant, guilty of the most horrible cruelties, very brave, so good a general that they call him the Mahometan Buonaparte . . . but as barbarous as he is successful, roasting rebels, etc.')*

26 August 1816

A list of grievances was sent to Plantation House, written by Count Montholon.

'Do you think this Governor will send it to England?' Napoleon enquired. I assured him there was not a doubt of it. The Governor had even promised to get it published. Napoleon said, 'He said he would send letters to Europe only if he approved of their contents.'

More *piquets* have been established and several additional sentries placed. Ditches of eight or ten feet deep nearly completed round the garden.

27 August 1816

I asked Napoleon if the King of Prussia were a man of talent. 'Who?' said he, 'the King of Prussia?' He burst into a fit of laughter. 'He, a man of talent! The greatest blockhead on earth.'

He then conversed for a considerable time about the Bourbons. 'They want to introduce the old system of nobility into the army. Instead of allowing the sons of peasants and labourers to be eligible to be made generals, they want to confine it entirely to the old nobility, to émigrés like that old blockhead Montchenu.

'When you have seen Montchenu you have seen all the old nobility of France before the Revolution. Such were all the race and such they have returned, ignorant, vain and arrogant as they left. After twenty-five years of exile and disgrace they have returned loaded with the same old vices and crimes. Believe me, in six or ten years' time that whole race of émigrés will be massacred and thrown into the Seine.

'The mass of the people,' continued he, 'now see the revival of the old feudal times. Every true Frenchman reflects with chagrin that a family so many years odious to France has been forced upon them by foreign bayonets.'

He then recounted a story, that when he returned from Italy, he met an old woman who did not recognise him. When he asked her as to why she was there she replied: '"I want to see the Emperor before I die." "Bah," said I, "He is a tyrant as well as the others." "That may

Dr Arnott (1771–1855) came to St Helena in 1819 and attended Napoleon from 1821 until his death.

be, monsieur," she replied. "But he is the King of the people, the Bourbons were Kings only of the nobles." There,' said he, 'you have the sentiments of the French nation expressed by an old woman.'

30 August 1816

Napoleon rose at three a.m. Continued writing until six when he retired to rest again. He then sent for Captain Poppleton, who was then in his morning dress, He wished to retire and change, but was informed to come 'sans cérémonie'. When he entered the billiard-room he found Napoleon standing with his hat under his arm.

'Well, *Monsieur le Capitaine*, I believe you are the senior Captain of the 53rd regiment?' 'I am.' 'I have the greatest esteem for the officers and men of the 53rd. They are brave men and have done their duty. I have been informed that it is said in camp that I do not wish to see the officers. Will you be so good as to tell them that whoever asserted this told a falsehood. '

5 September 1816

Major Gorrequer came up to Longwood to discuss the proposed reduction of the expenditure of the establishment. This was to be achieved by a great reduction in the number of persons composing it, by some of the general officers and other returning to Europe. From the 15th of this month the expenditure would not be allowed to exceed £1,000 a month. Should General Bonaparte be averse to the reductions necessary to bring the disbursements within this sum, the surplus must be paid by himself.

(This was the start of much undignified bickering about the expenses of the Longwood establishment. The original estimate had been that the Governor should have an establishment of £12,000 and Napoleon £8,000. On St Helena, however, the argument included detail of the amount spent on washing shirts and how much wine might be drunk or salt used. Napoleon rightly complained.) 'The Ministers go to the expense of £60,000 or £70,000 to send out furniture, wood and building materials for my use and at the same time send orders to put me nearly on rations, and oblige me to discharge my servants and make reductions incompatible with the decency and comfort of the house.'

8 September 1816

Napoleon enquired about General Meade, who had recently arrived on the island for a short visit. I told him I had been under his command in Egypt where he had been severely wounded in the unfortunate attack on Rosetta. Napoleon sent a letter, inviting the General and his wife to Longwood. General Meade did not come, saying that he understood that restrictions existed, and anyway his vessel was under weigh and he could not well detain her. Napoleon said later that he was convinced that the Governor prevented General Meade from coming to see him.

9 September 1816

Napoleon complained of a headache, colic etc. I wished him to take a dose of physic which he declined. General Gourgaud and Count Montholon complained of the wine, which they suspected contained lead, and desired me to get some tests to analyse it.

Young Las Cases and Piontkowski *(a member of the Polish Guard, formerly part of Napoleon's personal troops)* went to Jamestown and met the Commissioners. While they were speaking to 'the Rosebud' *(a very pretty young lady so called from the freshness and fineness of her complexion)* one of the Plantation House orderlies brought out their horses and said that their military servant was so drunk that if they did not all leave town immediately he would be punished. Young Las Cases coolly asked for written orders to that effect and threatened that he would horsewhip anyone who tried to lead their horses away.

10 September 1816

Sir Hudson Lowe asked me if Napoleon had made any observation relative to General Meade's not having accepted the offer to him? I replied that he had said he was convinced that he had prevented him. At this His Excellency exclaimed in a violent tone: 'He is a d—d lying rascal. None but a black-hearted villain would have entertained such an idea. Tell General Bonaparte that the assertion that I prevented General Meade from going to see him *e una bugia infame, e che un bugiardone chi l'ha detto.* Tell him my exact words.'

(Barry O'Meara translated this phrase as 'an infamous lie and the person who said it is a great liar'. He notes: 'It is unnecessary for me to say that I did not deliver this message in the manner I was directed.')

12 September 1816

Napoleon still unwell. Recommended him strongly to take a dose of Epsom salts. In a good-humoured manner he gave me a slap in the face and said, if he was not better tomorrow he would take his own medicine, crystals of tartar *(an emetic).*

I met Sir Hudson Lowe in town where I told of the complaint made about the wine and the request that I might procure some tests to analyse it.

13 September 1816

Napoleon much better.

A large quantity of plate weighed for the purpose of being broken up for sale. Complaints made by Count Montholon of the state of the copper saucepans. Found them on examination to be in want of tinning.

(It is typical of the hothouse atmosphere of Longwood that the colics the residents suffered from were ascribed to poison rather than defective saucepans. The breaking up and selling of his silver plate was a PR coup on Napoleon's part, necessary or not—even his English enemies thought it hard that a prisoner should have to supplement his sustenance in this way.)

17 September 1816

Sir Thomas Reade begged me to get him some of Napoleon's plate whole, which, he observed, would sell better in that state than if it were broken up. *(O'Meara was not in a position to do so.)*

19 September 1816

A large portion of Napoleon's plate broken up, the imperial arms and the eagles cut out and put by. The Governor ordered that the money from the sale of the silver should be deposited in the hands of Mr Balcombe, the purveyor, for the use of General Bonaparte.

21 September 1816

Sir Pulteney Malcolm came to Longwood to take leave of Napoleon, before his departure for Cape Town. Long interview; the conversation was chiefly relative to the Scheldt, Antwerp, battles in Germany etc.

Madame Bertrand gave a phaeton to Sir Pulteney and asked him, if possible to sell it in Cape Town on her behalf. Three of Bertrand's servants very seriously ill.

23 September 1816

Met Sir Hudson Lowe on his way to Longwood who observed that General Bonaparte had done himself a great deal of mischief by the letters he caused Count Montholon to write. That by conducting himself properly for some years the ministers might believe him to be sincere and allow him to return to England.

27 September 1816

The Commissioners came up to Longwood, but were refused admission by the officer of the guard. Their passes did not specify Longwood.

1 October 1816

Repeated to Napoleon what Sir Hudson Lowe had said to me on the 23rd. He replied, 'I expect nothing from the present ministry but ill-treatment. The more they want to lessen me, the more I shall exalt myself. It was my intention to have lived as a private person in England in some part of the country.' I observed that as long as he kept the title of Majesty, the English ministers would have a pretext for keeping him in St Helena. He replied: 'I wanted to assume an incognito on my arrival here but they insist on calling me General Bonaparte.'

Sir Hudson Lowe and his staff rode into Longwood, alighted in front of the billiard-room and demanded to see General Bonaparte. General Montholon informed the group that the Emperor was indisposed and would not see anyone. Sir Hudson Lowe sent again in rather an authoritative manner. An answer was sent that notice would be given to him when he could be received—Napoleon was suffering from tooth-ache. 'It is better that we should not meet,' said Napoleon, 'it is probably some *bêtise* of Lord Bathurst's which he will make worse by his ungracious manner of communicating it. Let him send Colonel Reade to explain what he has to say; I will receive and hear him.'

2 October 1816

Saw Napoleon in the morning. A toothache, he said, had prevented him from sleeping. After examining the tooth I recommended the extraction of it.

(This tooth was sold for 7 guineas at auction after Barry O'Meara's death in 1836 and for £11,000 in 2005.)

3 October 1816

Napoleon reiterated his decision never to see Hudson Lowe again. 'As to the Governor', says he, 'if he still insists on seeing me I will write myself in answer, "The Emperor Napoleon will not see you because the three last times you were with him you insulted him, and he does not wish more communication with you." I would sooner have an interview with the corporal of the guard than that *galeriano*.'

I wrote an account of what he had said for Sir Hudson Lowe, avoiding, however, repeating the strongest of his expressions.

4 October 1816

Sir Thomas Reade came to my room with new instructions from England.

The establishment was to be reduced by four persons. Those who remained were to be as amenable to the laws as if they were British subjects, and declaring the aiding and assisting him to escape a felony. Restrictions imposed on General Bonaparte pertained to all the French *(inhabitants of Longwood)* as well. If they disagreed with these instructions they will be sent to Cape Town. Any of them abusing, reflecting upon or behaving ill to the Governor or the Government would be forthwith sent to the Cape. There was also a demand for £1,400 for books which had been sent out. The whole was couched in peremptory language.

5 October 1816

Count Bertrand went to Plantation House where he learned that Piontkowski and three domestics were to be sent away.

9 October 1816

Sir Hudson Lowe arrived at Longwood. He spent over two hours in

Captain Poppleton's room. He often came out. He walked up and down outside the door, with the end of a finger in his mouth, as was his general custom when in thought.

Later, His Excellency said that it was my duty to tell him everything that occurred between General Bonaparte and himself. I replied that if there was a plot to escape or anything suspicious I should conceive it my duty to give him notice of it, but that I could not think of telling him everything abusive or injurious that might increase the unhappy differences between them.

Sir Hudson first agreed, but afterwards said that one of the means General Bonaparte had of escaping was vilifying him; that abusing and lowering the character of the ministry was an underhand and base way of endeavouring to escape and therefore he should be told everything of the kind instantly.

I replied that I had received letters from official persons returning thanks for my former letters which had been shown to Cabinet ministers *(and the Prince Regent)*, with a request to communicate circumstances relative to Bonaparte. The Governor was excessively uneasy at this, declaring that the Secretary of State *(Lord Bathurst)* was the only one who ought to know anything of the matter and all communication even to his Lordship should go through him only. *(The Governor here learns for the first time that O'Meara was in communication with the highest Cabinet authorities. This source of information, uncontrolled either by the Governor or his minister, introduced a new element into the relationship between him and O'Meara. The relationship worsens from now on.)*

10 October 1816

This evening Count Bertrand asked me to help him translate part of the new restrictions relating to the Emperor. Napoleon was henceforth prohibited from going off the high-road, from entering any house and from conversing with any person he might meet on his rides or walks. Prepared as I was, by the look on the Governor's face, I was thunderstruck. *(Napoleon had evidently been accustomed to greet the 'native blacks' on his walks, enter their cottages and give them tips, or, as Plantation House no doubt saw it, soften them with bribes.)*

11 October 1816

Sir Hudson Lowe sent for me to town. He confirmed the restrictions, and that any rule that applied to General Bonaparte applied equally to the other French. He stressed that the orders originated from the British Government, and that he was merely the person who carried them into execution.

12 October 1816

Napoleon spoke about the new restrictions and observed that Bertrand could not believe that he had rightly comprehended them. I explained as briefly and as delicately as I could.

A quantity of plate sent to town today and sold to Mr Balcombe.

13 October 1816

Napoleon in his bath. He railed against the island, complaining bitterly about violation of natural justice and particularly the new restrictions. 'They profess in England to furnish all my wants and in fact send out many things; this man then comes out, reduces everything, obliges me to sell my plate in order to purchase those necessaries of life which he either denies altogether or supplies in quantities so small as to be insufficient; imposes daily new and arbitrary restrictions; insults me and my followers; concludes by attempting to deny me the faculty of speech, and then has the impudence to write that he has changed nothing!'

14 October 1816

The French sign the submission papers to the new restrictions, only substituting 'L'Empereur Napoleon' for 'Napoleon Bonaparte'.

15 October 1816

The papers are sent back. Sir Hudson Lowe insists that if the papers are not signed in the original form, the officers and the domestics must all depart for the Cape of Good Hope instantly. The prospect of separation from the Emperor caused great grief and consternation, so they all signed the obnoxious paper (with the exception of Santini).

16 October 1816

Napoleon sent for me at half-past six in the morning. On my arrival he looked very earnestly at me and said, laughing, 'You look as if you had been drunk last night.'

I replied, 'No, but I had dined in the camp last night and sat up very late.' 'Quante bottiglie, tre?' he added, holding up three of his fingers.

He then told me that 'one half of the vexations I have experienced here have arisen from my title.' I observed that many were surprised at his having retained the title after abdication. 'As soon as I had em-

Ladder Hill, a sentry post above the town, reached by 699 steps, commands a stunning view of the South Atlantic.

This is the (much redecorated) room in Longwood which Barry O'Meara used as a bedroom.

This walkway was erected to provide Napoleon some privacy when he walked in the grounds of Longwood.

Napoleon brooding on St Helena, by Oscar Rex (1857–1929).

barked on the *Northumberland*,' he said, 'I was informed that I was a prisoner of war and that I was to be styled General Bonaparte. In self-vindication I was obliged to maintain on all occasions the title of Emperor. I had abdicated the throne of France, not the title of Emperor.'

I asked him later on whether Savary or Fouché had been the better Minister of Police. 'Savary,' said he, 'is not a bad man; on the contrary he is a brave soldier and a man of good heart. Fouché is a miscreant of all colours, a priest, a terrorist, and one who took part in many bloody scenes during the Revolution. He can worm your secrets out of you. His riches were badly acquired, by diverting taxes into his own pockets.'

I asked him why he had never given a dukedom in France to any person. He replied, 'because it would have produced great discontent. If I had created dukes with French titles it would have been considered as a revival of the old feudal privileges with which the nation had been cursed so long.'

He complained of his general health. I tried to feel his heart, but could not, which I attributed to obesity. His circulation was feeble, rarely exceeding fifty-eight or sixty a minute.

19 October 1816
Piontkowski, Santini, Rousseau *(lampist and oddjob man at Longwood)* and Archambault *(a groom)* to be removed from Longwood. They were each given a pension. Before embarkation their luggage was searched.

20 October 1816
Count and Countess Bertrand and family move from Hutt's Gate to Longwood.

26 October 1816
Napoleon out in the carriage for the first time for a considerable period. Said he had followed my prescription.

'English soldiers,' said the Emperor in the course of our conversation, 'are not equal in address, activity or intelligence to the French. When they get from under the fear of the lash, they obey nobody. In a retreat they cannot be managed; and if they meet with wine they are so many devils. In order to have good soldiers a nation must always be at war.'

Napoleon observed that the English seamen were as much superior to the French as the latter were to the Spaniards. I ventured to say I thought that the French would never make good seamen on account of their impatience and volatility of temper. 'I do not agree with you there, *Signor dottore*,' said he, ' but I do not think they will ever make as good seamen as yours. The sea is yours—your seamen are as much superior to ours as the Dutch were once to yours.'

'Pitt and his politics,' continued he, 'nearly ruined England by keeping up a continental war with France.' I remarked that if we had not carried on that war we should have been ruined and ultimately become a province of France. 'It is not true,' said Napoleon, 'England being at war with France gave the latter a pretence and an opportunity of extending her conquests under me, until I became Emperor of nearly all the world, which would not have happened if there had not been a war.'

Five p.m.

Napoleon sent for me. Seized with rigors, headache, severe cough. Tonsils swelled, cheek inflamed, pulse much quickened. He asked a great many questions about fever.

Saw him again at nine in bed. He imputed his complaint to the *ventaccio* continually blowing over the bleak and exposed site of Longwood.

27 October 1816

A free perspiration took place during the night and Napoleon was considerably better. Had some conversation with him relative to the Empress Josephine. His first acquaintance with her came in 1795. 'A boy of twelve came to ask me for his father's sword. I was so impressed by his touching request I ordered that the sword should be handed over to the youngster. He burst into tears when he saw it. A few days afterwards his mother came to make a visit of thanks. I was much struck with her appearance and still more her *esprit*. This impression was daily strengthened. Marriage was not long in following!'

Informed Sir Hudson Lowe of Napoleon's state of health and that he had expressed a desire to be moved from Longwood. His Excellency replied, 'The fact is that General Bonaparte wants to get his hands on Plantation House; but the East India Company will not consent to have so fine an estate given to a set of Frenchmen, to destroy the trees and ruin the gardens.'

30 October 1816

Napoleon consented to make use of a gargle of roses and sulphuric acid. He complained about the barbarous climate of Longwood and

Plantation House in 2005

again mentioned The Briars. Informed Sir Hudson Lowe of the state of Napoleon's health. He suggested that if General Bonaparte wanted to make himself comfortable he ought to draw on some of those large sums of money he possessed and buy a house.

1 November 1816

Napoleon better but has now developed swelling in both legs and enlarged glands in the thighs. More plate was broken up today and sent for sale in town.

2 November 1816

During the conversation I asked the Emperor his reasons for encouraging the Jews so much. 'I wanted to make them leave off usury and become like other men. There were a great many Jews in the countries I reigned over. By removing their disabilities and putting them on an equal footing with Catholics, Protestants and others I hoped to make them become good citizens.

'Moreover I wished to establish a universal freedom of conscience. My system was to have no dominant religion but to allow perfect liberty of conscience and of thought, to make all men equal, whether Protestants, Catholics, Mahometans, Deists, or others; so that their religion should have no influence in getting them employment under government. I made everything independent of religion. I wished to deprive priests of influence and power in civil affairs, and to oblige them to confine themselves to their own religious affairs and meddle with nothing else.'

5 November 1816

Hudson Lowe at Longwood. I gave my opinion that if Napoleon did not take exercise he would be attacked by a serious complaint. Sir Hudson asked with some degree of asperity: 'Why did he not take more exercise?'

The Governor required me to write a statement of General Bonaparte's health. Cautioning me that the life of one man was not to be put into competition with the mischief he might cause if he were to get loose. That my situation was very peculiar and of great political importance.

More plate was broken up and sent to Jamestown for sale.

7 November 1816

Napoleon much better and free from complaint.

8 November 1816

I made a few remarks about the Poles who seemed greatly attached to him. 'They are a brave nation,' said he, 'and make good soldiers. In the cold, the Pole is better than the Frenchman. If I had succeeded in Russia I would have made Piontkowski King of Poland.'

I then asked him why did he fail in Moscow? 'The cold, the premature cold, and the burning of the city,' replied Napoleon. 'I was a few days too late—I had studied the weather for fifty years before and the extreme cold never commenced before 20th December. When I was at Moscow the cold was at 3 degrees C which the French could bear; but on the march the thermometer sank 18 degrees and nearly all the horses perished. The soldiers lost their spirits and their senses and fell into confusion. The most trifling circumstance alarmed them. Some just lay down and fell asleep—soon blood would come from their noses and sleeping they died.

'Had it not been for the burning of Moscow, I would have succeeded. Two days before I entered Moscow my 90,000 French soldiers had beaten 250,000 Russians. There were provisions in the city for one year. Two days after our arrival fire was discovered, caused by the soldiers kindling their fires too near the houses. I was angry at this and gave every direction to extinguish it. The next morning a violent wind arose, and the fire spread, aided by Russian miscreants who dispersed about the city with tinders setting fire to as many houses as they could. This, with the wind, rendered it impossible to put the fire out. I retreated about a league away and you can imagine the intensity of the fire even at that distance when I tell you that you could scarcely put your hands on the walls or windows. It was a spectacle of a sea and billows of fire, a sky and clouds of flame—it was the most grand, the most sublime and the most terrific sight the world ever beheld!'

'*Allons, Docteur.*' This was Napoleon's general expression when he wished me to retire.

9 November 1816

Had some conversation with Napoleon about religion. 'There are so many religions or modifications,' said he, 'that it is difficult to choose. If one religion had existed from the beginning that should be the true one. As it is, I think every person should stick to the religion in which he was brought up.

'There is a link between animals and the Deity,' added he. 'Man is merely a more perfect animal than the rest. He reasons better. But how do we know that animals have not a language of their own? A horse has memory, knowledge and love. He knows his master from the servants, even thought the latter are more constantly with him. Who again could deny the sagacity of dogs?'

Speaking of English soldiers he observed, 'The English soldier is brave, nobody more so, and the English officers are men of honour, but I do not think them capable of executing great manoeuvres. If I were at the head of them, instead of the lash I would lead them by the stimulus of honour. When a soldier has been debased and degraded by stripes, he cares but little for the glory or the honour of his country.

'I would encourage young men of education and merchants to join the army and make them feel proud of their profession. Promotion would be by merit alone.

'When the Austrians invaded Italy, they tried to make soldiers of the Italians who either deserted, or would not fight. It was impossible to keep together a single regiment. I raised many thousands of Italians into the French army, and found that when properly stimulated, they fought as bravely as any good soldier!'

He then spoke of Sir Sidney Smith. 'He is a brave officer. At Acre he sent by flag of truce a letter containing a challenge to me to meet him at some place in order to fight a duel. I laughed at this. Notwithstanding this *sottise*, I like the character of the man.' (*According to Thomas Creevey,*

*Mrs Jane Balcombe, mother of the
irrepressible Betsy. Napoleon stayed at her
house The Briars in his early days on the
island.*

*Sir Sidney Smith's habit of retelling in minute detail the actions of the
siege earned him the nickname 'Long Acre', after a street in London's
Covent Garden area.)*

12 November 1816
Conversed with Napoleon, who was in his bath, for a considerable
time.

On asking his opinion of Talleyrand, '*Le plus vil des agitateurs,*' said
he. '*C'est un homme corrompu,* who has betrayed all parties and persons.
He is a man of talent, but venal in everything.'

Napoleon showed me the marks of two wounds; one a very deep
cicatrice about the left knee which he said he received in his first campaign of Italy. The other was on the toe.

Dined at Plantation House in company with the Marquis de
Montchenu who amused the company with the great importance he
attached to high birth.

17 November 1816
The allowances for Longwood diminished by order of Sir Hudson
Lowe *(two pounds of meat daily in consequence of the departure of a serv-
ant).*

25 November 1816

On my return from town to Longwood met Sir Hudson Lowe who observed, with an air of triumph, 'You will meet your friend Las Cases in custody.' It appeared that Las Cases had given a letter written on silk to James Scott, his servant, which he was to take to England.

The dragoons had also removed two large trunks from Las Cases's apartment containing his personal diary, and the history of the Italian campaign. Saw Napoleon in the evening who appeared wholly ignorant of Las Cases's intentions. 'I would have stopped him; not that I disapprove of his trying to make our situation known—on the contrary, but I disapprove of the bungling way in which he attempted it.'

26 November 1816

Napoleon in his bath. Asked if I had heard anything of Las Cases; professed his sorrow to lose him. 'Las Cases is the only one of the French who can read English well. Madame Bertrand understands English, but you know you cannot trouble a lady.' Besides, 'those Creoles are very susceptible. Josephine was subject to tuberculous attacks when in trouble. She was really an amiable woman—elegant, charming, and affable. *Era la dama la piu graziosa di Francia*. She was the goddess of the toilet; all the fashions originated with her. Everything she put on appeared elegant; and she was so kind, so human; she was the best woman in France.'

He then spoke of the distress prevailing in England. 'I think England, encumbered with a national debt which will take forty years of peace and commerce to pay off may be compared to a man who has drunk large quantities of brandy to give him courage and strength; but afterwards, weakened by the stimulus, his powers are exhausted.' *(The distress was primarily caused by the ending of the special economic conditions of the Napoleonic Wars. It is interesting to see that Napoleon had no sense of the development potential of the British industrial economy.)*

27 November 1816

Napoleon much concerned about the treatment Las Cases has suffered and the detention of his own papers. 'What guarantee have I that when I have nearly finished my history he will not seize it? With this *sbirro Siciliano* there is no guarantee or security. Tell him,' continued he, 'what I think of his conduct.'

He then sent for St Denis *(second valet at Longwood, who had excellent handwriting)* who had copied Las Cases's journal and asked him about it. St Denis replied that it was a journal of everything remarkable that had taken place since the embarkation of the *Bellerophon*, and contained anecdotes of different persons. 'Anything about the Governor?' 'A great deal, Sire,' said St Denis, who could not help smiling. 'Does it say that I said *C'est un homme ignoble*, and that his face was the most ignoble I had ever seen?' St Denis confirmed that it did, though certain expressions were moderated.

Later Napoleon conversed about his brother Joseph, who he described as being an excellent character. 'His virtues and talents are those of a private man; he is too good to be a great man.'

29 November 1816

Having been unwell for some days with a liver complaint, I called for Dr McClean of the 53rd Regiment. *(Sir Hudson Lowe returned Las Cases' papers.)*

In the afternoon I saw Napoleon in his dressing-room. He was much pleased at the return of the Italian papers and hoped he would reclaim the others.

While he was speaking my vision became indistinct, everything swam before my eyes, and I fell on the floor in a faint. When I recovered my senses, the first object I saw I will never forget. It was the face of Napoleon, bending over my face—with the expression of great concern and anxiety. With one hand he was opening my shirt-collar and with the other holding a bottle *de vinaigre des quatre voleurs (a favourite French concoction of herbs steeped in vinegar traditionally first used by four house thieves during the plague in Toulouse in 1630)*. He had taken off my cravat and dashed a bottle of eau de cologne in my face. 'I thought you had slipped,' he said, 'but seeing you remain without motion, and your face the colour of death, I concluded that it was either a fit, or your soul had departed.' Napoleon then ordered Marchand to give me some orange-water. He explained that in his anxiety he had broken the bell ribbon. He lifted me from the floor and placed me in a chair.

'I tore off your cravat and dashed water with eau de cologne into your face. I tried to prise open your collar. Did I do the right thing?' he asked.

I reassured him that he had done everything properly. When I was leaving the room, I heard Napoleon quietly ordering Marchand to follow me in case I had another fit.

1 December 1816

After some enquiries about my health, Napoleon said that he hoped that Las Cases would be sent back to Europe soon. 'The next to be removed will be Montholon. After they have been taken away, you will be sent off.'

3 December 1816

Napoleon sent for me at 1 a.m. Found him in bed suffering headache and general uneasiness, which had been proceeded by shiverings. Had a little fever during the night. I strongly repeated my advice about exercise, and my firm conviction that in the contrary case he would soon be seized with an alarming fit of illness. '*Tanto miglio,*' replied Napoleon, '*piu presto si finira.*' ('*So much the better, the sooner it will be finished.*')

4 December 1816

Wrote an account of the state of Napoleon's health and the advice I had given him for Sir Hudson Lowe. Napoleon somewhat better, talked at length about his various generals. 'Moreau was an excellent general but could not command a large army. He was very calm and cool under fire. He was often seen in action with a pipe in his mouth; however, he made the wrong decision—influenced by his young and pretty wife. He joined the conspiracy against France which will be forever a disgrace to his memory.' (*Moreau was a convinced Republican who initially aided Napoleon's rise but later turned against him.*)

'Desaix and Kléber were the best generals I ever had. Desaix loved glory for itself, but despised everything else. To him riches and pleasures were valueless. He despised comfort and convenience. I gave him a carriage with bed accommodation, several times, but he always seemed to lose it. He preferred to wrap himself in a cloak, throw himself under a gun and sleep as if it were a palace. For him, luxury had no charms. The Arabs called him "The Just Sultan". He was intended by nature to be a great general.

'Had Kléber lived, your army in Egypt would have perished. General Menou, who replaced him, was a fool and an idiot.' He then went on to explain that if Kléber had lived, Egypt would still be in French hands and could have destroyed the East India Company. (*Jean-Baptiste Kléber, perhaps the most brilliant of Napoleon's generals, was assassinated just after he had retaken Cairo in 1800.*)

'Lannes would have made a first-class general. He was cool in the rush of fire. He was ardently attached to me. He was far superior to Moreau or Soult. Masséna was at his best when cannon balls were landing all around him. He was, however, a thief. I offered him a substantial amount of money on condition that he stop. He could not stop. His soldiers hated him.

'Pichegru was my maths teacher when I was approximately ten years of age. He was a good general but eventually allied himself to the Bourbons. He was responsible for the death or capture of 2,000 French men.'

Later in the afternoon, Hudson Lowe came to Longwood and observed that General Bonaparte had adopted a bad mode of procedure by declaring war on the only person who had it in his power to make his situation comfortable. 'What can I do that would induce him to go out from his room?' I replied, an enlargement of the boundaries, taking off some of the restrictions, and giving him a house on the other side of the island. I observed also that the allowance of provisions was totally insufficient.

He explained that his directions were much more precise than those of the Admiral. He complained that his actions had been misconstrued and misrepresented and malicious constructions put on them. The British Government did not wish to render General Bonaparte's life miserable, to torment him. Indeed it was not so much he himself they were concerned with as disaffected people in Europe who would use his name to excite rebellion in France and elsewhere.

When I related all this to the Emperor, Napoleon said he did not believe a word of it. 'A government two thousand leagues off and ignorant of the localities of the island can never give orders in detail; they can only give general and discretionary ones. They have only directed him to adopt every measure necessary to prevent my escape. Instead of that I am treated in a manner dishonourable to humanity. To kill and bury a man is intelligible, but this slow torture, this killing in detail is much less human than if they had ordered me to be shot at once.'

5 December 1816

Asked the Emperor his opinion of Tsar Alexander. 'He has some talent, he is plausible, a great dissimulator, very ambitious; it is foible to believe himself skilled in the art of war. At Tilsit, Alexander and the King of Prussia fancied they were equal to the best generals in Europe because they knew how many buttons there were on a grenadier's jacket. I could scarcely keep from laughing when I heard them discussing on what button orders ought to be hung, with as much gravity as if they were planning an action between 200,000 men. Of course I encouraged them in this as I saw it was their weak point.'

Napoleon then recounted to me some part of his early life: 'What is most extraordinary,' he said, 'and I believe unparalleled in history, is that I rose from being a private person to those astonishing heights of power without having committed a single crime.'

Lady Lowe came up to Longwood to pay a visit to Countesses Bertrand and Montholon.

6 December 1816

Discussion of the meaning of Lady Lowe's visit. Napoleon inclined to think it was a blind by Sir Hudson Lowe to make it appear that even after the arrest of Las Cases, the Governor was well esteemed in Longwood.

'Yesterday,' he said, 'after his wife had been here, Madame Bertrand and family went out to walk. On their return they were stopped and seized by the sentinels, who refused to let them in because it was six o'clock. Now, in God's name, is this agreeable, or accommodating?'

7 December 1816

Had a long conversation with Napoleon about anatomy.

Afterwards he spoke about Robespierre. 'Though a bloodthirsty monster he was not as bad as others.' Latterly he wished to be more moderate, and actually some time before his death said he was tired of executions. 'Robespierre thought the King ought to have been despatched privately. "What is the use", said he, "of all this mockery of forms?" Actually the King ought to have said that by the laws he could do no wrong and that his person was sacred. It would not have saved their lives but they would have died with more dignity.' *(This was more or less the position adopted by Charles I of England—they both still died.)*

10 December 1816

Water very scarce at Longwood. The water in the tubs extremely muddy, green and nauseous. In Deadwood it is much more easy to get a bottle of wine than one of water. Parties of the 53rd are employed daily rolling butts of water to their camp.

Napoleon depressed and annoyed, having discovered that only three or four of the chapters of his Italian campaign writings have been returned. He supposed that Sir Hudson Lowe was having the others copied, and desired me to tell Sir Hudson Lowe this.

11 December 1816

Told Sir Hudson Lowe of Napoleon's opinion. His Excellency waxed very wroth and told me to write in my note book that Napoleon was unworthy of being treated like a man of honour and undeserving of the consideration of one gentleman to another. Later he asked me not to give this message to Napoleon and to rub it out of my note book.

When I was leaving he said, 'Tell General Bonaparte that it is very fortunate for him that he has so good a man for Governor; that others with the instructions I have had would have put him in chains for his conduct.'

12 December 1816

Sir Thomas Reade said to me, 'If I were Governor I'd be d—d if I did not make him feel that he was a prisoner. He is a d—d outlaw and a prisoner, and the Governor has a right to treat him with as much severity as he likes.'

13 December 1816

Napoleon conversed on the probability of a revolution in France. 'Before twenty years have elapsed, when I am dead and buried,' said he, 'you will witness another revolution in France. It is impossible that 29 millions of Frenchmen can live contented under the yoke of sovereigns imposed on them by foreigners. Can you blame the French for not being willing to submit to the yoke of such asses as Montchenu?' *(Less than ten years after Napoleon's death the July Revolution of 1830 finally ousted the Bourbons.)*

Napoleon had another 'sweating and fainting attack' today. St Denis threw eau de cologne in his face thinking that it was a glass of water. The perfume got into Napoleon's eyes, which gave him intolerable pain but it certainly cured his faint.

14 December 1816

Napoleon unwell. 'Doctor,' he said, 'I had a nervous attack last night with a severe headache and involuntary agitations. I verily thought and hoped that a more violent attack would have carried me off before morning.'

He afterwards spoke about funeral rites and added that he would wish that his body might be burned. 'It is the best mode,' said he, 'as then the corpse does not occasion any inconvenience; and as to the resurrection this must be accomplished by a miracle in any case.'

18 December 1816

Went with Dr Baxter to visit Count Las Cases and his son. Wrote a letter to Sir Hudson Lowe recommending the removal of the young Las Cases to Europe for his health's sake.

Informed the Emperor that the Governor had offered to allow Las Cases to return to Longwood, but that the Count had not decided whether to return or leave the island. Napoleon said that he left that decision to the Count; he had actually suggested to all his generals that they go so that they would no longer be at risk of ill-treatment from the Governor. 'I am not afraid,' he continued, 'that they will send *me* off the island.'

Told Napoleon that Sir Hudson Lowe had asked me to convey to him that he had orders from Government to treat General Bonaparte with all possible indulgence, which he had done. Indeed he had been very mild!

(Major Gorrequer records in his diary that during his discussion this day with O'Meara, Sir Hudson exhibited 'furious gusts of passion. He scarcely had breath to articulate at times. How often he repeated "dishonourable, shameful, uncandid conduct".)

23 December 1816

Sir Hudson Lowe came to Longwood. I reported Napoleon's fit of syncope from the previous evening. 'It would be lucky, 'replied Sir Hudson Lowe, 'if he went off some night in a fit of the kind.'

I remarked that it was very probable that he would be attacked with a fit of apoplexy if the restrictions were not modified.

Sir Hudson Lowe then went off to speak with Count Bertrand—meanwhile Mrs Balcombe and Jane came to visit Napoleon but they were not allowed in, as they did not have a proper pass.

Saw Napoleon afterwards: 'What a fool I was to give myself up to you.' Said he, 'I had a mistaken notion of your national character. I had a romantic idea of the English. There was also an element of pride in my decision. I did not want to give myself up to any of the countries I had already conquered. I decided to confide in you whom I had never vanquished. Doctor, I entered all the capital cities of Europe in triumph. I am now punished for the good opinion I had of you.

'I should have surrendered to my father-in-law *(Francis, Emperor of Austria)* or Alexander of Russia—they would have treated me with greatest respect.'

I observed that it was possible that Alexander would have sent him to Siberia. 'Not at all,' replied Napoleon. 'Alexander, in order to make himself popular, would have treated me like a King. My father-in-law, though not gifted, is still a conscientious man.'

25 December 1816
Napoleon in very good spirits.

26 December 1816
Sir Hudson Lowe sent for me. He observed that I had put too much political feeling into my letter about young Las Cases. I appeared to enter too much into the feelings of *those* people.

29 December 1816
Las Cases has decided to go back to Europe with his son. Napoleon wished to bid him goodbye, but today a letter arrived from Sir Hudson Lowe explaining that 'in consequence of the manner in which Count Las Cases had been removed from Longwood, the Governor could not permit him to take leave of General Bonaparte.'

About 3 p.m. Las Cases and his son embarked on the *Griffin* sloop of war. His journal and papers were detained by the Governor.

31 December 1816
Sir Hudson Lowe sent for me at six in the morning. Apparently Baron Sturmer *(the Austrian Commissioner)* had learned about the recent fit and the accident with the eau de cologne. His Excellency wanted to know how this information had leaked out. I replied that I did not know.

Returning, I was soon convinced by the questions put to me that half the town knew it.

1 January 1817
Saw Napoleon in the drawing-room and wished him a Happy New Year. He said he hoped that the succeeding one would find him better situated; and added, laughing, 'Perhaps I shall be dead, which would be still better. Worse than this cannot be.'

He was, however, in good spirits, and spoke about hunting the stag and the wild boar. Showed me the scar of a wound on the inside of the ring finger, which he had received from a wild boar. Count Montholon came in, to whom Napoleon whispered something after which he went out and returned with a snuff box which the Emperor presented to me with his own hands. 'Here, Doctor, is a present I make to you for the attention which you manifested towards me during my illness.' Napoleon also made some elegant presents to other members of the house-hold. *(Years later O'Meara showed this snuff box to Daniel O'Connell, who, in July 1823, described it to his wife: 'Gold with the N and Crown and many bees and stars. It was a beautiful article and the association of ideas made it really interesting.')*

5 January 1817

Napoleon spoke very highly of Lord Nelson and indeed attempted to palliate the only stigma on his memory, the execution of Caracciolo, which he attributed entirely to his having been deceived by that wicked woman Queen Caroline through Lady Hamilton. *(Napoleon is referring to Queen Maria Carolina of Naples, sister of Marie Antoinette, and after her sister's execution a cruel and inveterate hater of Republicans. Caracciolo was born in Naples but fought with the French navy; his execution was pushed through by Nelson. Napoleon deposed Queen Maria's husband in 1805.)*

8 January 1817

The Emperor breakfasted this morning in the English manner upon a little toast and tea.

12 January 1817

I asked if he had not been very thin when he was in Egypt. He answered that he was at that time extremely thin, although possessed of a strong and robust constitution. After his thirty-sixth year he began to grow fat. He told me that he had frequently laboured in state affairs for fifteen hours without a moment's cessation, or even having taken any nourishment. On one occasion he continued his labours for three days and nights without lying down to sleep.

When Napoleon was rising up from the table this day and in the act of taking his hat off the sideboard, a large rat sprang out of it, and ran between his legs.

17 January 1817

Madame Bertrand delivered of a fine boy at half past four o'clock. Her accouchement was followed by some dangerous symptoms.

Sir Hudson asked me if I had told General Bonaparte that he was at liberty to ride around by Miss Mason's unaccompanied? He added that 'he daily expected good news from England for the French and hoped he should be permitted by the Government to render their situation more comfortable.'

18 January 1817

Napoleon sent for me. Complained of severe headache and made many enquires concerning Madame Bertrand.

Went to town and procured some newspapers, which I gave to Napoleon on my return. Napoleon asked me to make sure that even if I could not procure a loan of any newspapers I should *see* all the newspapers, in case they might contain anything about his wife and child. 'For,' added he, 'one reason that the Governor does not send up a regular series of papers, is to prevent me from seeing any article which he thinks would give me pleasure.'

19 January 1817

Sir Hudson made me read out a passage from a recent *Quarterly Review* in which Bonaparte is described, among other abuse, as 'grossly and brutally ignorant'. During the time I was reading this he indulged in bursts of laughter. He then told me I might borrow any books I liked from his library. He took down a book called *Les Imposteurs* and with a peculiar grin said, 'you had better take this to General Bonaparte, perhaps he might find some characters in it like himself.' *(It was passages like these, verging on caricature, that allowed O'Meara's enemies to cast doubt on his book.)*

21 January 1817

Saw Napoleon and gave him the books I had borrowed, including *Amours sécrets de Napoleon*. He ran through the book, laughed heartily, but observed it was monstrous silly.

He sat up until late at night reading Pillet and I was informed that he was heard repeatedly to burst out into loud fits of laughter. *(Major-General Pillet was a prisoner of war in England for six years and his* Views of England *(1813) is a wild attack. Chapters include 'Machiavellism of the English ministry' and 'Habitual intoxication common among females', subjects designed to appeal to Napoleon.)*

23 January 1817

Napoleon in good spirits. He had no memory of Major-General Pillet. 'Probably,' he said, 'Pillet is someone who has been harshly treated by you in the prison-ships and is full of malice towards the English. There is only one statement in his book which I take to be correct. There is something horrid in the treatment of prisoners in England. The very idea of being put aboard a ship and kept there for several years has something dreadful to it.

In France all the English were treated well.'

I asked the Emperor about his campaign in Egypt. *(Two alleged incidents in the taking of Jaffa, now part of Tel Aviv, have been controversial. One was the shooting of a number of Turkish prisoners, and the other was the poisoning of French plague victims.)* Was it true that he caused between three and four thousand Turks to be shot some days after the capture of Jaffa? Napoleon answered: 'There were not so many. I ordered about a thousand or twelve hundred to be shot. The reason was that there was in the Turkish garrison a number of troops who had given me their parole not to fight against me; also, before I attacked the town I sent a flag of truce. Immediately we saw the head of the truce-bearer elevated on a pole above the wall. I could not spare enough troops to guard the prisoners; therefore, availing myself of the rights of war which authorise the putting to death of prisoners under such circumstances, I acted to protect my soldiers.'

Napoleon completely denied the poisoning story. 'As we were leaving, I was told that there were seven or eight men so dangerously ill that they could not survive 24 or 36 hours. Larrey *(surgeon-in-chief to the Napoleonic armies from 1797 to 1815)* told me that there was a chance that these poor fellows might live until the Turks arrived and then be subject to the tortures they were known to inflict on prisoners. Accordingly, I ordered four or five hundred cavalry to guard them until they died. As it happened, I have heard since that despite appearances one or two were still alive when Sidney Smith entered Jaffa.'

26 January 1817

Napoleon visited Countess Bertrand whom he complimented on her beautiful child, 'Sire,' said the Countess, 'I have the honour to present to Your Majesty *le premier français* who since your arrival has entered Longwood without Lord Bathurst's permission.'

27 January 1817

Napoleon talked on the numerous attempts to assassinate him. 'Shortly after I was made Consul there was a conspiracy formed against me by about fifty persons.' They planned to kill him while he was sitting for a statue; later, he and Josephine were nearly blown up by a street bomb while on the way to the theatre. He talked of other plots against himself.

I then asked Napoleon if he had really intended to invade England and if so what were his plans? 'Once the Channel was clear I would have hurried over the flotilla with 200,000 men landed as near Chatham as possible. I calculated we could be in London in four days. I should have proclaimed a republic, abolished the nobility, distributing the property of the lords among my partisans. I would have issued a proclamation declaring that we came as friends to the English, to free the nation from a corrupt and flagitious aristocracy. I think that with my promises and what I had accomplished I would have had the support of a great many; in a great city like London where there are so many *canailles,* I should have been joined by a formidable body. I should at the same time excite an insurrection in Ireland. There is no knowing what would have happened. Neither Pitt, nor you, nor I, could have foretold what would have been the result.'

30 January 1817

Napoleon directed me to take the following message to the Governor: 'Tell him that in consequence of his conduct I conceive him to be a man without honour and without faith. That he has broken his word to me.'

31 January 1817

Went to Plantation House and delivered the message in as moderate language as I could.

8 February 1817

The meat has been so bad for some days that the orderly officer has felt obliged to return it, with an official complaint.

9 February 1817

The servant of Las Cases called Scott—a native of St Helena—was released from prison today and handed over, on condition he would not leave his property. Mr Scott would be fined £100 if he ever went beyond the enclosure of his father's property.

10 February 1817

Had some conversation about Alexandria. 'Your ministers were most unwise by giving up Alexandria. Five thousand men would be a sufficient garrison to keep it under your control. It would pay for itself by the great trade you could establish between England and Egypt. You could prohibit the introduction of all other manufacturers except English. Alexandria is the only good port in that country. It would have been more important for you to keep Alexandria than Gibraltar or Malta. If Egypt ever got into possession of the French, farewell India to the

English. I do not know why you put such a great value on Gibraltar. You cannot prevent a fleet from coming into the Mediterranean. I was quite happy you held on to Gibraltar—because this always incensed the Spaniards against you.'

12 February 1817

Mrs and Misses Balcombe arrived at Longwood. I dined with Napoleon in company with them. He was extremely lively and chatty, and displayed a fund of *causerie (light chat)* rarely to be met with. He instructed Miss Eliza *(Betsy)* Balcombe how to play billiards.

Cipriani refused permission to go into the valley to buy sheep and vegetables from the farmers. The daily allowance of meat etc. being carted up in the sun to Longwood, many of the articles are unfit for use.

14 February 1817

Breakfasted with Napoleon with whom I had a conversation about Russia. 'If the Emperor Paul had lived there would have been peace with England, as you would not have been able to contend against the united northern powers. I encouraged him to continue building ships, and by all means to get a large Russian fleet into the Mediterranean.' *(Paul I, son of Catherine the Great, was Tsar 1796–1801. He was succeeded by his son Alexander 1801–1825.)*

Paul was brutally murdered in his bedroom. He hid behind the curtains but eventually he was discovered. He was dragged out; his captors insisted he sign a paper declaring his abdication. Paul refused to sign—they tried to suffocate him but he made a desperate resistance. He was pushed to the floor and was struck with the heel of his shoe deep into the socket of his right eye. Two others held Paul on the floor-while B— beat his head and brain into a pulp. In the struggle Paul had bitten a sizeable lump out of B—'s leg.' *(Count von Bennigsen, a Hanoverian general in the Russian service, was still alive at the time of the publication of O'Meara's book. This description of his role in the Tsar's murder is not accepted by all historians.)*

I asked if he thought Paul was mad. 'Latterly,' said Napoleon, 'I believe that he was. If Paul had lived you would have lost India. An agreement was made between Paul and myself to invade it. I furnished the plan. My 30,000 troops were to have gone to Warsaw to be joined by 30,000 Russians and 40,000 Cossacks. We would then all march together to the Caspian Sea. Some would cross by boat, others would proceed by land according to circumstances.'

I then asked if the Tsar Alexander intended to invade Turkey. Napoleon answered: 'Yes, all his thoughts were directed to the capture of Turkey. Initially, I agreed with him. It would have been an excellent idea to drive those brutes, the Turks, out of Europe. But reflecting I saw what tremendous power that would have given Russia, so I refused to consent. Those barbarians of the North were already too powerful. Probably in the course of time they will overwhelm all of Europe. I shall be revered as one who tried to stop that; I will be revered when the barbarians of the North possess Europe—which would not have happened but for you, *signori Inglesi.*'

Napoleon then expressed his worry that he felt that Count Montholon might be sent back to Europe. 'I should feel the loss of Montholon very much. I know it would grieve him to leave, though in truth it would render him a great service. He has nothing to fear in France—in fact he might readily find favour with the Bourbons if he chose.'

17 February 1817

Today we discussed the battle of Waterloo. 'Had it not been for Grouchy,' he observed 'I should have won the day'. *(Marshal Grouchy and 30,000 men were despatched by Napoleon to prevent Blücher and the Prussians from joining up with Wellington's army. For complicated reasons, mostly not his fault, and some Napoleon's, he failed to achieve this.)* I asked if Grouchy had betrayed him intentionally. 'No, no,' replied Napoleon, 'but there was a want of energy on his part. There was also treason on the part of his staff.'

Napoleon went on: 'When I came back from Elba there was no plot, no understanding with any of the generals. Not one of them knew my intentions. The proclamations were the whole of the conspiracy. But the enthusiasm of the troops was outstanding. I could have entered Paris with over 400,000 men if I so wished.' Napoleon continued: 'There never was yet a King who was more the noble sovereign of his people than I was. The mass of the French people hated the old nobles and the priests. I am not sprung from the ancient nobility, nor have I too much encouraged the priests. The French nation has an unconquerable passion for glory. They will as soon do without bread as glory. A proclamation will draw them on, unlike England where a county will follow the opinion of two or three noble families.

'Your nation,' Napoleon went on, 'is chiefly guided by interest. I have paid deeply for the romantic and chivalrous opinion which I had formed of you. Paoli (*President of the Corsican Republic*), who was a great friend of your nation said, on hearing the English praised, "They are not so generous or unprejudiced as you imagine; they are very self-interested; they are a nation of merchants and generally have gain in view." *Now* I believe that Paoli was right.'

18 February 1817

Saw Sir Hudson Lowe at Plantation House. Found him busy examining some newspapers for Longwood, several of which he put aside as not being proper to be sent. He explained that this was out of consideration, since 'articles written in his favour might excite hopes which could not be realised.'

24 February 1817

His Excellency told me, in order to show his good opinion, that the Commissioners were to be looked on with great suspicion. That they were in fact spies on everybody and everything. That I had better be cautious as in all probability they would report to their employers everything that I said. (*A more sophisticated man than Lowe would perhaps have involved the Commissioners in the day-to-day governance of Napoleon.*)

He also said that he had written to Lord Bathurst in the most favourable terms and suggested that my salary should be increased to £500 per annum.

28 February 1817

Napoleon had very little rest during the night. He awoke around 5 a.m. and walked for some time around the billiard-room. Found him lying on his couch. Looking low and out of spirits. Greeted me with a faint voice. Gave him a Portsmouth paper. On reading some remarks about international affairs he said 'Under the Bourbons, France will never be a first-rate power.

'I have been informed,' continued he, 'that the Balcombes were interrogated and cross-examined by the Governor and his privy councillor Reade about what they had heard and seen at Longwood, and that the father replied that his daughters had come here to have the honour of visiting us, not as spies.' (*Balcombe's firm was the somewhat inefficient food purveyor to Longwood, and he was suspected by Lowe of being a possible conduit of Napoleon's illicit correspondence with the outside world.*)

1 March 1817

Some iron railings have come out in the *Adolphus*. I explained to Napoleon that it was customary in England to put such rails around the country houses of gentlemen, at which he looked rather incredulous.

2 March 1817

I found Napoleon in his dressing-room, lying on the couch. He was rather low spirited and looked pale. He commented favourably on the fact that the Bourbons had employed men who had originally been employed by him rather than royalist ultras. I asked his opinion of Clarke. (*Marshal Henri Clarke was Napoleon's Minister for War 1807–1815. His family background was from Kilkenny, and his brother-in-law Colonel O'Meara was his ADC.*) 'He is not a man of talent, but he is useful and laborious in the bureau. He is, moreover, incorruptible. He pretends that he is descended from the ancient kings of Scotland or Ireland. I sent him to Florence as Ambassador, where he did nothing but turn over the musty records of the place searching for proofs of the nobility of my family which you may know came from Florence. He plagued me with letters on the subject, but I told him not to trouble his head or mine with such nonsense; I was the *first* of my family.'

3 March 1817

Saw Napoleon in very high spirits. Free from any complaints. Laughed and quizzed me about some young ladies and asked for the gossip of the town.

While walking about the room he asked: 'What sort of man did you take me to be before you became my surgeon?' I replied, 'I thought you a man whose stupendous talents were only equalled by your measureless ambition; that you would not hesitate to commit a crime when you found it necessary.' 'That is the answer I expected,' replied Napoleon, 'and is perhaps the opinion of Lord Holland and even numbers of French. The fact is that I am too much of a fatalist and have always despised mankind too much to have had recourse to crimes. As it is, though I have failed, I shall be considered an extraordinary man; my elevation was unparalleled *because* unaccompanied by crime.'

Napoleon afterwards walked down to Count Bertrand's. For two or three days he has taken much more exercise than formerly.

4 March 1817

Saw Napoleon in the billiard-room. He was in extremely good spirits. 'When I was on the throne,' Napoleon said. 'there were thirty clerks employed in translating English newspapers and books. Anything important was immediately sent to me. My English was so poor I did not know the article "the" at that time.'

The Governor declared today that when the railings were established around Longwood the gates would be locked at seven or eight o'clock in the evening and the keys then sent down to Plantation House until daybreak.

6 March 1817

Napoleon in very different spirits. He was reclining on his couch in a pensive attitude with his head resting in one hand, apparently melancholy.

He had his morning gown on, a Madras handkerchief around his head and his beard was unshaven.

'What news—has any ship arrived from England?' he asked.

I informed Napoleon that a book about him written by Dr Warden was recently published and had just arrived on the island. Napoleon was instantly interested. 'What is the nature of the work? Is it for or against me? Is it well written?'

I replied that it was a description of what had happened on board the *Northumberland* and at St Helena. (*Dr William Warden's* Letters written on board the Northumberland and St Helena *was not the first attempt to feed the British public's appetite for information about Napoleon. Lieutenant John Bowerbank's* Extract of a journal kept on HMS Bellerophon *was published in 1815. However, Warden's more substantial book gave Napoleon a chance to put his case to the British public. The anonymous publication* Letters from the Cape of Good Hope in reply to Mr Warden *was dictated by Napoleon to Count Bertrand over the next few months and published in 1817.*)

Napoleon asked how had the work been received in England? Were the Ministers pleased with it?

I then assisted him in reading over some extracts in *The Observer* which he admitted were correct. An article in the paper stated that Marie Louise had fallen from her horse into the Po. She had been saved with some difficulty.

General Gourgaud received a letter from his sister which included the news that Madame Dillon, Countess Bertrand's mother, was doing well. I never observed before the consolation afforded by a letter from distant relations or friends. A line of writing from Europe is, at Longwood, a treasure above all price.

7 March 1817

Some French newspapers sent up to Napoleon by the Admiral. Napoleon very anxious to hear further news about Marie Louise. The Governor sent up Dr Warden's book. Napoleon was highly amused to find a facsimile of his own handwriting in the book. Later that night Napoleon sent for me and asked me most earnestly to search the newspapers in Plantation House to get more news about Marie Louise and their son.

8 March 1817

Mrs Balcombe with Jane and Betsy came to Longwood. Napoleon sent for them and conversed for a few minutes. Hudson Lowe said 'they had no business speaking to General Bonaparte as the pass only specified Count Bertrand's family.'

(*Betsy Balcombe remembered: 'One day our pass from Sir Hudson Lowe only specified a visit to General Bertrand, but my anxiety to see Napoleon caused me to break through the rule laid down, and the consequences of my imprudence nearly proved serious, as my father all but lost his appointment. I caught sight of the Emperor in his favourite billiard-room and not being able to resist having a game with him, I listened to no remonstrances but bounded off leaving my father in dismay at the consequences. Instead of a game of billiards I was requested to read a book by Dr Warden. I had the task of wading through several chapters and making it as intelligible as my ungrammatical French permitted. Napoleon was much pleased with Dr Warden's book.'*)

10 March 1817

Napoleon in good spirits. Had some conversation relative to Warden's book. I asked his opinion of the book. He replied: 'The foundation of it is true, but he has misunderstood much that was said to him. Warden does not speak French. As a result he has often put into my mouth expressions that are unworthy of me and not in my style.

'He makes basic mistakes, for instance about Wagram where he puts Masséna near Esling where he never was, and about Jaffa, about the death of the Duc d'Enghien, about my return from Elba. Gourgaud in particular is very angry about what was said of him.'

Napoleon also stated that King Louis proposed to return to the throne of France after the battle of Marengo. 'Louis wrote to me saying that I delayed for a long time to restore him to his throne, but that the glory and happiness of the country needed both him and me. I sent back a handsome letter in which I stated that I was extremely sorry for his misfortune—but that he should abandon all thoughts of returning to France as a sovereign.'

A few moments afterwards Napoleon observed that it was true that the Belgians were sorry that the English had won Waterloo: 'They considered themselves as Frenchmen and in truth they were such. The greater part of the nation loved me and wished that I might succeed. *Millions* in Europe now *weep* for me. For instance, the Piedmontese preferred being a province of France rather than united to the Kingdom of Sardinia.'

Later this evening, we were informed that Count Bertrand's cook went to the camp and became so drunk as to be incapable of cooking. Napoleon, informed of this, sent some dishes from his own table to Countess Bertrand.

11 March 1817

Letters arrived on the sloop of war the *Griffin*. An official letter sent from Plantation House to Balcombe and Co. asking why 14s more than allowed had been spent on fish for Longwood; also to know why 2s 6d more than allowed had been spent on wine. Sir Hudson Lowe in a bad humour, railed at the *impudence* of Las Cases in presuming to send wine, oil and other articles from the Cape to Longwood. He said this was an insult to the British government.

12 March 1817

Saw the Emperor at 11 a.m. in very good humour. I asked if it were true that he had once been nearly captured by the Cossacks. 'At the battle of Brienne,' replied he. 'I remember 25 Uhlans, not Cossacks, got around the wing of my army—searching to destroy some artillery. It was beginning to be dark when the Uhlans stumbled upon me and my *état-major*. When they saw us they did not know what to do. They certainly did not recognise me. I thought they were some of our own troops. My staff began to fire on them. They became frightened and not knowing what to do tried to escape in all directions. One in particular came riding past and struck my knee with the wrong end of a spear. I pulled out one of my pistols but by the time I wheeled around— he was gone. The Uhlans were later cut to pieces.'

13 March 1817

Napoleon in his bath. In very good spirits. Some conversation about recent publications respecting him. 'I suppose,' said he, 'that when you go to England you will publish your book You certainly have a better right to publish about me than Warden. Truly no French physician has been about me as you have been. The world is more anxious to know such trifles about a man who has made a figure in it as how he eats, drinks, sleeps, his general habits and manners than to know what good and bad qualities he has.'

Captain Poppleton busy digging potatoes out of the little garden in front of the house.

14 March 1817

A letter appeared in the French newspapers stating that Napoleon had invited the Marquis de Montchenu *(Napoleon had refused to see him or the other Commissioners)* to dine and the Marquis had refused, saying that he had been sent to St Helena to guard Napoleon, not to dine with him. 'It is very likely that he has been *bête* enough to say that,' replied the Emperor, 'those old French *noblesse* are capable of any *bêtise!*'

16 March 1817

The Emperor in the drawing-room in extremely good spirits, joked with me on a supposed attachment to a fair damsel.

Napoleon spoke again about Talleyrand. 'The triumph of Talleyrand is the triumph of immorality. A priest united to another man's wife. A man who sold everything, betrayed everybody and every side! I forbade Madame Talleyrand the court because she was a disreputable character—a fine woman, English or East Indian, but *sotte* and grossly ignorant.' *(She was actually the daughter of a French official in India, and married a British civil servant there before becoming Talleyrand's mistress and eventually his wife.)*

He then described the canals he planned between the Red Sea and the Mediterranean. 'My surveyors found that the waters of the Red Sea were thirty feet higher than the Mediterranean at the highest. It would have prevented any problems with sluices.' *(This was, of course, wrong.)*

I asked how many had lost their lives on 13th Vendemaire *(the night of the 'whiff of grapeshot' by which Napoleon and Murat cleared an armed mob of anti-revolutionists and royalists from the National Convention.)* Of the people there were about 70 or 80 killed and between 300 and

400 wounded. On our side about 30 killed. The reason so few were killed was that after the first two discharges I made the troops load with powder only. They started with ball because to a rabble who are ignorant of the effect of firearms it is the worst possible policy to fire powder only at the beginning. The populace are frightened by the noise, but when they see nobody killed or wounded they pluck up their spirits. With a rabble everything depends on the first impression.' (*With typical clarity of thought combined with ruthlessness Napoleon reversed the normal course by opening with lethal fire first and then using the more humane powder only.*)

17 March 1817
Captain Poppleton wrote to His Excellency informing him that the horses had no hay for three days. The fresh grass recently cut contained 'cow grass' which horses will not eat. Consequently they were starving.

18 March 1817
Napoleon joked with me for quite some time about St Patrick. He tried to speak English and succeeded better than ever before. This was his best effort at the language so far. Napoleon laughed and pulled my ear. (*This curious physical gesture was a familiar one to Napoleon.*)

'I am told,' said Napoleon, 'that £20,000 worth of iron railings have been sent out. Before this railing can be fixed up here I shall be underground for I am sure that I shall not exist more than two years under the treatment I am now experiencing.'

Sir Hudson Lowe very busy inspecting ditches and other works he had ordered around Longwood.

19 March 1817
Saw Napoleon in his bath. He was reading a little book which I saw to be the *New Testament*. I explained that I was surprised, as most people would believe him to be an unbeliever. 'It is not true,' he said. 'I am far from an Atheist. In spite of the iniquities and frauds of the teachers of religion, when I was in power I did everything I could to re-establish religion. Man needs something wonderful. It is better he seeks it in religion than in fortune telling! Moreover, religion is a great consolation and resource to those who possess it, and no man can say what he will do at his last moments.'

(*Betsy Balcombe recalls a similar scene when she assumed he was a disbeliever. 'He seemed displeased at my observation and answered: "When you are wiser you will understand that no one could doubt the existence of a God."'*)

Napoleon then discussed Hudson Lowe, who he declared totally unfit for his situation. 'If he were,' said he, 'he could make it pleasant and interesting for himself. He could spend much of his time with me and get great information with respect to past occurrences. He would imperceptibly have opportunities of getting information from me which would be very desirable to his Ministers. If I had really any intention of escaping, instead of disagreeing with him, I would flatter him, endeavour to be on the best of terms, go to Plantation House, call on his wife and lull his suspicions asleep.'

20 March 1817

Saw Napoleon in his bedroom in his dressing-gown. He spoke at length about some statements in Warden's book.

Napoleon also discussed the various assassination attempts on him. 'On various nights throughout August, September and December of 1803 groups of men arrived in France under the command of a Captain Wright. Their names were Georges, Pichegru, Rivière, Coster, St Victor, La Hayes, St Hilaire and others. The last four named above were involved in a previous assassination attempt on me which failed. Pichegru was betrayed by one of his friends, so I declared the city of Paris to be in a state of siege. No one was allowed out except by day through certain barriers. Eventually they were all captured. All were put on trial. All were found guilty. Nine were executed. Rivière and others were pardoned. The Duc d'Enghien was waiting on the frontiers, waiting for news of my assassination on which he was to have entered France as the King's lieutenant. I caused the Duc to be arrested *(outside French national territory)*. He was tried for having borne arms against the Republic, found guilty and shot.'

23 March 1817

Napoleon dressed and in the billiard-room. In very good humour. Gave him some libels on himself. They were all in French and amongst them were *Mémoires sécrètes* and *Bonaparte peint par lui-meme* which excited his laughter.

I told Napoleon that Sir Hudson Lowe had suggested that Las Cases, Warden and others had stirred up bad blood between them. Napoleon replied, 'He deceives himself. In the first place it was the badness of his physiognomy; then a train of vexations which followed. He wants us to submissively demand pardon and to be his humble servants.'

24 March 1817

Napoleon complained of swelling in both legs. I recommended some simple remedies which he put in practice. He observed, 'These libels have done me more good than harm in France, because they irritated the nation both against the writers and the Bourbons who paid them by representing me and the government as monsters which was degrading to them as a nation.

25 March 1817

Napoleon in his bath. His legs much better. 'It appears, Mr Doctor,' said he, 'from the book you lent me, that when I was young I poisoned a girl; that I poisoned others for the mere pleasure of killing and that I assassinated Desaix, Kléber and the Duke d'Abrantes, and I know not, how many others! It's surprising what can be believed in the absence of communication. In France, if a house was burnt down, the vulgar attributed it to the English. "Pitt, Pitt," was the cry directly. Nothing could persuade the *canaille* that the fire at Lyons was not caused by the English.

'When I was at Elba,' added Napoleon, 'I was told that the sum of money allowed me annually by France would not be paid. Besides, my wife and child were seized, detained and never permitted to join me. By the treaty my mother and brothers were to receive pensions which were also refused. My own private property was confiscated. Moreover, assassins were sent out to Elba to murder me. There was even talk of my being sent to St Helena.'

I observed that the Allies feared that he aimed at universal domination. 'No,' replied the Emperor. 'I certainly wished to make France the most powerful nation in the world and no further. There are natural limits for France which I did not intend to overstep. (*This powerful idea was first promoted immediately after the Revolution—the limits being the Rhine, the Alps and the Pyrenees. As he says on 22 May, Napoleon well knew that French control of the harbours of Belgium and the Netherlands, only miles from the English coast, was regarded as too risky by the English.*) It was my intention to make Italy an independent kingdom. I wanted to prevent England from being able to go to war with France.'

Sir Pulteney and Lady Malcolm came up with two captains from the navy. One of them, Captain Stanfell, expressed astonishment at finding Napoleon so different from what he had expected. 'Instead of a rough, impatient, imperious character, I found him to be gentle in his manner and the pleasantest men I ever saw. I shall *never* forget him.'

Sir Pulteney Malcolm expressed to me his wish that matters might be accommodated between Napoleon and Sir Hudson Lowe, adding that the forthcoming arrival of Admiral Plampin and Lord Amherst would furnish an ideal opportunity.

26 March 1817

Napoleon conversed a good deal about the battle of Waterloo. 'Lord Wellington,' he said, 'allowed himself to be surprised. On the 15th I had beaten the Prussians without his knowing anything about it. I had gained 48 hours manoeuvres on him, which was a great object. And if some of my generals had shown that vigour and genius which they had displayed in other times I should have taken his army without a battle.

'The chief causes of the loss of that battle were first of all Grouchy's great tardiness and neglect in executing his orders, and next the grenadiers and the cavalry under General Gyot, which I had in reserve, attacked without my knowledge so that after the last charge I had not a single corps of cavalry to resist them. The youngest general of any army would not commit such a fault as fighting without a reserve.'

Napoleon than spoke about the libels which I had collected for him. 'You have not produced one that is worth an answer. They are contemptible and absurdly false. Silence is the only answer—there is just one report that is quite true. It concerned a young officer, on the field of battle. I saw his young face covered in blood. I said "*Oh, comme il est beau!*" My enemies had made my admiration of the gallantry of a brave soldier into a crime and a proof of delighting in blood.'

I then told the Emperor that Lord Amherst, the late British Ambassador to China, was expected here in a few days. (*Lord Amherst's embassy to China in 1816–1817 had famously come to grief when he had refused to kow-tow to the Emperor*). He said he thought that the British had done wrongly in not complying with the customs of the place he was sent to. 'If I,' he continued, 'had sent an Ambassador to China I would have ordered him to make himself acquainted with the ceremonies performed before the Emperor by the first Mandarins, and, if required, to do the same, and no more. Now, perhaps you will lose the friendship of the nation and great commercial advantages through this piece of nonsense.'

29 March 1817

The Emperor conversed about the English manufacturers. 'I gave up near 500 convents to individuals on the sole condition of establishing a manufactory in them.' I observed that the prevalence of machinery was one cause of the distress in England. 'But,' replied Napoleon, 'you were obliged to have recourse to machinery because the necessaries of life are twice as dear in England as on the Continent and taxes six times greater.'

31 March 1817

I was invited to a dinner at Plantation House with many other guests. The Commissioners very anxious to know something about Napoleon *(to have something to report in their despatches).*

2 April 1817

Napoleon in tolerable spirits. I asked him if he was forced to quit Egypt because of fear that the Directory proposed to have him assassinated there. 'No,' replied the Emperor, 'I never thought so. I had to return because my presence was necessary in France.'

Apparently Sir Sidney Smyth sent papers to Napoleon under a flag of truce with letters and newspapers stipulating the imminent collapse of the government in France. 'This,' he said, 'decided me to return'.

Many people who arrived at St Helena wished to be introduced to Napoleon. If they were pretty and spoke French, Napoleon, who is very partial to female society, was only too delighted to see them. However, Sir Hudson Lowe effectively prevented their meeting by sending Sir Thomas Reade to be an attentive listener close by their side.

Captain Cook and his midshipman, a Mr McKenzie, were able to obtain an interview. McKenzie was on board the *Undaunted* when Napoleon sailed to Elba. Napoleon observed that he had grown much since he had seen him before. He enquired from Captain Cook what actions he had participated in. Captain Cook mentioned among others Trafalgar. When they were leaving, Napoleon learned they were to dine at the camp. 'Then take care,' he said, 'that you do not get drunk.'

3 April 1817

I told Napoleon how the midshipman had said that the ship's company of the *Undaunted* had liked him very much. 'Yes,' replied Napoleon, 'I believe they did. I used to go amongst them. Speak to them. My freedom in this astonished them as it was so different from what they had been used to from their own officers. You English are *aristocrat*s. You keep a great distance between yourself and the people.'

I replied that at sea 'it was imperative to keep seamen at a distance in order to maintain proper respect for officers.' Napoleon replied that on the field of battle he often walked among his men, conversed with them and took an interest in their plans. 'This I found was of great benefit to me.'

Napoleon then mentioned that a book recently published declared him to be an 'imbecile' and his army nothing more than robbers. 'It says that I foolishly engaged Wellington with a forest at his back—actually it was a great fault in Wellington to engage me with a forest at his rear and only one road; in case of defeat he could not have retreated.'

Napoleon then asked if we kept Good Friday sacred, if we fasted? I replied that we did observe it, but that Protestants seldom fasted, though when we did we abstained altogether from food. That we did not consider avoiding animal food and gorging with fish as fasting. *(As an Irish Protestant O'Meara could not resist a small anti-Catholic dig.)*

Napoleon then spoke about General Hoche. 'He was one of the finest generals that France ever produced. He was brave, intelligent, abounding in talent, decisive and penetrating! If Hoche had landed in Ireland he would have succeeded. He possessed all the qualifications to ensure success. He was accustomed to civil war and knew how to conduct himself under such circumstances. He was well adapted for Ireland. He had a fine handsome figure, a good address—just the right man. But by some stupidity he was placed on board a frigate which never reached Ireland. The rest of the expedition of about 18,000 men reached Bantry Bay where they remained for some days but could not land. Grouchy, the second in command, was uncertain what to do, so after some days of indecision he returned to France. Had Hoche been there he would have succeeded. England would have lost Ireland!

'If the Irish,' added he, 'had sent over honest men to me, I would certainly have made an attempt upon Ireland. But I had no confidence in either the integrity or the talents of the Irish leaders that were in France. They could offer no plan, were divided in opinion and continually quarrelling with one another. I had but a poor opinion of the integrity of that O'Connor who was so much spoken of amongst you.' *(Arthur O'Connor 1763–1852, a leading United Irishman and friend of Lord Edward Fitzgerald, came to France in 1803 and was appointed General-de-division by Napoleon. He married Grouchy's niece. He lived in France for the rest of his long life.)*

4 April 1817

Napoleon in very good spirits, comparing English rule with French. 'I do not deny that the old Constitution of France was a very bad one, and required to be newly modelled. But the Constitution which I gave them when I returned from Elba was excellent. Indeed, its only fault was that it left too little power in my hands, and perhaps too much in those of the Senate. I could not imprison a man without a decree, order a fine, impose taxes, or levy them by conscription; and there was a law for the liberty of the press.'

Went with Captain Poppleton and others of the 53rd to a rat hunt in the camp. Fourteen killed in less than half an hour.

6 April 1817

Napoleon in good spirits. Mentioned the Marquis Cornwallis. 'He was the first man who gave me a good opinion of the English. His integrity, fidelity, frankness and the nobleness of his sentiments impressed me. There was a man of honour, a true Englishman.' *(Cornwallis, who died in 1805, met Napoleon while negotiating the Treaty of Amiens in 1802, not long after an active few years in Ireland crushing the 1798 rebellion and using his reputation as a supporter of Catholic emancipation to secure the passing of the Act of Union.)*

He also stated that Lord Castlereagh *(British Foreign Secretary 1812–1822)* offered him asylum in England before he went to Elba. Castlereagh said, 'Why go to Elba? Why not come to England?' He would be received in London with the greatest of pleasure. Let him give himself up without making any pre-conditions and he will be received with the greatest joy!' 'This had great influence with me later,' Napoleon said.

A pause now took place. Napoleon walked a few paces, stopped, looked at me and said in an expressive manner: 'No one but myself ever did me any harm. I was, I may say, the only enemy to myself. My own projects, the expedition to Moscow and the accidents which happened there were the cause of my fall.'

I asked him if he had ever said this of Metternich: 'One or two lies are sometimes necessary, but Metternich is all lies. Nothing but lies, lies, lies from him.' Napoleon laughed and said '*C'est vrai.* He is composed of nothing but lies and intrigues.'

'I always had a high opinion of your seamen,' he said later. 'On one occasion,' he explained, 'I was returning from Holland with the Empress Marie Louise and I wanted to cross the river Meuse during a violent storm. My own sailors said that the waters were so high it would be impossible to pass for two or three days. There were some British prisoners in the barracks. I asked them if they could join a number of boats so I could get across. They said it was possible, but hazardous. In the course of a few hours they had succeeded in what the *imbeciles* said was impossible, and I crossed before the evening was over. I ordered those who had worked on the bridge to be given money, clothes and their freedom.'

8 April 1817
Races were held at Deadwood. General Gourgaud had long conversations with the Commissioners without any British officer overhearing them.

Napoleon went to Madame Bertrand's house and watched all the events through the upstairs window.

Following the races, Mrs Younghusband *(wife of one of the officers of the 53rd)* invited some of the French to her home for refreshments. The Commissioners, Madam Sturmer, Baron Gourgaud and others all accepted. Later on that evening Sir Thomas Reade expressed great anger for extending such an invitation to the French. He also suggested that the Governor ought to turn her off the island for it.

9 April 1817
Napoleon walked out for some time with Counts Bertrand and Montholon. Saw him at mid-day. He asked many questions about the races. Observed that from what he had heard Montchenu had made use of very improper language before Lady Lowe when the breeze interfered with some lady's dress. 'In general,' said Napoleon, 'Frenchmen at his time of life are proverbially polite, but he could never have been brought up in good company.' *(We know from unedited versions of other memoirs—particularly Gourgaud's—that Napoleon's conversation could be extremely 'barrack-room'. The limitations of what could be published give us no hint of this in O'Meara's account.)*

15 April 1817
Napoleon anxious in his enquiries about the health of Madame Bertrand and the two Montholon children, Tristan and Napoleone, both of whom were very unwell, especially Tristan who had severe dysentery. Bleeding afforded the child great relief.

16 April 1817

Napoleon has been for some days in very good spirits.

Had a long conversation with him on medical subjects. Napoleon was convinced that in internal medicine the patients had an equal chance of dying by the physician's misdiagnosis or by the remedies prescribed operating in a manner different to what was intended. He was for trusting entirely to Nature. With surgeons he had a far different opinion and acknowledged the great utility of that science.

I proposed that in some complaints Nature was a bad physician, and mentioned in proof the cases of Countess Montholon, General Gourgaud and Tristan who, if left to Nature, would certainly have gone to the other world. Napoleon was sceptical and inclined to think that if they had taken no medicine, abstained from food and drunk plenty of water they would have done as well. *(How right he was.)* Eventually Napoleon said, 'Well, perhaps if ever I have a serious malady I may change my opinion. I would like to know what sort of patient I should make— tractable or otherwise—I am inclined to think the former.'

'Are you a fatalist?' he asked. I said I believed a man's dissolution to be inevitable, but if in a battle he saw a cannon-shot coming towards him he would naturally step aside, and with certain complaints medicine is the same. I told him of a most unusual death of a young man on board the *Victorious* when they fought and captured the *Rivoli*.

'The man who had been slightly wounded hid himself among the cables where it appeared no shot could reach him. Towards the end of action a shot struck the ship low down, penetrated the wings, bounced off the cable, rose upwards, struck a beam and, being spent, rebounded and fell on the man's chest (he was lying on his back). He was found later with a 36-pounder lying on his chest!'

Napoleon replied 'That confirms what I say to you—that man cannot avoid his destiny!'

The Emperor during the course of conversation spoke about eunuchs; a most disgraceful and horrid practice. 'I suppressed it in all countries under my dominion. In Rome I prohibited it under pain of death. There was one Crescentini, an excellent singer who often sang before me. I conferred upon him the Knighthood of the Iron Crown (*an Italian order initiated by Napoleon in 1805 predominantly for nobles and military officers*). Many people were displeased with this. Madam Grassini silenced their objections when she said "The Emperor is quite right. The poor man merits it—if it were only on account of his wounds."'

The St Helena landmark 'Lot's Wife' in the south-west of the island, photographed by the author in April 2005. At first the mist can be seen beyond the rock, in the distance; ten minutes later it has swept over the island.

23 April 1817

Napoleon remained in his bedroom and ate nothing. He told me that he rose at three in the morning and dictated all day.

He spoke of the time he was in the habit of dictating to four different secretaries at once, and sometimes five, each writing as fast as he could. Made some comments on the Emperor of Austria *(his father-in-law)*. The Emperor he pronounced to be a good and religious man but an old blockhead, always led by the nose by Metternich. As long as he had a bad minister his government would be bad as he entirely trusted to him and only paid attention to botany and gardening.

24 April 1817

Napoleon in good spirits. Very curious in his enquiries about Murat's expedition against Sicily. 'That foolish fellow Murat!' exclaimed Napoleon. 'He lost me 1,300 men, by that rash disembarkation he made in Sicily! If I had really intended to take Sicily I would have pushed out the Toulon fleet with 30,000 men to effect a landing near Palermo. But the object was really to keep your army occupied in Sicily lest it be employed against me elsewhere.'

He then spoke about Corsica and the Corsicans and observed that they were brave and revengeful by nature, the best friend and the most dangerous enemy in the world. 'Their prominent national characteristic,' he said, 'is never to forget a benefit or an injury. For the slightest insult in Corsica *una archibugiata*. Murders are consequently very common.'

25 April 1817

Count Bertrand stopped by the sentinel when going towards Dr Wilton's cottage. Napoleon said that he supposed that the soldiers had instructions to stop all *suspicious* persons and that obviously the French were the only suspicious people on the island. Told him that a report had arrived of war having been declared between Spain and America and Russia and America. 'Russia and America?' said he. 'Impossible. If it takes place I shall never be astonished again at anything.' *(Why would Russia bother with America, with its population of fewer than ten million, when the rich pickings of Europe were available?)*

29 April 1817

Dined with Sir Pulteney Malcolm in town. The Russian Commissioner joined us to explain *(no doubt with a view to this being passed on to Longwood)* that he felt very awkward in respect of the French. He felt he was an object of suspicion to the Governor. He would therefore have to decline further conversation with General Gourgaud, however unpleasant it was to do so in a place where there was so little French society, until he got instructions from Russia as to how he was to act.

Cipriani was in town today to buy provisions. Sir Thomas Reade had been very busy and helpful in procuring hams and other provisions.

30 April 1817

Napoleon has been occupied for some days dictating and writing his observations on the Great Frederick. *(Frederick II of Prussia, 1712–1786, by military triumphs and economic reforms brought Prussia into the front line of European states.)* Told me that when finished it would comprise of six or seven volumes. His writing much more legible than before. Napoleon said that in the past he wrote very quickly—writing only half or three quarters of the word and running them into each other. His secretaries had become well accustomed to it.

Napoleon then observed that I had made considerable progress in French. 'Though you have a very bad accent,' said he. 'I know you English say that I speak Italian better than French. This is not true. Although I speak Italian frequently it is not pure *Toscian*. I cannot write a book in Italian nor do I speak it in preference to French.'

Speaking of Chateaubriand's attacks upon him, he observed: 'He is one of those insects who prey on a corpse, which while it is still living they dare not approach!' *(Chateaubriand, who had briefly worked in the Napoleonic diplomatic corps, refers to Napoleon in his 1814 pamphlet* De Buonaparte et des Bourbons *as having 'the sword of Attila and the maxims of Nero', and condemned the invasion of Spain as' impious, sacrilegious, odious and above all anti-French'.)*

Among other conversations I asked him if there had been sufficient provisions on the retreat from Moscow, the loss might have been smaller. 'No, the cold would have destroyed them in any case. Those with food died by hundreds. Even the Russians themselves died like flies.'

2 May 1817

General Montholon very ill. Napoleon expressed much anxiety about him.

6 May 1817

During our conversation Napoleon said, 'The Admiral *(Sir Pulteney Malcolm)* held a long conversation with me the other day. He praised the Governor; said I was mistaken in him, that he was extremely well-informed and at bottom a good heart. He was very anxious that I meet as if nothing had previously occurred. I told him that until he changed his conduct I would not see him, unless by force. As long as he treats me "*à la* Botany Bay" I will not see him.'

Napoleon told the Admiral that 'England had been the first to violate the Peace of Amiens. Conscious of this, Lord Whitworth offered me 30 million and to help me become King of France if I would let them have Malta. My reply was that I would owe nothing to strangers or to their interference. If the French nation did not want to create me King—foreign influences should never be employed.'

Captain Meynell was very ill. General Montholon much better. *(Meynell was Captain of the* Newcastle *and a frequent visitor to Longwood. He was MP for Lisburn 1826–1847.)*

I then asked him about Captain Wright *(who was the commander of the cutter that landed Pichegru and the other conspirators in the assassination plot. He was captured in an unrelated incident a year later and subsequently—while Napoleon was fighting in Austria—found in his cell with his throat cut. His death is a favourite anti-Napoleon theme.)* 'He should have been tried by a military court and then shot within twenty-four hours,' replied Napoleon. 'What would your Government do if a French captain was found in London trying to murder King George—would they have been so lenient as I was with Wright?' *(Elsewhere Napoleon suggests that in fact Wright had heroically killed himself to avoid compromising his government under torture.)*

7 May 1817

Napoleon very particular in enquiring after Captain Meynell. Had some further conversation about prisoners made at the commencement of the war. We discussed the exchange of prisoners. Napoleon could not remember the exchange of ships but he did remember an occasion when he wanted to exchange 2,000 Spanish and Portuguese plus 1,000 English prisoners for 3,000 French soldiers. The British wanted the English to be released first, even though the Portuguese and Spanish were their allies. At the same time the French prisoners in England wrote to Napoleon protesting that when the 10,000 or so English prisoners were released the British would break off these exchanges on some pretext and subject them to ill-treatment and brutalities. 'I could not ask for a better testimonial,' he said, 'of the way English prisoners were treated than that many of the English sailors did not want to be released and returned to their ships.'

11 May 1817

Told Sir Hudson Lowe what Napoleon said of the restrictions on his exercise excursions around Longwood, and the Commissioners, etc.

His Excellency observed that the principal cause of the difficulty was that Sir George Cockburn had given much more indulgence than he had any right to; not only had he not the right, but it was contrary to instructions.

He then complained about the letter sent by Madame Bertrand to the Marquis de Montchenu—which he seemed to consider a very heinous offence. I explained that when the letter was written there had been no prohibition against correspondence between people on the island. His Excellency did not appear well pleased with this explanation.

12 May 1817

After some conversations about the Governor, Napoleon said, 'When I was at Elba, the Princess of Wales informed me of her intention to visit.' *(Princess Caroline, the estranged wife of the Prince Regent, was at that time living a somewhat rackety life in Italy.)* 'I sent back an answer begging her to defer her visit for some weeks that I might see how matters turned out,' he explained. 'I knew that such a visit could not fail to injure the Princess, so I put it off. I was quite surprised, as her father and her brother had been killed fighting against me. She went afterwards to see Marie Louise and I believe they are great friends.

'Prince Leopold,' continued he, 'was one of the finest young men in Paris; he was near to being one of my aides-de-camp for which he had solicited, like many of the young princes in Germany. Luckily for him he did not succeed, as probably if he had he would not have been chosen to be a future King of England.' *(Leopold was married to Princess Charlotte, the Regent's heir. Charlotte, however, died in childbirth in November 1817. Leopold became 'King of the Belgians' in 1831.)*

13 May 1817

Permission granted to let a local farmer (Mr Breame) to supply Longwood with two calves each month; the farmer to be paid by the French themselves.

14 May 1817

Napoleon in very good spirits. Asked me why I had dined in the camp yesterday? I replied, 'because there is nothing to eat at Longwood.' He laughed heartily at this.

16 May 1817

Napoleon complained of a headache and had his feet immersed in hot water. At first he was rather melancholy but subsequently became lively. He asked if a three decker could enter the harbour at Alexandria without being lightened? I replied that I thought it might, and if not it could easily be lightened sufficiently. Napoleon discussed in detail how the fleet had been destroyed at Aboukir. 'The attack took place at night,' he explained—'when the French fleet were at anchor.' Brueys should have fortified the island at the entrance to the harbour.' *(In the 1798 Battle of the Nile, as it is also called, Nelson smashed the French fleet by manoeuvring behind the island, thus, for a time at least, locking Napoleon and his 30,000-strong army in Egypt.)*

He then went on to discuss how some men are born to lead while others are born to be led. 'Breuys was a man of undoubted talent, but lacked that decisive resolution which is the most essential quality in an admiral or general. I myself was a commander of the army at the age of twenty-two, but Nature made me different from most others,' he said.

'The French soldiers had great contempt for the English troops at the beginning of the war, caused by the failures of the expeditions under the Duke of York. In this they were fools, but it is difficult to conceive how little the French soldiers thought of yours until they were taught to the contrary.

'When I went to see the King of Prussia, instead of a library I found he had a large room like an arsenal, furnished with shelves and pegs on which were placed fifty or sixty jackets of various modes. Every day he changed his costume. He was a tall dry-looking fellow—he would have made an excellent Don Quixote. He attached more importance to the cut of a dragoon or hussar uniform than what was necessary for the salvation of his kingdom. At Jena his army performed the finest and most intricate of manoeuvres possible—but I put a stop to their *coglionerie* and taught them that to fight and to execute dazzling manoeuvres and wear splendid uniforms were very different affairs.'

The Emperor observed that we allowed too much baggage and too many women with our armies. 'Women, when they are bad,' said he, 'are worse than men, and more ready to commit crimes. The soft sex when degraded fall lower than others—witness the *tricoteuses de Paris* during the Revolution.

'When I was crossing the Alps, I gave strict orders that no women were allowed—it was far too dangerous. I put two captains on guard at the bridge with instructions—under pain of death—that no women should pass. I went to the bridge myself and found a crowd of women who shouted and reviled with me— "Oh, *petit caporal*, it is you who will not let us pass!" (I was then called *petit caporal* by the army). Some miles further on I found many women up the mountainside. I discov-

Count Bertrand (1773–1844) Grand Marshal. Having been with Napoleon on Elba as well as St Helena, Bertrand lived long enough to accompany Napoleon's coffin to Les Invalides in 1841.

ered that they had hidden themselves in barrels and casks on the way through.'

18 May 1817

Major Fehrzen *(who commanded the 53rd Regiment in St Helena)* came to Longwood. Being asked why he did not call on the Bertrands, the Major replied that the Governor had signified that no communication between the 53rd Regiment and the French should take place.

22 May 1817

Had some conversation with Napoleon about Montchenu who he said would perfectly justify the idea that the English formerly held of the French, viz. that they were a nation of dancing-masters.

Napoleon (who had just come out of his bath) spoke about Russia and said that the European nations would eventually find that his policy of re-establishing the kingdom of Poland was the only effectual means of stopping the increasing power of Russia. 'It puts a barrier against that formidable empire which one day could overwhelm Europe! I will not live to see it, but you may. I think you will see Russia invade India or enter Europe with 400,000 Cossacks and 200,000 real Russians. Alexander will be obliged to prevent revolution in Russia by this means.'

'A great object for England,' added Napoleon, 'is to keep Belgium always separated from France. If France had Belgium then it might be said in the case of a war with England to have Hamburg etc.' *(Which would mean easy access not only to potential invasion sites across the Channel, but also to the British Royal family's ancestral lands in Hanover.)*

'If I had succeeded in Russia I would have been able to compel England to make peace.' He added that he was tired of war. if there had been peace he would have employed himself doing nothing more than improving France, educating his son and writing his history. 'At least the Allied powers cannot take from me the great public works, which I have executed. They cannot take from me the code of laws, which I formed, and which will go down to posterity. I pity the poor King of France. He is just a prisoner in the hands of the Allies and the population hate it. The Bourbons will not survive long.'

23 May 1817

Sent for to attend the Governor at Plantation House. He complained that I had received newspapers which I had lent to General Bonaparte without his knowledge, in contravention of the Act of Parliament. I replied that I was not included in the Act since I should not be treated or considered as one of the French, and that I would resign immediately if I was required to hold my position on those terms. General Lowe then asked me not to give any newspapers or books or be the bearer of any information—without first consulting him. I replied that this put me in a very difficult position as Napoleon was bound to ask me about news.

Hudson Lowe then proposed that 'as soon as any ships arrived, both Captain Poppleton and myself should be locked up in Longwood until he vetted all information and newspapers arriving on the island.' I replied that I would not remain one hour in my situation subject to such a restriction.

I observed that 'Sir George Cockburn never considered it necessary to keep back newspapers from Napoleon, and the only instruction had been not to show him anything personally offensive.'

(However tactless and unimaginative, technically Sir Hudson was in the right. In the Parliamentary debate in April 1816 on the 'Act for effectually detaining Napoleon Bonaparte' and the associated 'Act for regulating the intercourse with the island of St Helena' it is made quite clear that the Ministers intend that Napoleon be treated as a prisoner of war, and that all letters and other communications to and from 'the general and his attendants' shall go via the Governor, and there be opened before being passed on.)

26 May 1817
Napoleon indisposed, with catarrh, inflammation and swelling of the right side of his face and gums with headache, caused probably by exposure to the cold wind in the garden.

27 May 1817
Napoleon better.

'In the course of a few years,' said he, 'Russia will have Constantinople, the greatest part of Turkey and all Greece. Once mistress of Constantinople, Russia gets all the commerce of the Mediterranean, becomes a great naval power and God knows what might happen. The powers that can oppose it are England, France, Prussia and Austria. England is falling. Even Prussia prohibits your goods. In my opinion the only thing that can save England will be abstaining from meddling in continental affairs. You are superior in maritime force to all the world united; by your present mode of proceeding you forfeit all those advantages.'

28 May 1817
A servant, William Hall, dismissed from Longwood. He underwent a long interrogation at Plantation House as to what he had seen and heard at Longwood.

Sir Hudson Lowe told me with some embarrassment, that 'his conduct had undergone a parliamentary investigation. An account of these proceedings was in the newspaper'. This report, he assured me, 'might be incorrect and unfaithful'. This I was to report to General Bonaparte, if he ever read the article. *(In March 1817 Lord Holland, while admitting that 'the opinion of the country went along with ministers' in respect of Napoleon's captivity, nonetheless raised the allegations of 'harsh, cruel and unjust usage', saying if untrue they should be refuted; if true they should be corrected. The Minister, Lord Bathurst, admitted nothing.)*

30 May 1817

Napoleon asked me to translate the *Times* report of Lord Bathurst's speech, in which he said that changes in the conditions had only been made for his benefit, that the reason for reducing the limit had been his tampering with the inhabitants, that communications with officers and inhabitants was unrestricted.

Napoleon replied, 'I am consoled that the minister feels obliged to justify his atrocious acts to parliament and the people by lies. This is a miserable resource, which cannot be sustained. In the meantime I have ordered Bertrand to make a full translation and to consult you about any doubtful phrase.'

31 May 1817

Gave Napoleon a translation of a letter in the *Courier* newspaper He expressed his opinion that it had been written by the Governor.

'You were greatly offended with me for having called you a nation of shop-keepers. Had I meant you were a nation of cowards, you would have had reason. All I meant was that you were a nation of merchants. All your riches and your grand resources came from commerce. You are ashamed of yourselves and want to be a nation of nobility and *gentlemen*. All these things did very well for me in France because they are conformable to the spirit of the nation. But, believe me, it is contrary to the spirit and the interest of England. Stick to your ships, your commerce and banks, and you will prosper.'

2 June 1817

I was ordered to Plantation House. His Excellency asked what were General Bonaparte's remarks on the discussions in Parliament. I repeated Napoleon's expressions. Sir Hudson Lowe was visibly embarrassed and attempted to justify Lord Bathurst's remarks. Then he stated that he had never heard any complaints of a deficiency in the quantity of provisions for Longwood, and that the quantities supplied were as requested by Count Montholon. Major Gorrequer confirmed that only the wine quantity had been specified by Count Montholon; the provisions were on a scale laid down by His Excellency himself. Sir Hudson Lowe persisted in asserting that he was ignorant of the insufficiency of the allowance; I then listed the number of days on which I, Mr Balcombe, and the *maître d'hôtel* had complained. I also observed that the fact that Sir Thomas Reade had spent so much time procuring various eatables for Longwood would have left him in no doubt as to the wants of the

French. The Governor sneeringly observed 'it appeared that I would be the best witness *those* people could call.'

4 June 1817

An increase of 28 pounds of meat per day was now furnished to Longwood by order of the Governor.

5 June 1817

Count and Countess Montholon went to town shopping and to pay a visit to Admiral and Lady Malcolm. An officer was ordered to follow them into the Admiral's and pay attention to their conversation.

6 June 1817

Napoleon in very good spirits. Told me that a person who had seen the Grand Llama had arrived on the island. 'I am,' said he, 'very curious to get some information about this Grand Llama. I have never read anything I could rely on, and have sometimes doubted his existence.'

Saw Sir Hudson Lowe in town; mentioned to him that Napoleon had remarked when speaking of Lord Bathurst 'almost all ministers are liars. Talleyrand is their corporal, next come Castlereagh, Metternich, Hardenberg.' (*These were respectively the French, British, Austrian and Prussian representatives at the Congress of Vienna.*)

A report current in town that a marble bust of young Napoleon was brought out in the *Baring*, and that Sir Thomas Reade had recommended that the captain throw it overboard and say nothing about it.

8 June 1817

By order of Major Gorrequer the liveries of the servants of Longwood must be changed from green to blue and the quantity of gold lace on the coats diminished.

10 June 1817

In the evening Napoleon sent for me and said that he had heard that a sculptor at Leghorn had made a bust of his son which he had forwarded to St Helena by the *Baring*. Napoleon asked me if I knew anything about the bust? I felt confused and said I expected that the Governor would have it sent up.

11 June 1817

This day a beautiful white marble bust of young Napoleon was sent up, about life-size and very well executed. 'Look at that,' said Napoleon, 'Look at that image. The countenance would melt the heart

Napoleon II (1811–1832)

of a ferocious wild beast. The man who gave orders to break that image would plunge a knife into the original if he could.'

He gazed at the bust for a long time with great satisfaction and delight. No man who had witnessed this scene could deny that Napoleon was animated by the tender affection of a father. *(Betsy Balcombe remembered that 'Napoleon gazed on [the bust] with proud satisfaction, and was evidently much delighted at our warm encomiums on its loveliness . . . my mother said she never saw a countenance so interestingly expressive of parental fondness.')*

13 June 1817

Saw Napoleon in the billiard-room. He was in very good spirits. Spoke about the possibility of remaining in France after Waterloo. 'I could not have done so,' said he, 'without having shed the blood of hundreds. The Legislative Body were frightened and divided; Lafayette was one of the chief causes of the success of the enemies of France.' *(A hero of 1789 and of the American Revolution before that, Lafayette made a famous speech in the Chamber of Representatives declaring that three million Frenchmen had died fighting for Napoleon, and that was enough.)*

'Many were of the opinion that I ought to have fought to the last. Others said that fortune had abandoned me. The smiles of fortune were at an end. I ought to have died at Waterloo, but when a man seeks death most, he cannot find it. Men were killed around me, before, behind, everywhere, but there was no bullet for me.'

19 June 1817

Colonel Fagan, formerly Judge-Advocate in India had an interview with Napoleon. The Colonel spoke French like a native, so they had a long conversation concerning his profession.

Napoleon said he had asked Colonel Fagan many questions about the military penal code. 'On this subject, I am master,' he said. 'I am a Doctor of Laws and while the Code Napoleon was forming, the lawyers were astonished at my knowledge of the subject. I also originated many of the best of its laws.' *(The credit for the Civil Code is usually given to Jean Jacques Régis de Cambacérès, later Duc de Parme, whose fourth process of codification the Code was.)*

20 June 1817

An official report made to His Excellency of the quality of the bread supplied to Longwood which has been so bad that for a considerable time Napoleon has been obliged to make use of biscuit.

30 June 1817

Lord Amherst paid a visit to Count and Countess Bertrand. Napoleon observed: 'When the Governor came to Bertrand's with Lord Amherst, he merely introduced him and then, without sitting down or conversing like a gentleman, turned and took his leave, like a gaoler who points out his prisoners to visitors, turns the key and leaves.'

3 July 1817

The new Admiral Plampin arrived on *Conqueror* from the Cape. He came to Longwood today with his flag-captain and his secretary. They were introduced by Sir Pulteney Malcolm. Napoleon remarked to me afterwards on the singular difference of appearance between Sir Pulteney and his successor. 'Few men,' said he, 'have so prepossessing an exterior and manner as Malcolm; but this new Admiral reminds me of those drunken little *schippers (bargemen)* I have seen in Holland.'

On my return from town, dined with the Emperor *tête-à-tête* in his writing-room. He was in very good humour. Dinner was served on a little round table. The Emperor sat on the couch and I on a chair opposite. I was very hungry and did great justice to what was presented to me. The Emperor made some remarks on the late attacks on the validity of his title to the throne.

'If I was not a legitimate sovereign, then William the Third was a usurper of the throne of England, as he was brought in chiefly by the aid of foreign bayonets. George the First was put on the throne by a faction, composed of just a few nobles. I was called to the throne of France by the votes of over four million Frenchmen. In fact, calling me a usurper is absurd. If my title to the crown of France was not legitimate—what is that of George the Third?'

Napoleon then said he would like to see me drunk and ordered Marchand to bring a bottle of champagne. He took one glass and made me finish the rest, calling out in English, 'Doctor, drink, drink.'

4 July 1817
Sir Pulteney and Lady Malcolm sailed for England.

The affair of the bust is being whispered about the island. It was reported that the bust had been executed at Leghorn by orders of the Empress Marie Louise. Napoleon is inclined to believe this.

Some days later when he was better, Napoleon agreed to see Lord Amherst and his staff. Lord Amherst was alone with Napoleon for nearly two hours.

9 July 1817
Packages and cases arrived at Count Bertrand's house for Napoleon (including a superb set of chessmen) from the Honourable Mr Elphinstone in gratitude for saving the life of his wounded brother the day before Waterloo. It appeared that on the presents was engraved the letter N, surmounted by a crown, which His Excellency considered highly objectionable and dangerous.

17 July 1817
Saw Sir Hudson Lowe and had a long and disagreeable conversation. He complained that I had failed to convince General Bonaparte of the justice of his (Sir Hudson's) conduct. I informed him that both Sir Pulteney Malcolm and I had done everything to conciliate matters. His Excellency said that Napoleon had caused Bertrand to write him the most impertinent letter he had ever received, and remarked that he

*Rear-Admiral Plampin, commander-in-chief of
the St Helena and Cape of Good Hope naval
stations from July 1817 to July 1820*

had it in his power to turn General Bertrand off the island whenever
he chose.

18 July 1817

*(Napoleon was very angry about Sir Hudson Lowe's actions about the
bust of his son.)* 'He says that according to the rules he was not authorised to send up those presents. Where are those regulations? I have
never seen them. To a dungeon, to chains on his arms and legs a man
may accustom himself, but not to another's caprice. I do not desire any
favour from him. Perhaps he requires that I should write him a letter of
thanks daily for the air I breathe.

'I told Lord Amherst,' he continued, 'that neither your prince, nor
both your Houses of Parliament can oblige me to see *mon geolier et mon
bourreau.' (My jailer and executioner.)*.

The Emperor was so firmly impressed with the idea that an attempt
would be made forcibly to intrude on his privacy that he always kept
four or five loaded pistols and some swords in his apartments, with which
he was determined to despatch the first who entered against his will.

19 July 1817

Sir Hudson Lowe accuses me of not supporting him during my conversations with Napoleon. 'Means have not been taken,' he said, 'to justify my character to him.' He ordered me to tell him of Napoleon's discussion with Lord Amherst. 'Napoleon informed Lord Amherst that he was prevented from speaking with anyone and leaving the road.' His Excellency started and with a degree of violence that considerably impeded his utterance exclaimed: ''Tis false! 'Tis false!' When he had recovered a little of his power of speech he reproached me in a violent manner for not having contradicted these assertions. After he expended most of his wrath, I observed that I had attempted his defence to the best of my ability.

Eventually he ordered me not to speak with General Bonaparte unless upon professional subjects. He ordered me to come to town every Monday and Thursday in order to report to him General Bonaparte's health and habits.

21 July 1817

Had another conversation with Sir Hudson Lowe of a nature similar to yesterday. A long and disagreeable discussion took place. Eventually I requested him to remove me from my situation. *(Now Sir Hudson Lowe was in a quandary. If O'Meara left the island Napoleon would probably refuse any medical help from the English and particularly any doctor recommended by Lowe himself. If Napoleon became acutely ill then Sir Hudson could be held responsible for his death.)*

24 July 1817

Went to town according to Sir Hudson Lowe's orders. His Excellency made me undergo an interrogation before Sir Thomas Reade and Major Gorrequer during which he expressed much anger, because my sentiments did not accord with his own.

Finding that Sir Hudson Lowe made me, in a manner, responsible for all of Napoleon's actions and expressions and took every opportunity of venting upon me all the ill humour he could not possibly discharge upon his prisoner, I determined to confine myself to my medical duties.

10 August 1817

Had some conversation with Napoleon about a report in one of the papers relating to his removal to Malta. He did not give it any credit, observing that he would cause less alarm in England than in Malta.

11 August 1817

Told Sir Hudson Lowe that Napoleon wished to have the garden freed of spurge, a weed by which it is now overgrown, and desired that it be converted to grass.

14 August 1817

Went yesterday to Plantation House. I now have to go there on Tuesdays and Saturdays, instead of Mondays and Thursdays. He asked me to repeat the words used by Napoleon in conversation with Lord Amherst. I warned Sir Hudson that my report might upset him again, nevertheless he insisted. I repeated that Napoleon had said that 'neither your Prince nor your House of Parliament can oblige me to see my jailer and executioner'. Sir Hudson Lowe walked about for a few minutes, looking very angry. He asked why General Bonaparte should use such expressions? I replied that I did not know. He then began to vent upon me all the ill-humour which he entertained towards Napoleon. He ended by saying, 'You are not authorised, Sir, to communicate with General Bonaparte on any other than medical subjects. If you hold any other communication with him it is at your own peril, unless you make them known to me and thereby free yourself of responsibility.'

Napoleon took a walk of two hours and appeared to be in good spirits. Saw him on his return. He discussed the Egyptian campaign and some of the individuals who accompanied him there.

15 August 1817

Napoleon's birthday. *(He was forty-eight.)* He was dressed in a brown coat. All the generals and ladies dined with him at two o'clock, also the children were brought in for a short time. He gave them each a present and amused himself for some time playing with them.

17 August 1817

Saw Napoleon at two o'clock He was in extremely good humour and very pleasant, joking and rallying me about a young lady on the island.

Napoleon then made some observations about *(the possibility of his being transferred to)* Malta. 'The Government should have made a treaty with me binding me to remain in Malta for a number of years. After a certain length of time I would then be received in England where I would live for the rest of my days. This would save the English nation six or eight million francs a year.' (*'Hope deferred maketh the heart sick'—poignantly, Napoleon's hopes for leaving St Helena are constantly being refreshed.*)

'It would,' added he, 'have been more humane to have had me shot on the *Bellerophon* than to have condemned me to be exiled to such a rock as this.

'I really think that Lord Bathurst imagined that by a series of ill-treatments and humiliations they would induce me to commit suicide, and for that purpose found *son homme*. The very idea of this, if I ever had any thoughts of doing so, would effectually prevent my putting it into execution.'

22 August 1817

Saw Napoleon at twelve o'clock. He has continued to rise at four o'clock in the morning and to employ his time reading and writing. Pointed out to me that he had been obliged to cause his coat to be turned, there being no green cloth on the island.

'What do you think,' he asked, 'would give me the greatest pleasure?'

I was about to reply 'removal from the island of St Helena', when he said, 'to be able to go about incognito, in London and other parts of England and dine with a friend in many cafés and restaurants—and just listen to the conversations.

'This and the education of my son would form for me my greatest pleasure. It was my intention to have done this had I reached America.

'The happiest days of my life were from sixteen to twenty when I went about various restaurants with very little money, just listening to the conversations of other people. I was never truly happy on the throne. Not that I have to reproach myself with doing evil while seated there— on the contrary—I restored 50,000 families to their country and the improvements I made in France speak for themselves. I made war, certainly, but in almost every instance I was either forced into it, or I had some great political object in view.

'Had I died in Moscow,' continued he, 'I should have left behind me a reputation as a conqueror without parallel in history. A ball ought to have put an end to me there.

'My greatest mistake was not having made peace at Dresden'. *(A tactically brilliant victory by Napoleon over much larger Allied forces in 1813.)*

I asked him what was the most rewarding time in his life.

'The march from Cannes to Paris!' *(on his escape from Elba)* he said without hesitation.

I asked why Marie Louise had not made 'some exertions on his behalf?' 'I believe,' he replied, 'that Marie Louise is just as much a state prisoner as I am myself. I have always had occasion to praise the conduct of my good Louise and I believe that it is totally out of her power to assist me; moreover she is young and timorous.

'Perhaps,' he went on, 'I should have married the sister of Emperor Alexander—as proposed by him at Erfurth. But I did not like to have a Russian priest as a confessor of my wife as he would have been a spy for Alexander. My union with Marie Louise was first proposed by Emperor Francis himself and by Metternich.' *(Alexander's sister had not yet reached puberty. Napoleon was forty-one; he needed an heir. Marie Louise was eighteen.)*

23 August 1817

General Gourgaud informed me that at the close of the battle of Waterloo English cavalry came within 300 yards of where the Emperor was standing. Napoleon ordered some shots to be fired to drive them away and one of these shots carried away the Marquess of Anglesea's leg.

Napoleon was prevented from throwing himself amongst the enemy by Soult who laid hold of his bridle exclaiming that he would not be killed but taken prisoner.

25 August 1817

Napoleon in high spirits. Saw him in the dining-room dressed in a grey double-breasted coat.

'When at Lyons in 1786 I gained a gold medal for an essay on the sentiments necessary for happiness. When I was on the throne I mentioned this to Talleyrand who immediately acquired the theme from the college. He presented it to me, but I immediately put it on to the fire. It was too visionary, abounding with Republican ideas and exalted sentiments of liberty.

'Robespierre,' said Napoleon, 'was by no means the worst character in the Revolution. He opposed the trial of the Queen. He was not an atheist; on the contrary he sincerely believed in the existence of a Supreme Being. He was a monster, but he was incorruptible and incapable of robbing. Marat and others were infinitely worse. One, for example, maintained that to ensure the liberation of France, it was necessary that 600,000 heads should fall. Astonishingly, those fanatics bathed up to the elbows in blood but would not have taken a piece of money or a watch belonging to the victims they were butchering.'

'Not so Talleyrand, Danton, Barras and Fouché, who would have taken any side for money. When I was commander of the army in Italy, Barras charged the Venetian Ambassador 200,000 francs for a letter he sent to me begging me to be favourable to the Republic of Venice. I threw this letter in my waste paper basket. I never paid any attention to such letters.

'Fouché,' he added, 'was never my confidant. Never did he approach me without bending to the ground. He was a terrorist but I kept him on as Chief of Police, because in that way I knew he would betray all his friends. We were able to imprison over 200 of his friends. Talleyrand really possessed my confidence for a long time and was frequently acquainted with my projects a year or two before I put them into execution. He is a man of great talent but wicked, unprincipled and covetous of money. His rapacity was so great that I was obliged several times to dismiss him from my employment.

'Madame Campan,' said Napoleon, 'had a very indifferent opinion of Marie Antoinette. She told me that a person well known for his attachment to the Queen *(Count Fehrsen)* came to see her on the 5th or 6th of October. The palace was stormed that night. Marie Antoinette fled undressed from her own chamber to that of the King for shelter, while her lover descended from the window. Looking for the Queen, Madame Campan entered the Queen's bedroom to find she was absent but discovered a pair of breeches which the favourite had left behind in his haste and, which were immediately recognised. *(Madame Campan was a lady-in-waiting at Versailles and later ran a school established by Napoleon for the daughters of members of the Légion d'Honneur. The sex life of Marie Antoinette was a favourite topic of speculation among revolutionists; it is extremely unlikely that this anecdote came from the devotedly Royalist Madame Campan.)*

1 September 1817

The *Marie* transport ship arrived from the Cape with mail. A letter from young Las Cases to Madame Bertrand states that he at last obtained permission to quit the Cape. His father is very unwell and since there was no medical officer on the brig it might be better if they did not sail at all. Also, there was a letter for Count Bertrand from Baring Brothers & Co. of London informing him that two years ago the sum of £12,000 had been deposited with them for his use.

Dr Baxter, Deputy-Inspector of Hospitals on St Helena, and an ally of Hudson Lowe. He never saw Napoleon as a patient. He left St Helena in 1819.

Napoleon has been in good spirits for several days. Yesterday he went out to look at the progress of the new road, greatly to the surprise of the sentinel who stood gazing at him at the distance of a few yards.

In one of the newspapers, there was an *(untrue)* article stating that his sister Caroline had married General MacDonald. Napoleon remarked that he did not think that his sister would remarry. 'She is a woman arrived at an age when her passions are no longer *brûlants*; that she has four children and is possessed of a strong, masculine understanding. However, there is no accounting for the actions of a woman.

'Have you heard,' said he, 'that Lord Wellington was the person who first proposed to send me to St Helena?' I replied that I had but did not give the report any credit. 'If it be true,' said he, 'it will reflect but little honour upon him.' *(It is much more likely to have been Talleyrand.)*

2 September 1817

Madame Bertrand wishes Mr Brooke *(Secretary of the St Helena Council)* to sign some papers. Due to her illness and the inclement weather, she could not travel the five miles to Jamestown. Sir Hudson Lowe saw some ulterior motive. Why, he asked, did they not come to him as Chief Magistrate?

'He wants to get the Marquis de Montchenu in conversation in front of Mr Brooke who does not understand French.' I replied that it never occurred to them that such was their intention. 'Then it does you little credit, Sir. You are very sharp at finding out everything to their advantage,' and added that I was an instrument in their hands.

Sir Hudson said very gruffly that the less communication I had with them *(the French)* the better. He repeated his surprise that I should not have spotted their motives in wanting to see Mr Brooke. I could have told him it was no more than the invincible repugnance everybody at Longwood had to his presence.

3 September 1817

Found the Emperor in the drawing-room reading the *Old Testament* aloud. In very good spirits. He made some observations about the way in which the Governor examines every little bill, receipt and account. 'Even the bills and salaries of the servants are minutely examined, and every trifling sum obliged to be accounted for. Useless vexations, for it could not be by small sums which I get here that I could escape. But if he had his will he would order me to breakfast at a certain hour, dine at another, go to bed at a time prescribed by him, and see himself it carried into execution. But all this will recoil on him. He does not know it but everything that passes here will be recorded in history.' *(On the contrary, Sir Hudson was in fact acutely aware of this. His minutely detailed papers referring to his time on St Helena run to nearly 90 volumes.)*

Napoleon then said that 'Cipriani informed me that the Governor took some great pains to have me understand that the Burgundy sent here some time ago came from him. I ordered him never to bring me any more of it. I do not blush to drink the wine and eat the bread of John Bull but I will accept nothing from the hands that have become so odious to me.'

4 September 1817

The weather has been extremely wet for several days and Napoleon has ordered that a fire should be kept in the four rooms he uses. He cannot stand the smell of coal and there was a great deficiency of wood on the island. Found Noverraz *(third valet at Longwood)* breaking up a bedstead and some shelves to burn.

Saw Napoleon in his bath. He remarked that Northern people required the stimulus of the bottle to develop their ideas. The English appeared in general to prefer the bottle to the ladies as was exemplified by our allowing them to go away from the table and remaining for hours to intoxicate ourselves. I remarked that although we did sit sometimes for hours after the ladies withdrew it was more for the sake of conversation than for wine of which there was not so much drunk as formerly. Our conversation after dinner frequently turned on politics and other matters with which ladies seldom meddled. He maintained that it was a custom which could not be justified—that women were necessary to civilise and to soften the other sex. *(The reputation of the English, and the Irish, for hard-drinking had certainly been earned, but it is interesting to see O'Meara confirming the change historians have detected at this time to more sober habits.)*

5 September 1817

Had some conversation in the morning with Napoleon on the deficiency of wood.

Went to Plantation House by order of Sir Hudson Lowe. Explained that there were 23 fires at Longwood, which he thought too numerous. 'They had no business with so many,' he answered. I had explained that Longwood was very damp, and that French ladies and children required constant fires. He said that 'Lady Lowe had no fire in *her* room.' I observed that the French were natives of a more southerly climate than ours. I also told His Excellency that Napoleon could not bear the smell of coals, and suggested that instead of sending wood to the camp coals might be furnished, and the wood sent to Longwood; to which he replied that 'he did not like to humour any person's whims'.

Napoleon said that he had seen Admiral Plampin who had explained how a 74-gun ship could take 80 tons more water in tanks than in casks. 'Had I had known this in 1806,' he said, 'I would have sent an army of 30,000 men to invade India. I had made several calculations about sending so large a body of men to India but my calculations always found that they would have been short of water for a month. The plan was to fill 46 line-of-battle ships with 800 troops in each. They would have proceeded to India, disembarked in time to allow the Mahrattas to join them. They would then proceed in different directions, and do you all possible mischief. Had I known of the tanks, I would certainly have made the attempt.

'One of the greatest errors I ever was guilty of,' continued the Emperor, 'was sending that army out to St Domingue. *(Stimulated by the rhetoric of the Revolution, the slaves of the French colony of St Domingue, now Haiti, rose up in 1791; Napoleon sent an army to return them to colonial control in 1801.)* I should have declared St Domingue free, acknowledged the black government and sent some French officers to assist them. This would have done you incalculable mischief; you would have lost Jamaica and your other colonies would have followed. But after the peace I was continually beset by proprietors of estates in the colony, merchants and others. Indeed the nation was crazy to regain St Domingue.'

6 September 1817

Informed Count Montholon that Sir Hudson Lowe stated that he had regulated the quantity of fuel necessary for Longwood by a comparison with that consumed in Plantation House. Montholon replied that both his and the Countess's clothes were spoiled by the damp, in spite of the fires which were used. *(Playing cards became stuck together because of the damp and had to be heated before they could be separated.)* As to asking for more, he did not like to subject himself to slights or refusals.

Napoleon for some days has eaten no dinner. Told me he intends to accustom himself to only one meal a day. Mentioned he once proposed the invasion of Surinam. 'You have been there, Doctor—would I have been successful?' he asked. I replied that 'I thought not. Large ships would have to anchor 17 miles offshore and the channel for lighter vessels was only practical at high water (for vessels not drawing more than 18 feet). The country itself was full of marshes and very inaccessible.'

The weather has not been so bad this day as for some time past. Napoleon went out as far as Count Bertrand's. *'Veramente,'* said he, *'non e paese Cristiano.'*

7 September 1817

Napoleon complained of rheumatic pains and slight headache. He blames the dampness of the climate and the house.

He made some remarks on the *Manuscrit venu de Ste Hélène (a book published in England in April 1817 purporting to be written by Napoleon),* and observed that there was such ignorance and so many mistakes as to time and place that it would make a corporal in the French army laugh. Notwithstanding this, 'what he says on the Nobility is true. The Nobility I formed was of the people. I took the son of a peasant and made him a Duke or Marshal when I found he had talents. I wanted to introduce a general system of equality, so that every person should be eligible to every situation, provided he had talents to fill it. I wanted to do away with all the ancient privileges of birth.'

Speaking about the badness of the house Napoleon observed that 'with all Cockburn's activity construction of a new house would take three years, and with this man six; I shall be dead long before that time. Plantation House is the only one on the island fit for me. The Governor having a house himself in town could easily live there in winter and here in summer.'

Count Montholon called for Captain Blakeney *(the new Orderly Officer who had replaced Captain Poppelton)* and myself to look at the state of his apartments. The rooms were in a shocking state. The walls were covered in a green fur and mould—despite the fact that fires were kept constantly lit in every room. I never saw a human habitation in such a mouldy and humid state with which opinion the orderly officer agreed.

8 September 1817

Saw Napoleon who informed me that he had found himself very unwell yesterday with headache and pain in the limbs; and had taken a warm bath following which he felt much better.

He was in very good spirits and asked many questions about the number of bottles of wine we drank at our party the night before. Blamed Mr Boys' conduct for having preached in allusion to the Admiral. *(Rev. Boys was chaplain to the East India company in St Helena; not only was Admiral Plampin notoriously living with a woman not his wife, but he rarely attended church. Boys was a notoriously righteous man; he became unpopular when he insisted that the full names and positions of the fathers of illegitimate children—including some of Lowe's most trusted lieutenants—be written clearly in the baptismal register.)* Napoleon said that a man's conscience was not to be amenable to any tribunal; that no person ought to be accountable to any earthly power for his religious opinions. 'Had you not persecuted the Catholics in Ireland,' added he, 'in all probability the greatest number of them would before now have become Protestants.'

9 September 1817

Races at Deadwood. The Commissioners all present. None of the French from Longwood attended except the children and some of the domestics.

During the interval between races, Sir Hudson Lowe sent for me and asked if 'some of General Bonaparte's horses were not on the race course?' I replied that I had borrowed two horses from General Gourgaud, one of which I lent to Miss Eliza Balcombe and the other to the surgeon of the *Conqueror*. Sir Hudson Lowe immediately broke out into not the most moderate expressions, and his gestures attracted the attention of many of the spectators. He characterised my daring to lend those horses without his permission as the greatest presumption he had ever witnessed. I replied that I had to come to St Helena to learn it was a crime to borrow a horse for the use of a young lady, and that neither had I known that it was necessary to go to Plantation House to ask permission to borrow a horse belonging to Longwood. Sir Hudson replied that 'I had no business to form any opinion about it'.

Napoleon in high spirits; looked out of a window at the races, with which he was much pleased. Told me he had done everything in his power to establish races in France.

12 September 1817

Went to Plantation House. After some conversation about the quantity of fuel allowed to Longwood, Sir Hudson Lowe asked me in an abrupt manner if I had not received some books from Dr Warden? I replied that I had received some monthly publications. 'It is very extraordinary,' said Sir Hudson Lowe, 'that you did not inform me of it.' I replied that I was not bound to inform him of any or every book I received or purchased. Sir Hudson asked if any of the French had seen them. I replied that to my knowledge they had not. He said, 'I might have books in my room of a very improper tendency, which they might read in my absence.'

14 September 1817

Napoleon was in very good spirits. Asked many questions about the horses that had won at the races and how they had trained our horses; about how much money I had won or lost; about the ladies etc. 'You had a large party yesterday,' continued he. 'How many bottles of wine had you? Who dined with you?' I mentioned Captain Wallis *(who was lieutenant with the unfortunate Captain Wright)*. 'What does he say about Wright's death?' I said, 'He believes that Wright was murdered by Fouché for the purpose of ingratiating himself with you.' Napoleon replied, 'I would never allow that. If he was put to death it could only have been by my orders. Fouché knew me too well. He was aware that I would have hanged him directly if he attempted it. Wright ought to have been brought before a military commission and the sentence executed within 48 hours. Why this did not happen, I do not recollect.'

Rallying me on my supposed attentions to Miss —, Napoleon recounted some of his own love adventures. 'The most beautiful woman I ever saw,' he said, 'was an Irish girl, Mademoiselle G—s; whether she was born in Ireland or was of Irish family, I am not certain. I met her one day while hunting in St Germain. I met her afterwards three or four times. Her mother was an old intriguer, so although I was undoubtedly smitten by her, I gave orders that prevented her from ever again being admitted to my presence.'

19 September 1817

Went to Plantation House to report on the state of Napoleon's health. I said that apart from slight catarrh, his health had been tolerably good. The Governor then observed that Madame Bertrand had told the Commissioners that Napoleon was extremely unwell; I repeated that he had suffered some indisposition but not of a serious nature. *(The real state of Napoleon's health was a constant puzzle to Plantation House. Was he really ill? Or was he shamming to gain international sympathy? Either could be a prelude to his removal from St Helena. Sir Hudson believed that O'Meara was controlled by Napoleon, but did that mean his reports were worthless?)*

20 September 1817

Saw Napoleon in his bath. At first he was dull and out of spirits. Complained of pain in the right cheek. Great want of sleep. I recommended exercise on horseback in as forceful a manner as possible. Napoleon replied that under the present restrictions, liable to be insulted if he budged off the road, he would never stir out.

He then made some observations about Mr P— on the island having sold his wife, which he said reflected little credit on the Governor. *(Up to the late 19th century wife-selling was a tolerated, extra-legal, folk form of divorce in England.)*

I asked Napoleon where did he consider himself to have been in greatest danger?

'At the beginning, at Toulon and Arcola,' he replied. 'At Arcola my horse was shot and, rendered furious by the wound, galloped towards the enemy line. In the agonies of death he plunged into a morass and died, burying me up to my neck, in a swamp. I was helpless. I thought the Austrians would come and cut off my head which at this time was just above the water level. But the enemy were afraid to enter the swamp—as they all would sink. Eventually my own soldiers were able to extract me.'

I asked if he had not been frequently slightly wounded. He replied, 'several times, but only once I needed surgical assistance. At Marengo, a cannon took away part of the boot of my left leg and a little of the skin. This was treated with a piece of linen—dipped in salt water.' I asked about a wound of which there was a deep scar on the inside of his left thigh. He said it was from a bayonet. *(In fact this was inflicted at Toulon, by an Irishman.)*

I then asked him how many horses were killed under him in battle. He replied 'Eighteen or perhaps nineteen. When I was about seventeen I narrowly escaped being drowned in the Saône. While swimming, cramp seized me and after struggling, I sank. I experienced at that moment, the sensation of dying and lost all recollection. However, the current carried me to a sand bank where I lay senseless for, I know not how long. I was eventually restored to life by some of my young companions.'

One of the newspapers had reported that Lord Castlereagh had purchased a great amount of land in Northern Ireland. 'Ah,' said Napoleon, 'some of my money has gone to pay for those estates! Upwards of 40 millions of francs, my private property, was seized as "state property" in 1814 and divided amongst Talleyrand and others, including Castlereagh.' *(Castlereagh, who had been Foreign Secretary for ten years, committed suicide not long after the publication of O'Meara's diaries, prompted, some believed, by this accusation.)*

The talents required in a good general came under his observation. 'Turenne was the greatest, then Luxembourg. Marshal Saxe was a mere technician without spirit; Marlborough was a great general; Wellington, however, is a man without spirit, without generosity or soul. I think that history will pronounce him *un homme borné.*'

(Borné means limited, narrow-minded. When asked, before 1815, whether he had ever been engaged against Napoleon in person, Wellington replied, 'No, and I am glad I never was! I would sooner,' he added, 'hear that 40,000 French reserves had appeared rather than Napoleon had arrived to take command.')

21 September 1817

At about six minutes before ten o'clock last night three distinct shocks of an earthquake were felt at Longwood. The whole house was shaken with a rumbling, clattering noise. The whole might have lasted for sixteen or eighteen seconds. No mischief was done. Everybody appeared calm, including Tristan de Montholon—who complained that someone was trying to throw him out of bed! The soldiers who were sleeping on the ground felt it more than others.

22 September 1817

Saw Napoleon in his bedroom. 'Well M. Doctor, *tremblement de terre* last night. At first I thought the *Conqueror* had taken fire and blown up, or else some powder magazine on the island had exploded.' *(When this remark was reported to Admiral Plampin he exclaimed 'Ay, ay, the damned rascal supposed so, because he wished it!')*

I mentioned that previous earthquakes had been felt on the island in 1756 and 1782, but I said it was likely that the fanatics and superstitious on the island would attribute the earthquake to his presence; for the Portuguese had said that the strong and destructive storm at Madeira when I arrived there in 1815 had been produced by his arrival. Napoleon laughed very heartily at this, and observed that the story would have been better if the earthquake had occurred immediately on his arrival on the island.

Napoleon then said he had learned that Lord Moira had demanded 20,000 extra European troops for India. 'I always entertained hopes of driving you out of India. Every year I received ambassadors from the Nabobs and other Indian princes especially of the Mahrattas imploring help from me to drive you out. The hatred they expressed against you was astonishing.'

25 September 1817

Napoleon sent for me this evening at eight o'clock. He complained of headache and swelling at the right side of his face. He asked me of what temperament I took him to be—what was necessary to keep him in a good state of health? I replied that I conceived him to be of a temperament that required much activity, both mental and physical. 'You are right,' replied the Emperor, 'such has been necessary throughout my life. I exercise the mind every day by my writings—and exercise for the body I should take even on this island were I not in the hands of *boja*.'

26 September 1817

Saw Napoleon at nine o'clock. He complained of soreness in both legs.

He ate his breakfast before me, which consisted of two or three radishes, a little toast and butter followed by café au lait.

28 September 1817

Saw Napoleon at 11 a.m. Appeared to be in nearly the same state as yesterday. Ankles swelled; appetite bad; I proposed to call in Mr Baxter *(Deputy-Inspector of Hospitals in St Helena)* for medical advice.

Napoleon replied, 'There is no necessity for it. If all the colleges of medicine in France and England were assembled, they would give the same advice as you have—viz. exercise on horseback. But as long as the present system is in place I shall not stir out.' He then repeated the conversation he had had with Lord Amherst on the subject.

'The only one of us,' added he, 'who goes out is Gourgaud, and he has been stopped upwards of fifty times. Once during the Admiral's time I was stopped but he turned the island topsy-turvy on account of it. Now this brute here would be pleased with it, or with anything else, to lower or degrade my character.' *(Admiral Cockburn's short period in charge was becoming in retrospect a golden age—the last thing Napoleon would have admitted at the time.)*

Soon after this Sir Hudson Lowe came to Longwood and made me repeat all the above conversation. He asked 'If I had made any reply?' I said 'No.'

After a tolerably long harangue in which His Excellency accused Napoleon of having delayed seeing the Ambassador in order that he (Sir Hudson) should not have a chance of refuting calumnies, he concluded by saying: 'Do you not think, Sir, that General Bonaparte has treated me shamefully in that business?' I replied that Napoleon had been unwell, and that anyway Lord Amherst had seen and conversed with him for some hours after his conversation with Napoleon!

This reply excited His Excellency's wrath, who, looking at me with an expression of countenance I shall never forget said: 'If it were not that it would be made a subject of complaint, I should, without waiting for an order, have you expelled immediately from the island, Sir!'

29 September 1817

Sent my report of Napoleon's health to Plantation House by Captain Blakeney and made an application for sea-water to be sent to

Longwood for a bath for the use of Napoleon.

Saw Napoleon who was in much better spirits. After some talk about my patron saint he exclaimed, 'St Napoleon ought to be obliged to me, and do everything for me in the next world. Poor fellow, nobody knew him before! He hadn't even a day in the Calendar. I persuaded the Pope to give him the 15th August as a feast day—my birthday.'

Napoleon then began to rally me on my profession.

'You medical people,' said he, 'will have more lives to answer for in the next world than even we generals. What will you say for yourselves?' asked he, laughing. 'Think of all the poor sailors and soldiers you have despatched to the other world. Given the wrong medicine, mistook their complaints, or bled too much! Or, you were at the theatre when you were needed or with a fine girl or after drink?' I replied that my conscience was clear. I very likely have made some mistakes—but not intentional ones. I have done everything to uphold the honour of my profession. Napoleon replied that physicians dispatched many through ignorance to the other world. Surgeons, on the other hand, 'you do not work in the dark—your senses guide and assist you.'

'Larrey was the most honest man and the best friend to the soldier that I ever knew. He would be seen on the field of battle long after the action had ceased, accompanied by a train of young surgeons, endeavouring to see if there was a sign of life in any soldier. He tormented the generals and woke them up at night whenever he wanted accommodation or assistance for the wounded or the sick.'

30 September 1817

Napoleon in much the same state. Told Sir Hudson Lowe that there was nothing immediately dangerous, but that the swellings of legs and ankles in a man of Napoleon's time of life were always suspicious and frequently the primary symptoms of dropsy. Sir Hudson Lowe said he had had an interview with Count Bertrand, who had been very violent in his language, 'insisting that everything should be put back on the same footing as during the reign of Sir George Cockburn's time, and that he would write and hold correspondence with whomever he liked and in fact do what he liked in the island without restriction.'

1 October 1817

Napoleon's legs still swollen. There was some relief following a salt bath. *(Sir Hudson has responded promptly enough to the request of a couple of days before.)* He would have taken another bath but there was no water. Had eaten scarcely anything. Slight headache.

3 October 1817

Napoleon complained of pain in his right side. This had been present, he said, for the past two months. On examination his liver was swollen and tender to touch. He asked if the pain was due to an enlarged liver. *(Here O'Meara has written into his diaries that he would not tire the reader with details of Napoleon's medical history. He would only include them when absolutely necessary).*

4 October 1817

I was called to see Sir Hudson Lowe who had read my medical report on Napoleon, said that there were too many details in it, and that I must make one out which could be made public', he said. Said he had received a letter from Count Bertrand alluding to Lord Liverpool *(Prime Minister 1812–1827)*. I said Napoleon always declared that Lords Liverpool and Sidmouth were better disposed to him than other ministers. That indeed I never heard him speak ill of any of the English ministers except Lords Bathurst and Castlereagh. *(Sidmouth, formerly Henry Addington, was as Home Secretary responsible for most of the political repressions of the time.)*

6 October 1817

Napoleon nearly the same. Again recommended him exercise and told him that if he deferred it the swellings might increase so as to render him incapable of taking it. He assented to this but declared that until things were put on the same footing as had been in Sir George Cockburn's time he would not go out.

I took the liberty of observing that he was 'like a man tumbling down a cliff who would not lay hold of a rope within your grasp!' He laughed at this comparison, and said, 'when the dice are cast, our days are complete.'

7 October 1817

Napoleon nearly the same. Observed that the Governor had insinuated that he is trying to kill himself. 'Had I intended this,' he said, 'I would have fallen upon my sword a long time ago. I am not fool enough to attempt to kill myself by the slow agonies of a lingering disease. I never loved tedious warfare. But there is no death that I would not prefer to dishonouring my character.'

Reported the substance of what Napoleon had said to Sir Hudson

Lowe. He said that his measures had been approved by the British Government.

8 October 1817

Napoleon walked for a short time in the garden, but being unaccustomed to exercise was obliged to sit on the steps before the veranda. He was, however, in better spirits and had benefited from the salt-water baths.

9 October 1817

The Emperor not so well. Got cold yesterday. 'I was going to send for you early in the morning,' said he, 'but then I considered this poor devil of a doctor has been up all night at a ball and has need of sleep. If I disturb him now he will have eyes so heavy and his intellect so confused that he will not he able to form a correct opinion. Soon after this I fell into a perspiration and later felt much better.'

10 October 1817

Napoleon in rather bad spirits.

Had some conversation. 'When I returned from Italy, I went to live in a small house in Paris—and a few days later the street was renamed "Rue de la Victoire". Everyone wanted to give me money, houses, estates, etc. etc. I had sent more than 30 million francs to the Treasury and yet I was scarcely worth 300,000 francs myself. The Directory were quite jealous of my success and said "that my services were such that it could not be rewarded by money."

'Everyone tried to see me—I refused. I attended only two gala balls, and I only spent a short time at both. One I remember was given by Talleyrand. I was afterwards nominated to the command of the Army of England, which was so named to deceive your Ministers as to its real destination, which was Egypt.

'To show the confidence I had in the army,' said he, 'I need only recount this. Five or six days after my landing at Cannes *(from Elba)* in 1815 the advance guard of my little army met a division marching against me. I went to them myself, with a few of my Guard and called out "The first soldier who pleases may come forward and kill his Emperor." It operated like an electric shock—"*Vive l'Empereur!*" resounded through all ranks; the division and my Guards fraternised, all joined me and all advanced together to Grenoble.'

12 October 1817

Sir Hudson Lowe had a long interview with Count Bertrand; the latter explained that they considered being obliged to send all letters through him, open, a needless humiliation. Count Bertrand also mentioned that the Emperor considered a free intercourse with the inhabitants as the only guarantee of his life. When Major Gorrequer was at Count Bertrand's on the 10th the latter told him that some of the officers had assured him that in the 53rd Regiment, there were neither assassins not executioners to be found. *(In London, ministers and their associates undoubtedly joked among themselves about how much easier things would be were Napoleon dead. In 1816, for instance, John Wilson Croker, Admiralty secretary, wrote to Robert Peel in Ireland: '[Admiral] Cockburn is come back in good health and spirits; he gives us no hope of Buonaparte's dying. He eats he says enormously, but drinks little, takes regular exercise and is in all respects so very careful of his carcass that he may last twenty years . . . Sir Hudson Lowe is as strict as Cockburn without any of his liveliness and little of his activity and talents.')*

14 October 1817

This morning, on presenting myself according to custom to call upon Napoleon, I was informed that he was asleep, and had left word for me to go down to Count Bertrand. The latter said that the Emperor had been given to understand that I was in the habit of writing bulletins of his health daily, and that it was his desire that such bulletins should be shown to him before being sent.

Saw Napoleon afterwards who told me that he had thought that I might be required to make reports as to his health, and he had taken no notice of it. Some days ago, however, Montholon and Gourgaud were asked *(by the Commissioners)* about certain symptoms the Generals never knew he had. It was stated that such symptoms were described in the bulletins sent to the Governor.

I informed Napoleon that I had often made reports on his health. I brought one of the 10th. Looking over it he perceived the word 'General' and said he would never consent to be so styled by his physician in reports that were likely to be sent to Europe; it would appear to be an acquiescence on his part to such title, which he would rather die than consent to. As to verbal reports, he did not care if I referred to him as *tiranno Bonaparte*. For the future he insisted I should submit to him all reports of his health before sending them to the Governor.

I replied that I would never be permitted by the Governor to style him *l'Empereur* and suggested that I might use Napoleon Bonaparte. After further discussion I proposed dropping all titles and using the word 'personage'; he approved this but proposed 'patient'.

15 October 1817

Sir Hudson Lowe did not object to my showing the reports to the Emperor, but insisted that he be referred to as Napoleon Bonaparte or General Bonaparte.

17 October 1817

Napoleon was lying on his sofa, looking low and melancholy. Marchand told me he had been very unwell in the morning. He would not answer the inquiries I made relative to his complaints.

18 October 1817

Napoleon in his bath. Still persisted in refusing to consult me on his complaints. Told me that were it not for the confidence he had in me he would have dispensed with my services. 'The fact is,' continued he, 'that all this is only an artifice to deprive me of medical assistance.' Communicated this to Sir Hudson Lowe who, after some hesitation, agreed that for the future no more bulletins would be demanded without having made him acquainted that such were asked for.

19 October 1817

Reported this reply to Napoleon and assured him that I would not send any bulletins without having shown them to him. After which he entered into particulars touching his malady.

28 October 1817

Went to Plantation House where Sir Hudson Lowe demanded to know if I had any remarkable conversations with General Bonaparte. This led to a discussion in which His Excellency was more than ordinarily violent and abusive. Amongst other elegant expressions he said that he conceived me as a jackal and running about in search of news for General Bonaparte. I said I would neither be a jackal nor a spy nor an informer for him or for anyone else. 'What do you mean, Sir,' said he, 'by spy, or informer?' I said that if I complied with his orders to inform him of any conversation that passed between Napoleon and myself, I would conceive myself to be both. In a paroxysm of rage, he shouted at me that I was prohibited from holding any conversations with Napoleon except on medical subjects. I asked him to give this order in writing. This Hudson Lowe refused and after some further abuse ordered me to wait outside the door for some time. *(O'Meara's account certainly makes out Sir Hudson to be an almost comically choleric man.)*

When I re-entered the room Sir Hudson Lowe informed me that he only authorised me to hold medical communications with General Bonaparte that as to other subjects I was myself responsible. I was not of course to refuse to answer General Bonaparte, but I was not to ask any questions other than medical.

He then told me in future he would dispense with my attendance twice a week but that I should give verbal reports to Dr Baxter.

2 November 1817

Napoleon reclining on the sofa with some newspapers lying before him. He looked very melancholy and low. *(A newspaper had arrived, via Plantation House, confirming that his son was not to inherit the Duchy of Parma from Marie Louise. This was not in fact a total surprise, since it had been part of the deliberations of the Congress of Vienna.)* 'From another this would be nothing, but he culls all the pieces of news that might be agreeable and sends only what might wound my feelings. You can see,' added he with emphasis, 'that he lost no time in sending me that news. I expected something of the sort from the wretches of the Congress. They are afraid of a prince who is the choice of the people. As for me, I may be considered dead. I am certain that before long this body will be no more. I feel that the machine struggles but cannot last.

'I suppose,' added he, 'that Montchenu is very glad to hear of my illness. By what channel does he send his letters to France?' I replied that he sent them through Lord Bathurst. 'Then they are all opened and read in London.' I replied that I was ignorant of such practices. 'Because,' said Napoleon, 'you have never been in a situation to know anything about it. I tell you that the despatches of all the Ambassadors that pass through the Post Office are opened. Otto *(French diplomatist stationed in London 1802–1804)* ascertained this to be a fact beyond doubt.

'In France,' continued the Emperor, 'all letters sent by the Ambassadors were sent to a secret department of the Post Office in Paris where they were opened and deciphered. By these means I knew the contents of despatches before they arrived at their destination. How often have I laughed within myself to see them licking the dust from under my feet at my *levée* after reading in the morning the *bêtises* they had written of me to their Sovereigns. *(The innocence of the foreign ambassadors in trusting to their codes and the Post Office suggests that the French practice was more sophisticated in this respect than other nations.)*

Napoleon told me that he had resolved to have one regular meal daily.

5 November 1817

Napoleon remained in bed very late, not having had any sleep during the night. Found him not risen at eleven.

8 November 1817

Napoleon observed that I walked lame and asked if I had gout. I said that it was caused by a tight boot, that I never had the gout and never had been confined to my bed a day in my life by illness. *(Evidently not believing this)* he asked if my father ever had the disease. And said he would prescribe for my present complaint to eat nothing, drink barley-water and keep my leg up on the sofa during the day.

He then made some observations on the disinheritance of his son. 'If he lives,' added he, 'he will be something.' *(Napoleon II was never strong, and died of TB in Austria in 1832, where he had been a virtual prisoner since 1818.)*

'The Emperor Francis,' added he, 'whose head is crammed with ideas of high birth, was very anxious to prove that I was descended from some of the old tyrants of Treviso, and after my marriage to Marie Louise he employed people to search into musty records of genealogy. He imagined that he had succeeded at last, and asked to publish an account of his findings. I refused. I preferred being the son of an honest man to being descended from any little tyrant of Italy.

'There was formerly one Buonventura Bonaparte who lived and died monk. The poor man lay quietly in his grave until I was on the throne of France. It was then discovered that he had had many virtues and the Pope proposed to canonise him. "For the love of God," I said, "spare me the ridicule. People will say that I forced you to make a saint out of my family."'

(About this time Napoleon wished to give his son one of his most personal items, the small spyglass which he had had with him at every battle. He constantly used the instrument—it gave him enormous pleasure. Afraid, however, that he might damage this wonderful souvenir, he asked Barry O'Meara to look out for a telescope. As luck would have it, Mr Solomon had just one in his store. Leaving a deposit Barry asked him to clean it up

and assemble it properly. But when Barry called the telescope was gone.
The Governor had used his superior rank to demand the telescope.)

25 November 1817

Signal made for me to go to Plantation House where I found Sir
Hudson Lowe who interrogated me on various matters that had taken
place at Longwood. I replied that I had formed a determination not to
meddle with what did not concern me and only troubled myself about
my professional pursuits. He said that I must have had some non-medical conversations with him and demanded to be informed of their subjects. I replied that I did not think myself bound to repeat the subjects
of such conversations unless Napoleon permitted, or unless matters came
to my knowledge of importance to the Government.

Sir Hudson replied, 'You are no judge, Sir, of the importance of any
conversation you had with General Bonaparte. I might consider several
subjects of great importance which you would consider trifling.' I observed that if I was not at liberty to use my own discretion or judgement
I must necessarily repeat everything I heard, which would place me in a
most dishonourable and disgraceful situation.

The Governor replied 'that it was my *duty* to inform him. It was a
duty I owed to the English Government.' I answered that it would be
acting as a spy, an informer , and a '*mouton*'. My duty did not require
me to commit dishonourable actions and I would not do so.

Sir Hudson Lowe remained silent for a few moments and then asked
what was the meaning of '*mouton*'? I replied '*mouton* means a person
who insinuates himself into the confidence of another for the purpose
of betraying it.' Sir Hudson Lowe then broke out into yet another paroxysm of rage and said that I had given him the greatest possible insult
in his official capacity that could possibly be offered. He walked about
in a frantic manner, repeating in a boisterous tone, 'Leave the room,
Sir!' which he continued bawling out for some moments after I had
actually quitted it. (*How infuriating it must have been for Sir Hudson to
have the most interesting man in Europe, the key to the history of the
previous twenty years, on his doorstep and be unable to talk to him. And—
what was worse—to be aware that the uncooperative Irishman in front of
him was engaging in just those long and detailed discussions.)*

4 December 1817

Miss V—, a pretty girl, and *femme de chambre* to Lady Lowe, came
from Plantation House this day mounted on one of the Governor's

horses. She went to Longwood House where she remained for near two hours. During which time she passed through almost every room; the French domestics were much enchanted with the apparition of this young and pretty girl that their gallantry could refuse her nothing. She was, however, prevented from seeing Napoleon, although she was allowed to peep at him though the keyhole. *(A few months afterwards the young woman left the island; rumour whispered that she was pregnant by one of the inmates of Plantation House.)*

7 December 1817

Napoleon had at last agreed to take some medicine, by which he temporarily benefited. Mr Baxter agreed as to the propriety of affording some other winter abode than the dreary and exposed situation of Longwood.

9 December 1817

Signal made for me to proceed to Plantation House. Soon after my arrival Sir Hudson Lowe said, with a serious air, that he had grave occasion to censure my conduct. He then asked me if I was not a medium of communication for the French—with persons on the island? I replied that if going into shops buying articles for Countess Bertrand and Montholon could be construed as carrying correspondence, I must certainly plead guilty. He then asked 'had I not written to town to a person to send up some articles?' I replied, certainly, some articles of household use.

The Governor said that it was a breach of orders. 'If Madame Bertrand wants anything of the kind, let her apply to the orderly officer.' Sir Hudson Lowe then demanded 'what business had I to do so. It was a breach of orders to bring any messages if it were not medical.' I replied that cleanliness was necessary to prevent sickness and consequently everything relating to it was medical. The orderly officer was absent from Longwood when the requirements were made; even if he had been present, delicacy would prevent the ladies from making demands to him for articles she could mention only to her surgeon.

His Excellency, as usual, flew into a violent passion and said that he would not allow me to insult him in his capacity as Governor. I asked for written instructions in order to prevent the possibility of a mistake, which he refused to give. I then asked if the ladies required me to purchase articles for them in the shops, what reply was I to make? After some hesitation he said if they wished me to purchase things myself I need not refuse, but I was not to comply with instructions from a third party.

The Emperor observed around this time, that General Masséna had lost himself in Portugal, because the state of his health did not permit him to sit on horseback, or to inspect himself what was going on. 'A general who sees with the eyes of others,' added he, 'will never be able to command an army as it should be.'

14 December 1817

Sir Hudson Lowe came to Longwood. Asked me several questions about Napoleon's health. Observed that it was very extraordinary that he did not take exercise. He enquired if the want of sleep was caused by mental or by bodily disease. I said that no active man, leading such a life as Napoleon did, could possibly remain long in a state of health. The Governor said with a sneer that *he* believed that *laziness* was the cause of his not taking exercise.

In the course of conversation this day Napoleon expressed his disapproval of our custom of shutting up shops and prohibiting people from working on Sundays. 'To oblige a poor man who has a large family, without a meal to give them, to leave off labouring to procure food is the height of barbarity. If such a law be enforced, Government should feed those who could obtain food if permitted to labour; or your greedy priests could give a portion of their own dinners—they would have less apoplexy and indigestion.'

Speaking of the possibility of amalgamating the negroes and the whites Napoleon observed that it had often occurred to him that the only way of reconciling the two colours would be to allow polygamy in the colonies, and that every black and white man should be permitted a wife of each colour. In a generation, jealousy and bad feeling would disappear. He added that it would have been easy to have obtained a dispensation from the Pope to that effect.

Saw Napoleon in the evening. He had seen the Governor passing by his windows today. 'Every time I see that Governor,' said he, 'I can only think of the man heating the poker for your King Edward II at Berkeley Castle! Like Cain, his nature is written on his face. If he were presented to me in London and I were asked "whom do you conceive this man to be?" I would answer "the public hangman". It is not that I have anything against your nation. I had every confidence in Admiral Cockburn, even after we differed—but all this man does is send for shiploads of iron railing to cage me in. If I had such a physiognomy, the world

would say "look at the countenance of the scoundrel, look at the murders of thousands stamped on the face of the monster!"' *(Although, as
Count Montholon said years later, 'an angel from heaven could not have
pleased us as Governor of St Helena', there was something visceral about
Napoleon's dislike for Lowe's appearance. Around this time Major Gorrequer
records that Lowe spoke disapprovingly of 'the French style of diplomacy,
that provided the end was attained, it did not signify by what means it was
done'.)*

1 January 1818

Napoleon nearly in the same state as yesterday.

*(Byron's friend John Cam Hobhouse had sent a book to Napoleon which
Sir Hudson Lowe had confiscated because it was inscribed 'To the Emperor
Napoleon'. This book had been seen in the library of Plantation House.)* 'It
was a *bêtise* in the Governor,' said he, 'to leave it where any person
might see it.'

'Years ago,' said Napoleon, 'in Cardinal Richelieu's time, a young
nobleman was ushered into the Cardinal's private office. While he was
there a great man called, and after some conversation took his leave.
The Cardinal escorted him out. On his return he rang a bell and one of
his confidential secretaries entered, to whom he whispered something.
He then very amicably finished the conversation and bade the young
nobleman goodbye. As he was going outside the door he was arrested
and conveyed in secret to the Bastille where he was kept for ten years.
After that time the Cardinal sent for the prisoner and explained the
situation. The fact was that he had left a paper on the table containing
State secrets of vast importance which he was afraid he might have
perused in his absence. The safety of the kingdom obliged him to take
measures to prevent the possibility of them becoming known. As soon
as the safety of the country permitted he had released him and would be
happy to make some amends.

'The French Revolution,' said he, 'was a general movement of the
mass of the people against the privileged classes. The nobles retained
the administration of justice and other feudal rights enjoyed the privilege of being exempt from taxes and exclusively possessed all honourable employments. The chief object of the Revolution was to destroy
those privileges and abuses. It established equality of rights. Any citizen
might succeed to any office according to his talent. Before this, France
was composed of provinces unequal in extent and population. They
had a great variety of legal customs and peculiar laws. France was an

assemblage of several states without amalgamation. The Revolution destroyed all these little states and formed a single territory. There was now one France, with a homogenous division of land. They had the same civil and criminal laws and the same regulation for taxes throughout the land.

'Subsequently, the French nation established an Imperial throne and placed me upon it. No person ever ascended a throne with more legitimate rights. The throne of France was granted—a long time ago—by a few bishops and nobles to Hughes Capet. The Imperial throne was given to me by the desire of the people whose wishes were three times verified in a solemn manner. The Pope crossed the Alps to crown and anoint me.

'Kings hastened to acknowledge me. Before she violated the Peace of Amiens, England offered to acknowledge me as King of France if I would agree to the cessation of Malta. If Mr Fox had lived, peace would have been made.' *(Charles James Fox died in office as Foreign Secretary in 1806, after years in vocal opposition. Although he had been an ardent supporter of Napoleon in the past—a stance inherited by his nephew Lord Holland and his wife—indications are that he had begun increasingly to see him as a threat to Great Britain.)*

2 January 1817

Went to Plantation House by order of the Governor, whom I saw in the library. He asked a great many questions concerning my appointment as surgeon to Napoleon and concluded by asserting that I was not his surgeon, but only *tolerated to visit him*. I observed that the bills which I drew for my pay on the Navy Board were worded 'as surgeon to Napoleon Bonaparte and suite'.

He asked me 'if I conceived myself to be independent of him as Governor?' I replied that no British officer could be independent of the Government of his country. He then asked 'whether I conceived myself independent of *him*, and if it were not in his power to send me away if I pleased?' I told him that he knew best what the extent of his authority was. This answer did not please him.

Saw Napoleon. Had some conversation relative to the capture of Rome by the French. 'That incapable but intriguing Court of old women at Rome,' said Napoleon, 'excited the populace by all means of bigotry and superstition to massacre the French. But since I believed that a rupture with Rome would inevitably lead to one with Naples *(and so leave Mediterranean bases open to the English)* I decided to punish but not destroy her. The Directory, however, decided that we should march against the Pope and said that the time had come to overturn that idol. Berthier was sent with an army to revolutionise Rome and establish a republic, which was done. At first the people were delighted, but they changed their minds when the troops plundered the Vatican and the palaces of the nobles.

'The Venetians,' continued Napoleon, 'thinking that Joubert's army had been defeated and cut to pieces, armed a number of peasants and all the French in Verona were massacred. The sick and wounded in the hospital were barbarously murdered. In other towns in the Venetian territories similar cruelties were practised. When they discovered that the French army had not been destroyed their fright knew no bounds. They waited on me, making the most submissive proposals, pledging themselves to agree to everything I wanted—and offering millions if I would grant their prayers. But I ordered the French to leave Venice and declared war.' *(Napoleon invaded Venice in May 1787. After 1,070 years of independence, the Venetian Republic was later handed over to Austria.)*

9 January 1818

Another series of interrogations in Plantation House, partly about Napoleon's interview with Lord Amherst. Sir Hudson Lowe mentioned that Count Bertrand had told him that General Bonaparte was influenced by the persons about him, amongst whom I was one. I could scarcely help smiling at the supposition that I could have influenced such a person as Napoleon and contented myself with replying that as far as I knew him he was not a man to let himself be guided by the opinions of others.

13 January 1818

More interrogations at Plantation House. Sir Hudson Lowe took out of his pocket a *Morning Chronicle* of 17 September 1817 containing details of a conversation between Napoleon and some English gentlemen. Sir Hudson Lowe deduced from the text that either Admiral Malcolm or myself was the author. I replied that I had neither written nor communicated it and reminded him that others beside the Admiral and myself saw Napoleon. The Governor seemed to want to saddle it on the Admiral. I saw from the first glance that it must have come from Mr Ellis *(secretary to Lord Amherst).*

15 January 1818

Saw the Governor at Plantation House to whom I reported that Napoleon's indisposition had rather increased. Communicated same to Mr Baxter.

16 January 1818

Saw Napoleon who felt somewhat relieved by physic.

20 January 1818

Went to Plantation House according to orders. While I was speaking with Dr Baxter in the library Sir Hudson Lowe came in, looking very angry, and asked in a rough and abrupt manner what communication I had to make respecting General Bonaparte's health? I replied that there had been no permanent improvement.

'Has he been out of the house?'—'He has not.'—'Has he been in the billiard-room?' — 'He spends a considerable portion of his time there every day.'—'How does he employ his time there?'—'I cannot tell, Sir.'—'Yes, you can, Sir,' replied the Governor, regarding me in his customary manner, 'you well know what he does there; you do not do your duty to Government.'

Sir Hudson Lowe then demanded to know the name of the person who told me that Lord Liverpool had interfered to prevent my removal from the island. *(Lowe was not unreasonably anxious to know the channel by which the Prime Minister's name had been involved; O'Meara is unenthusiastic about naming names, but has offered to show the orderly officer at Longwood the letter so as to exculpate various people.)* I repeated my offer to show the letter to a third person, but Sir Hudson took this an insult to him. I said then that as my replies only brought on me bad language and bad treatment I must decline giving him any more answers on this subject. 'Put down, Major Gorrequer, that Mr O'Meara refuses to answer,' was the Governor's reply. After a long abusive harangue about my conduct, I was permitted to depart.

28 January 1818

Saw Napoleon, who was feeling better.

Had some conversation about Chateaubriand. 'He is an old emigré,' he said, 'while I was in power he was one of the most abject of my flatterers. Now he is a characterless blaggard, with a grovelling soul, a writer's itch.'

I asked about Bernadotte's conduct *(Count Bernadotte, one of Napoleon's marshals became Prince-Elect of Sweden in 1810; in 1813 he fought against Napoleon with the Coalition. He became King of Sweden in 1818 and his heirs are still on the throne.)* 'Bernadotte,' said he, 'was ungrateful to me—I was the author of his greatness, but I cannot say that he betrayed me. Although he was once a Marshal of France and by marriage to Desirée, my sister-in-law *(and ex-mistress)*, he in a manner became a Swede. Neither Murat nor he would have declared against me had they thought that it would lose me my throne. Their wish was just to diminish my power—not to destroy me altogether.'

30 January 1818

Went to Plantation House. Sir Hudson said that he had learned that General Bonaparte was in a much worse state of health than I reported. He desired therefore that whenever I came to town I would give Mr Baxter or Sir Thomas Reade a report on the state of his health.

I applied for a small still in order to make orange-flower water for Napoleon *(this request was never complied with, though frequently repeated.)*

3 February 1818

The *Cambridge* store-ship arrived today with the melancholy news of the death of Princess Charlotte. *(Princess Charlotte was the Prince Regent's only child and heir apparent. Her death, in childbirth, eventually cleared the way to the throne for Queen Victoria. Her accoucheur, Sir Richard Croft, was blamed for the death, and subsequently took his own life.)*

Napoleon expressed his sorrow at the event, not only at the fate of a princess cut off in the prime of youth and beauty, but also he said that he had not been without hope that she would have caused a more liberal attitude to be adopted to himself. He inveighed against the accoucheurs and expressed his surprise that the populace had not stoned them to death. 'Had it not been for me, Marie Louise would have died in a similar manner. Dubois *(Dr Antoine Dubois, premier accoucheur of the Empire)* came to see me with alarm on his countenance "the Empress is in great danger—there is a wrong presentation". I told him to treat her as you would the wife of a petty shopkeeper in the Rue St Denis. Dubois asked "If it were necessary to choose, which should be saved, the mother or the child?" "The mother, certainly," I replied. "It is her right."'

10 February 1818

No improvement in Napoleon's health. Had some conversation about the British Princess Royal whom Napoleon met in Stuttgart. 'I had the pleasure of interfering when her husband, who was a brute though a man of talent, had ill-treated her. The English royal family,' said he, 'is crowded with little petty princes to whom I would not have given a second lieutenant's commission.' *(Very few people were polite about George III's sons. Wellington described them as 'the damnedest millstone round the necks of any Government that can be imagined.')*

16 February 1818

While in Jamestown, I was asked by Mr Barber of the *Cambridge*, who had opened a shop in town, 'How did Bonaparte like the portraits?' He had brought out two engravings of young Napoleon for sale, thinking it would please the French and induce them to give him some custom. Mr Barber appeared much surprised and disappointed when he learned that they had not reached Longwood.

17 February 1818

Went to Plantation House. After some enquiries on the state of Napoleon's health Sir Hudson Lowe reverted back to the letter in which Lord Liverpool was mentioned. I replied that it was a long time ago and that I had offered to show the letter at that time. This was refused. I then said that as I do not know why I am now requested to show this letter, I declined to do so. His Excellency was not pleased with this and began to abuse me in his customary manner. Saying that 'I constantly insulted him as Governor,' I replied that it had never been my intention, in word or deed. I was very sorry if constructions so foreign to my intentions, should have been put upon them.

Sir Hudson Lowe then got up and looking at me in a menacing manner said, 'Upon your word of honour, Sir, I ask if you have had any conversations with Napoleon Bonaparte upon other than medical subjects for the past month?' I replied, 'Perhaps there may have been on other subjects, not interesting!'—'I do not allow *you*, Sir, to be a judge of whether they were interesting or otherwise. You have no authority for holding any conversation with Napoleon Bonaparte unless upon medical subjects. Have you had any communication with any other persons in his household?'—'Certainly, Sir, I have had.' Without waiting to learn whether these were medical or otherwise, he burst out with, 'You have no authority, Sir, to hold any conversation whatsoever with any of his household unless on medical subjects. You have no business to go amongst them unless for medical purposes and when you finish you will leave them immediately.

'You go to town when ships arrive—which I do not approve of. You go to collect news for General Bonaparte.' I replied that I was an English officer and as such would not give up my rights. Moreover, I wanted to buy essential things as soon as they landed, before the monopoly took place to increase the price. That if he intended to prohibit me from going to town I had to request orders to that effect in writing.

This Sir Hudson refused, saying with a sneer: 'The request is worthy of the place you came from and the people with which you associate. I do not think a person under a pledge to Napoleon Bonaparte ought to be received in society. You are a suspected man. You are suspected by *me.*'

18 February 1818

Napoleon more lively than he has been for a few days.

He spoke of his plans to invade England. 'Had I succeeded in effecting a landing,' said he, 'I have very little doubt that I should have accomplished my views. Your fleet having been decoyed away, 3,000 boats, each to carry twenty men and one horse, with a proportion of artillery, were ready. Four days would have brought me to London. I have no doubt your troops would have done their duty, but one battle lost and the capital would be in my power. You could not have collected a force sufficiently strong to beat me in a pitched battle. I would then offer you a constitution of your own making. I would have declared the King fallen from the throne, abolished the nobility and proclaimed liberty, freedom and equality. Think you that in order to keep the house of Guelf on the throne your rich citizens, merchants, and others of London would have consented to sacrifice their riches, houses, their families and all their dearest interests, especially when I had made them comprehend that I only came to give them liberty? No, it is contrary to history and to human nature. You are too rich. Your principal people have too much to lose by resistance and your *canaille* too much to gain by a change. If they supposed that I wanted to make England a province of France then indeed *l'espirit national* would do wonders. But I would have formed a Republic according to your wishes.' *(At the time he expressed himself differently. In the glorious enterprise, he told Admiral Villeneuve, of 'destroying the Power which for six centuries has oppressed France, we can all die without regret.')*

'You talk of freedom! Can anything be more horrible than your pressing of seamen? Our conscription included everyone—it wounded your pride because it fell upon all ranks. Oh, how shocking that a gentleman's son should be obliged to defend his country just as if he were one of the *canaille*! And that he should be compelled to expose his body, or put himself on a level with a plebeian!' *(Napoleon, of course, judged the class relations in England by what he knew from pre-Revolutionary France.)*

20 February 1818
Underwent a few more interrogations from Sir Hudson Lowe in which I had the good fortune to leave the house without having been assailed with any outrageous language.

23 February 1818
Cipriani complained this day of inflammation of the bowels which from the moment he made it known to me presented the most formidable appearances. Recourse was had to all the vigorous remedies usually employed in such cases. It was soon evident that his life was in imminent danger; other professional men were called in. *(Cipriani had a ruptured appendix, followed by peritonitis. In the days before antibiotics this was nearly always fatal.)* All was useless and the complaint was rapidly hurrying him on to dissolution. Cipriani himself, although conscious of his danger, preserved the greatest composure. Napoleon was extremely anxious and frequent in his enquiries.

24 February 1818
This morning at four o'clock poor Cipriani was numbered among the dead. His corpse was followed to the grave by Count Bertrand, Count Montholon, by myself, and by all the household who could attend. So much was he esteemed at St Helena that several of the most respectable inhabitants and some of the officers of the 66th Regiment joined the funeral procession. Had he been buried within the limits, Napoleon himself would have been able to attend the funeral.

Immediately after his death I reported the circumstance to Napoleon, who remarked: 'Where has his soul gone? Gone to Rome perhaps to see his wife and child, before it undertakes the long final journey.'

Some days before his demise Cipriani told me that not long after the Governor had put into execution his rigorous measures, Santini, who was normally of a merry disposition, had been observed to be much altered and apparently thoughtful and melancholy. One day he came into Cipriani's room and avowed his intention of shooting the Governor as soon as the latter came to Longwood. Cipriani said he was mad, and tried to dissuade him. Finding his arguments fruitless, he went to Napoleon to whom he communicated the whole affair. The Emperor immediately questioned Santini and commanded him to drop all thoughts of injuring Sir Hudson Lowe, and succeeded, not without some reluctance on Santini's part, in making him abandon the project.

6 March 1818

The progress of disease in the Emperor slowly continues its advance.

Found him reading Corneille. He observed that to the sentiments which he inspired France was indebted for some of her glorious deeds, adding that if Corneille had lived in his time, he would have made him a prince.

He then conversed about himself, saying that he believed that Nature had destined him for great reverses—he had a soul of marble.

'Maitland *(Captain of the* Bellerophon *that first took Napoleon from France),*' said Napoleon, 'was not an accomplice in the snare that was laid for me by your ministers when they gave him orders to receive me on board his ship. He was deceived as well as myself and probably thought, in bringing me to England, that I should have been allowed to live there, subject to certain restrictions.'

He then gave some explanation of his fall. 'I planned that France should retain her natural limits of the Alps and the Rhine, but at Châtillon the powers insisted that France should be reduced to the limits she had previous to 1792, which I rejected. Had it not been for the subsequent treachery of Talleyrand, Marmont, and Augereau, the Allies would not have succeeded in forcing upon the throne a detested family against whom for twenty-five years the nation has combated; and France would not have been degraded by the spectacle of a King upon the throne who had the baseness publicly to declare that he owed it to the Prince Regent of England.'

28 March 1818

Thirty-four volumes of books were sent to Longwood by Sir Hudson Lowe, being the whole supply of books sent out by the ministers since the arrival of the *Phaeton* in 1816. It has been a rule for some time that all captains are obliged to submit a list of their books, newspapers etc. to Sir Hudson Lowe under the pretext of desiring to forward them to Longwood, where however, none of the books have arrived and very few of the newspapers.

4 April 1818

Some days ago one of the foreigners informed Count Montholon that the Commissioners had seen an account of Napoleon's health in the bulletin of that day. Montholon, knowing that no bulletin had been issued by me, asked for an explanation. It appeared that fictitious reports were made up by a person who never saw Napoleon and sent to the Commissioners for transmission to their courts. *(Evidently the verbal reports given by O'Meara to Dr Baxter were being written up by Baxter—thus getting over the 'Emperor/General Bonaparte' problem—and distributed generally.)*

10 April 1818

Sir Hudson Lowe, having failed in the application that he made in London to procure my removal from St Helena, had recourse to an expedient which ensured him success. He informed me that I was not to pass out of Longwood. Thus the Governor imposed on me restrictions even more arbitrary and vexatious than on the French; for he deprived me of English society while at the same time prohibiting me from holding intercourse with the French other than on medical matters.

As soon as I received this letter I went to The Briars, intending to lay the affair before Admiral Plampin, but he would not see me. I then wrote a letter to Sir Hudson Lowe tendering my resignation and another to Count Bertrand in which I explained the step I had been compelled to take.

14 April 1818

Napoleon sent for me prior to my departure, during which he declined receiving any more medical advice. 'Well, Doctor,' he said, 'you are leaving us. Would the world believe that he would have had the cowardice to meddle in this way with my doctor? Unfortunately, you are only a lieutenant, subject to the arbitrariness of military discipline and do not have the independence to help me. However, I thank you for your care. Leave as quickly as possible this place of shadows; I will die here, in this miserable hut, eaten with disease and without help; and your country will be dishonoured for ever.' He then bade me adieu. *(O'Meara was now confined in Jamestown, and prevented from going to Longwood. Major Gorrequer records Sir Hudson talking of O'Meara: "What a complete, villain, O'Meara is. There never was such a damned rascal." These expressions repeated three times, and worse.' 16 April 1818)*

9 May 1818

Sir Hudson Lowe, finding that he could not succeed in his plan of establishing another surgeon with Napoleon, and having been made to comprehend by the Commissioners that if Napoleon died while I was excluded, strange surmises would arise in England and in Europe regarding his death, accordingly he released me, having kept me in confinement 27 days. In the letter containing the order for my release His Excellency acknowledged me as Napoleon's private surgeon, a point which he had contested before.

10 May 1818

In order to put a stop to the fabrication of bulletins, Napoleon required that I make a report on his state of health once a week. Sir Hudson, however, absolutely prohibited me from making any written report.

Napoleon's state of health had become worse since last month; the pain was constant and severe.

16 May 1818

A proclamation issued by Sir Hudson Lowe and placarded in the most conspicuous places forbids all officers, inhabitants and other person whatever from holding correspondence or any communication with the foreign persons under detention on the island. Considerable indignation was excited on the island at the conduct which had been pursued towards Napoleon.

18 May 1818

Captain Blakeney read the proclamation to the English servants. Informed of this, Napoleon ordered that the English servants should be discharged.

11 June 1818

Napoleon's state of health has become much worse. He has been confined almost entirely to his apartments for nearly six weeks. Extracted two more teeth.

20 June 1818

The officers of 53rd Regiment had done me the honour of electing me an honorary member of their Mess, and on their departure, the officers of the 66th did the same. Sir Hudson Lowe sent Sir Thomas Reade to tell Colonel Lascelles that I had become displeasing to the Governor, who had turned me out of his house and consequently I was unfit for their society; insinuating that my expulsion would be very agreeable to Sir Hudson Lowe, who, he observed, had said that he should consider any person who was seen to associate with me as his personal enemy. Colonel Lascelles asked Lieutenant Reardon to persuade me to withdraw privately from the mess as my presence was obnoxious to the Governor, though personally he had a great esteem for me. I requested a full and open investigation, but Sir Hudson Lowe sent an order to Colonel Lascelles to exclude me from the mess, without assigning any reason.

25 June 1818
Sent a letter to Deadwood camp thanking the officers for their courtesy whilst an honorary member of their mess.

26 June 1818
The officers replied that my conduct had always been perfectly consistent in every respect with that of a gentleman and thanked me for my letter.

27 June 1818
Napoleon had a severe catarrhal infection. Discontinued some of the remedies he was taking and reported on his state of health to the Governor.

15 July 1818
Several cases of wine sent by Princess Borghese *(Napoleon's sister Pauline)* arrived in Jamestown. A few were sent to Longwood and the remainder deposited in Government stores. Napoleon expressed great affection towards his sisters Eliza and Pauline, adding that he thought Pauline would try to come out to St Helena *(she had lived with Napoleon in Elba.)* He expressed a very strong sense of the attention and kindness shown him in his misfortune by Lady Holland and other members of the family of the great Fox.

20 July 1818
Went to town to procure a copy of Lord Bathurst's speech. Captain Bunn of the *Mangles* told me that Sir Hudson Lowe had taken five copies of the pamphlet saying that they wanted to send two or three to Longwood. *(They never arrived.)* They had been very particular in requiring him to render an account of all the books he had brought out.

25 July 1818
Captain Blakeney delivered a letter which informed me that by instruction from Earl Bathurst I was to withdraw from attendance on

General Bonaparte and to have no more interviews with the inhabitants at Longwood. I was to leave Longwood immediately on receiving the letter without holding any further communication whatsoever with the persons residing there.

Humanity and the duties of my profession forbade compliance; Napoleon's health required that I should prescribe a regimen for him and prepare the medicines which it would be necessary for him to take in the absence of a surgeon, as I was perfectly sure he would accept no one recommended by Sir Hudson Lowe. I accordingly went instantly to Napoleon's apartment. 'I have lived too long for them,' said Napoleon. After I had given him such medical instructions as I could, he then presented me with a snuff box and a small statuette of himself. He asked me to see all his family in Europe, but he did not wish any of them to come out to St Helena. 'You will express these sentiments which I preserve for them,' he added. 'You will bear my affection to my good Louise, to my excellent mother, and to Pauline. If you see my son—embrace him for me. May he never forget that he was born a French prince! Adieu, O'Meara, we will not meet again. Be happy.' *(Napoleon gave O'Meara various other messages to carry to his family, including one to his brother Joseph, to make public various confidential and potentially embarrassing letters written to him at the height of his power by the Emperors of Russia and Austria and the King of Prussia. They were never found. This was of course exactly the kind of message that Lowe had attempted to prevent.)*

In his book Expositions of the transactions that have taken place on St Helena *(1819) O'Meara describes how when he left Longwood 'my baggage had been secretly rummaged and my papers examined'. Money, jewellery and papers disappeared. He was hustled on board the* Griffin, *and 'several respectable inhabitants were refused permission to come on board' to see him.*

A few months after O'Meara's departure, in October 1818, at the Congress of Aix-la-Chapelle, the Great Powers formally approved the measures taken for Napoleon's safe custody.

Chapter 6. Napoleon's last days

One by one Napoleon's entourage left the island: Las Cases was the first to go, expelled in December 1816; Gourgaud and the Balcombe family left in March 1818; Barry O'Meara in August 1818; Madame de Montholon (who, rumour suggests, may have been Napoleon's mistress) and her children left in July 1819. The Bertrands were apparently planning also to leave. In the meantime, the Conference of the Allies at Aix-la-Chapelle confirmed the terms of Napoleon's captivity, and seemed to reduce to nil the chances of his ever leaving St Helena. Napoleon seemed now to close in on himself. He saw fewer visitors, apparently having decided that the earlier strategy of making his plight known to as many people as possible had not worked. At the same time, he was becoming sicker. He took little exercise and remained in his bedroom for most of the day.

One of the very last of his visitors was Charles Ricketts, a relative of the Prime Minister Lord Liverpool. Napoleon arranged for the young man to be ushered into his bedroom where he lay on a camp bed, unshaven and apparently in pain. The room was so poorly lit that Ricketts could barely make out the Emperor's features. During the course of a long interview, Napoleon presented him with a paper detailing his requests: to leave the island because of his hepatitis, to have his doctor O'Meara returned, to have 'a man of honour' put over him instead of Sir Hudson, etc. The requests were not treated sympathetically, Lord Bathurst reporting that Ricketts had seen though 'all the manoeuvres which were practised to impose on him'.

Napoleon became increasingly invisible to all but his immediate entourage. The orderly officer Captain Nicholls had been given strict instructions to see General Bonaparte physically twice every day. If Napoleon refused to leave his room, this became extremely difficult. Nicholls spent frustrating hours each day trying to catch glimpses of the captive. Eventually, Lowe exasperatedly said that, if need be, Nicholls could force Napoleon's door. Incensed, Napoleon immediately ordered that the doors and windows be barricaded, and loaded pistols and guns placed near his bedside. He was determined to kill anyone who attempted a forcible entry.

As he increasingly closed in on himself, Napoleon had these spyholes in the shutters made, one for use from a sitting position, one from a standing position.

At the same time, rumours about a possible rescue attempt organised in America were rife (one of the wilder ones talked of a plan to approach St Helena by submarine). Other rumours said that Count Montholon had hanged himself, and there had been a fire in Longwood (in fact there had been a small fire, which was easily controlled). Hudson Lowe could not sleep.

As a replacement to O'Meara, in September 1818 Dr James Roche Verling, surgeon to one of the island's artillery detachments, had been sent up to Longwood. Although he was young, French-speaking, approachable and, as it happened, Irish, Napoleon refused to see him, simply because he had been appointed by Hudson Lowe. This was rather a pity as, not alone was Dr Verling an excellent physician, but he had also written his MD thesis on liver disease. Dr Verling remained in Longwood until replaced, as we shall see, by the Italian physician Antommarchi in September 1819. Although he attended to the Bertrand and du Montholon families while in residence, he never saw Napoleon for a medical consultation.

In November 1817 O'Meara had introduced a young surgical friend of his, John Stokoe, to the Emperor. Dr Stokoe was an agreeable young naval officer, who had applied for, and had been granted an extended posting at the St Helena station. Rumour connected his name romantically with Jane Balcombe. After an alarming seizure, Napoleon allowed Bertrand to call in Dr Stokoe. He first visited Longwood on 17 January, and made four further visits in the next few days. After a thorough examination the doctor diagnosed hepatitis. His report to Sir Hudson went as follows: 'I found him in a very weak state, complaining of considerable pain in the right side in the region of the liver and shooting pain in the right shoulder . . . it will be highly necessary that a medical man be near his person . . . for the daily treatment of chronic hepatitis which the above symptoms indicate.'

Lowe received this report with considerable distrust, fearing, as he believed of O'Meara, that the French had somehow suborned Stokoe. The following week Napoleon became quite ill. The doctor had again to wait for hours before permission to visit Longwood was granted. At 2 a.m. there was a torrential downpour, just as Dr Stokoe set off up the mountain. When he arrived at Longwood, Napoleon was asleep. Stokoe remained with him all day in Longwood. When he eventually examined the Emperor he confirmed his diagnosis of hepatitis. His report went as follows: 'The patient passed a restless night but without any alarming symptoms. It appears from the symptoms of chronic hepatitis that this is the principal cause of the derangement in his health . . . I do not apprehend any immediate imminent danger, although in a climate where the above disease is so prevalent, it will eventually shorten his life.'

Lowe decided that Stokoe had to go. The doctor was ordered back onto his ship and told to remain there, on the grounds that the naval service could not do without him. This had been expected, as Lowe's attitude became plainer. Stokoe informed General Bertrand: 'I have every reason to believe that my visits will soon come to an end, either because my superiors will forbid them or because the situation will become so disagreeable to me that I shall be obliged to discontinue them. In either event I beg you to urge the illustrious patient to follow the treatment I have prescribed.'

Life became extremely difficult for the naval surgeon. Wisely, he requested permission to return to England. This was granted, but no sooner had he arrived home than he was faced with a demand that he return immediately to St Helena to face court-martial. The poor doctor returned to St Helena, clocking up 144 days at sea. The court enquiry lasted for four days. Charged with 'having evinced a disposition to thwart the intentions and regulations of the Rear-Admiral and to further the views of the French prisoners in furnishing them with false pretences for complaint', Dr Stokoe was, of course, found guilty. Somewhat harshly he was, after twenty-five years' service, cashiered from the navy. He was returned to England in disgrace. He was eventually given the miserable pension of £100 per year. (It was lucky for him that no one knew of the bank draft for £1,000 that Napoleon had given him for his services, a serious breach of service regulations. This fact only emerged from the archives one hundred years later.)

Corsican arrivals

In September 1819 two Corsican priests and a Corsican doctor, sent by Napoleon's family, arrived on the island. Napoleon had written to his uncle, Cardinal Fesch, the previous year, requesting a good cook, an intelligent priest and (knowing that Barry O'Meara's time was running out) a doctor with a good reputation. The new arrivals were a disappointment. One of the priests was old and infirm (he was just recovering from a stroke), and the other (a Fr Vignali) was not very bright and too young. The cook sent by Pauline 'could not even brew a cup of coffee', Napoleon said.

The physician was a Dr Francesco Antommarchi, an anatomy demonstrator from the University of Padua. Aged twenty-eight, he was described by an English visitor as 'a common-looking young man whose conversation betrayed both ignorance and vulgarity'. He was excellent at post-mortems but not a very good physician. Although he had taken the precaution of meeting O'Meara in London before coming to the island, to learn about the case, Antommarchi did not inspire confidence. Napoleon did not like him: 'I would give him my horse to dissect, but I would not trust him to cure my foot,' he said. Antommarchi paid his first visit to Napoleon on 23 September. He would remain as the Emperor's physician to the end of Napoleon's life.

The Emperor knew that he was ill. His father had died from gastric (stomach) cancer; now he was sure that something similar would happen to him. He became preoccupied with death. He wrote his will. He had the dining-room turned into a chapel where he heard mass on Sundays. 'We have become Christian again,' he said with a smile.

In July 1820 Napoleon developed acute pain over his liver. 'It stabs like a penknife,' he said. Antommarchi diagnosed hepatitis and prescribed enemas every day. He suggested that the Emperor take more exercise, in particular in the Longwood garden that had become his latest interest. There was no improvement. Napoleon started to lose weight. Occasionally he became delirious. When Fanny Bertrand decided to return to France, claiming that her children needed European education, Napoleon was furious. He had the greatest affection and respect for Madame Bertrand, but now that she was leaving he could not forgive her. He refused to see her again.

Despite his discomfort he was adamant that he would not see any physician appointed by Hudson Lowe. He took to his bed. He had frequent shivering attacks, which often worried Antommarchi. The doctor knew that Napoleon disliked and did not trust him; this antipathy was dutifully reflected by the other French citizens at Longwood. Antommarchi's casual dress sense also offended the Marshal (Bertrand) and the other grandees of Napoleon's little court. As a result the doctor felt much more comfortable in Jamestown surrounded by strangers. So he was often not available when Napoleon needed him most. Antommarchi's cavalier attitude towards his patient reinforced Hudson Lowe's view that Napoleon was not as ill as he made out to be. It was most probably 'a subterfuge to get off the island and get back to Europe', he surmised.

In August 1820 Napoleon knew he was much worse. As the Governor was so unhelpful, the Emperor decided to write in person to Lord Liverpool stating that 'he had chronic hepatitis for the past two years and that medical remedies can no longer help. It is imperative that he return to Europe to lessen his suffering'. There was no reply.

On 18 September 1820 Napoleon went out for a horse ride. It so exhausted him that he was forced to stay in bed all the next day. In October, however, he felt fit enough for a long ride down to the house of an old native of the island, Sir William Doveton, on the southern part. On arrival he was invited indoors and offered breakfast. Instead, they shared the meal the French had brought, set out on a table on the lawn shaded by magnificent cedars and cypresses. Suddenly Napoleon felt extremely tired; he painfully remounted his horse and began the long ride back to Longwood. He had to be helped up the steps on his return. His eyes were closed, his face was ashen grey.

A few days later Napoleon fainted while getting out of his bath. He complained of headache and pain in his right upper abdomen. He was extremely constipated and the daily enemas weakened him. Sunlight hurt his eyes so the curtains were drawn. He spent most of the day dozing in bed. General Montholon suggested that they might call in the English physician Dr Archibald Arnott (the fifty-year-old surgeon to the 20th Regiment). He spoke Italian quite well and had a reasonable knowledge of French. Napoleon resisted the idea, saying, 'I will be better in a few days.'

News arrived that his sister Eliza had died from carcinoma of the stomach. She was aged forty-three. Napoleon was distressed by the news. 'Well, Doctor,' he said to Antommarchi, 'Eliza has shown us the way. Death seemed to have overlooked our family. Now it is beginning to strike. My turn cannot be far off.'

On New Year's morning 1821 Marchand entered the Emperor's bedroom and, after opening the curtains, wished Napoleon a happy new year. Napoleon replied that it would be his last year on earth. Later that day, leaning on the arm of Marchand, he went for a short walk; however, this exhausted him so much that he was forced to return to his bed, where he lay down to catch his breath. Occasionally he was hungry, but when he put soup to his mouth his appetite would quickly disappear.

On 17 March Napoleon went out for his last carriage drive. Very quickly however, he developed severe lower abdominal pain and was forced to return home. Dr Antommarchi prescribed an emetic, which Napoleon quite correctly refused to take.

However, the following day he felt so unwell that he was eventually persuaded to accept the prescribed emetic. Immediately afterwards he started to vomit and became 'racked with abdominal pains so much that he rolled around the floor groaning aloud'. As a result of this ill-judged intervention Napoleon refused to see Antommarchi for two days. Montholon began to urge him to supplement the latter's incompetence by consulting Dr Arnott. Finally, Napoleon agreed to see him. Before he called, Arnott met Antommarchi and discussed the symptoms.

On arrival at Longwood he was shown into a darkened room. He could just see the outline of a bed in the corner, but little more. Napoleon appeared to be in some pain. In the darkness Arnott felt his pulse, palpated the abdomen and limbs. In his report to Lowe he revealed the continuing scepticism of the English party: why, if there was no intent to deceive, was such darkness necessary? He declared that, assuming that the body he had felt had been Napoleon's, there was 'nothing that indicated immediate danger'. Subsequently, Dr Arnott became a more frequent visitor to Longwood. He informed the Emperor that he had a stomach inflammation but that his liver was quite healthy and not the cause of his pain. He prescribed various medications, which Napoleon refused to accept.

Napoleon now developed rigors every few hours. He was sweating so much that his bed linen had to be changed several times throughout the day and night. Fanny Bertrand abandoned her plans to leave the island with the children. Marchand and Montholon took it in turns to stay up with the Emperor.

Napoleon decided to write his will. He had about 6 million francs of his own, plus, as he supposed, 200 million in various properties. His body he wished to 'be returned to France and buried on the banks of the Seine'. He dispensed his wealth to his family, some marshals and faithful friends. To his son he bequeathed his sword, saddle and spurs, but, in knightly tradition, he left him no money. He called Fr Vignali and ordered the priest to set up an altar in the next room for the exposition of the Blessed Sacrament. 'You will hear my confession and say prayers for the dying.'

He was unable to swallow solid food, and was losing weight. He could only tolerate jelly, milk or soup. Arnott did nothing more than encourage Napoleon to cheer up, although Napoleon knew that he was seriously ill. Arnott reassured him that there was no tumour—'neither hardening nor swelling'—as he repeated. In his opinion, the organ was simply 'sluggish'.

During one of his more lucid moments Napoleon added a codicil to his will. He began by saying: 'I die in the Roman Catholic faith, in which I was born some fifty years ago. I am proud of my dear wife Marie Louise, and I beg her to take care of my son. I urge my son never to forget that he was born a French Prince. He is never to avenge my death. I die prematurely—murdered by the English oligarchy and its hired assassin.'

There followed a long list of bequests, in total amounting to considerably more than was held in his bank. He stipulated that the residue of his estate would be given to the wounded of Waterloo.

The next day Napoleon had shivering attacks followed by violent sweating and vomiting. With dawn there came some improvement. When Arnott arrived he informed the Emperor that he could find no hardening of the liver. Again there was much vomiting and restlessness all night. Napoleon complained of pain over his liver like 'a knife cutting into him'.

On 18 April, after vomiting most of the night, Napoleon woke to a beautiful day. He asked Montholon to open the doors into the garden. 'Let me take in a breath of the air God made.' He asked Bertrand to go and pick him a rose. He inhaled the perfume with voluptuous delight. He then gazed at the clear blue sky for a considerable time in silence. He appeared happy and content—almost resigned to the situation.

The end

Occasionally he seemed better, but he did not believe in any long-term recovery: 'Don't fool yourselves, I am better today but my end is not far off. When I am dead you will all have the sweet consolation of return-ing to your families in Europe.' From now on it became obvious to all, except the English doctor Arnott, that Napoleon was dying. He had difficulty in hearing people speak. He could not tolerate food—it made him vomit.

Within a day or two he started again to vomit copious amounts of black liquid. He had a raging fever all night but when the dawn came he was somewhat better. In a confused state he gave out to Bertrand. He spent most of the night in stupor. Around 3 a.m. he started to hiccough—this continued until morning. It quite exhausted him. His mind became confused, mistaking Antommarchi for O'Meara, and ask-ing for Dr Baxter, who had long left the island. His bed was moved into the larger sitting-room.

On 1 May Fanny Bertrand saw Napoleon for the first time in six weeks. She was shocked by his appearance. They had a most agreeable conversation. Fanny told him that she would have liked to nurse him back to health. He invited her to visit him each day and in particular to bring her children with her.

Napoleon called for Antommarchi and instructed him as follows: 'After my death you will carry out the post-mortem. Do not let the English carry this out. While you are operating on me pay particular attention to my stomach. Please remove my heart, place it in a silver container and bring it to Marie Louise. I want you to make a clear precise examination overlooking nothing.' Antommarchi agreed to carry out this request.

By early May even Dr Arnott had become convinced that Napoleon was in a serious condition. He conveyed his feelings to the Governor. Lowe promptly offered that 'English medical science should have the chance of saving his life'. Dr Thomas Shortt and Dr Mitchell moved into the New House beside Longwood. They wished to be 'as near as possible to the dying man'.

Dr Arnott now insisted that Napoleon be given a purgative, and suggested 10 grains of calomel. This was much too strong for Napoleon's weakened state. A most reluctant Marchand was ordered to mix the powdered calomel in water with a little sugar added. Napoleon swallowed it with difficulty. He tried to vomit it up but was unsuccessful. He turned to Marchand and gently said: 'You are deceiving me also!'

Over the next two days his fever rose and sank; he took a little soup and sweetened water, most of which he vomited up. Occasionally he spat black, chocolate-like mucus. At two in the morning of 5 May he spoke for the last time, incoherent words interpreted by Montholon as 'France—army—army head—Josephine!'

The bed was pulled into the middle of the room and the windows were opened. In the small hot room all the French, including for a while the Bertrand children, sat watching around the bed. All that could be heard was the ticking of a clock, and the occasional sigh from the Emperor. Two silver-plumed doves, of the species peculiar to St Helena, landed on the windowsill and started to coo. They were pushed away, but later they returned and again perched on the windowsill.

Towards evening the room became bathed in a bright orange-red glow of the sunset. Napoleon's breathing became quite irregular. Antommarchi put a finger to his artery, and Dr Arnott scribbled on his pad: '5.30. He is worse, the respiration has become difficult'. It was obvious to all that the end was near. His breathing stopped. Everybody waited. Then Antommarchi gently leaned over and closed the Emperor's eyelids. It was 11 minutes to 6 on Saturday 5 May 1821. The Emperor Napoleon Bonaparte was dead. Count Bertrand reached up and quietly stopped the pendulum on the little clock.

There were tears in everyone's eyes. The men wept in silence. The women quietly sobbed. Even Dr Arnott was seen to brush a tear from his eye. Bertrand went down on one knee and kissed Napoleon's hand. Each one in the room followed suit. Arnott now wrote a note to the Governor stating that 'he has at this moment expired.'

Lowe insisted that two British doctors be admitted to confirm the death. Reluctantly they were allowed into the room. Captain Crokat, the orderly officer, paused at the end of the bed and saluted. Then followed Drs Shortt and Mitchell who confirmed the death of Napoleon Bonaparte.

At midnight they washed the body in eau de cologne. His face was shaved and a chin bandage put in place. He was dressed in a white shroud. A crucifix was placed on his chest. The room was aired and tidied up. Most of the furniture was removed, apart from a small bedside table upon which a number of candles were burning brightly. Signals to Plantation House confirmed the death, and Lowe, discussing the situation with his staff said, with a characteristic mixture of fatuous self-importance and respect: 'Well, gentlemen, he was England's greatest enemy and mine too, but I forgive him everything. On the death of a great man like him we should only feel deep concern and regret.'

The following day Sir Hudson Lowe arrived, dressed in all the finery his office could command. His highly-coloured feathered helmet glinted against the burning sun. All stood as Lowe entered. He removed his helmet and stood in silence at the end of the bed gazing at the Emperor for the first time without fear or amazement.

Post-mortem

The damp, hot climate demanded that if there was to be an autopsy it should be soon. So it was decided to hold a post-mortem the afternoon after the death. The body was placed on the billiard table. Dr Antommarchi (as requested by Napoleon) started the post-mortem. This was what he could do best. He took pride in his work. He could now show the English doctors just how good he was. Deftly he made the incision from the sternum to the pubis.

Multiple adhesions were found between the stomach and the liver. Almost two-thirds of his stomach was cancerous. The tumour had eaten its way through the entire coat of the stomach and directly into the left lobe of the liver. There was a large ulcer on the lesser curvature of the stomach, quite near the pylorus, which had penetrated directly into the liver. It was obvious to all that this was the cause of death. Dr Antommarchi said so during the operation. All six other doctors agreed. He then wished to open the skull but Bertrand and Montholon objected, so it was left intact.

The heat and stench from the open abdomen in that crowded room was overpowering. They all agreed—a diagnosis had been made: death was undoubtedly from the stomach cancer, but the liver was also infected. It was time to go. As instructed by Napoleon his heart was removed and placed in a silver container, which had been filled with alcohol. Antommarchi excised the entire gut and placed it in a large tin container. To make the air in the stifling heat somewhat more agreeable he poured eau de cologne freely into the abdominal cavity. He then carefully stitched up the incision.

When Hudson Lowe read the post-mortem report he was furious. The report suggested that 'the liver was enlarged and densely adhered to the stomach. There was a large ulcer on the lesser curvature (of the stomach) which had perforated into the liver. This in turn had become so adhered to the liver that it had prevented the contents of the stomach from spilling over into the peritoneal (abdominal) cavity.' Lowe however insisted that the liver be reported on as 'normal'—otherwise Dr O'Meara would have been correct in his diagnosis during all those years.

In a rage he furiously scratched out the offending paragraph. He insisted that all the doctors reconsider their findings and present him with a new post-mortem report with no mention of any problems in the liver. After considerable deliberation, reluctantly, all the British surgeons signed—even Dr Shortt who initially had been adamant that he would not sign. The harsh treatment of Dr Stokoe was still very fresh in their minds. Dr Antommarchi, who had carried out the most excellent post-mortem, absolutely refused to sign the second report.

After the autopsy Napoleon was laid out in his little bedroom, and crowds of islanders queued to file past the bed.

Funeral

Hudson Lowe, no doubt reflecting both British and French official opinion, would not consider allowing Napoleon's body to return to Europe. Neither would he allow Marie Louise to have the Emperor's heart. He decided, however, on having a military funeral. On 8 May he wrote to Montchenu as follows: 'Sir, I do myself the honour to inform you that the remains of Napoleon Bonaparte will be interred with all honours due to a General officer of the highest rank, at 12 o'clock tomorrow.'

Fr Vignali celebrated mass in the small room for the last time. Adding incense to the turifer, he sweetened the air around the coffin, and recited prayers for the dead.

Eight Grenadier officers from the 20th Regiment lifted the heavy coffin shoulder high and with the greatest difficulty made their way out through the billiard-room, down the veranda steps, onto the lawn, and to the waiting hearse. The coffin was covered with a large, rich, purple velvet cloth. On top of the coffin, Bertrand placed Napoleon's cloak of Marengo and his sword.

It was a beautiful, bright, clear, silent morning. Two thousand soldiers lined either side of the road from Longwood to Talbot Springs. With bowed heads, and rifles reversed, each soldier stood to attention in the warm quiet air.

Fr Vignali, reciting prayers, led the way accompanied by young Henri Bertrand carrying the holy water. The band played a funeral march. Four horses slowly pulled the heavy black carriage along the road. A young boy led a grey, riderless horse. Then came General Bertrand and General du Montholon. Behind them came the staff of Longwood. At some distance Hudson Lowe and his staff followed. They were met at Hutt's Gate by a carriage bearing Lady Lowe and her unmarried daughter, Susanna, dressed suitably in black. Last of all came the islanders.

When the cortège reached Talbot Springs, the coffin was placed beside the large, open grave. Napoleon's tomb was deep and wide. As the coffin was lowered into the grave, volleys of musketry were echoed by the great guns from the fleet in the harbour and from the forts across the island. After a moment's silence, Lowe asked Montholon and Bertrand if they wanted to say anything—they declined. The soldiers reformed and marched back to camp, the plangent fife music hanging in the air.

In an undignified last-minute squabble, Sir Hudson refused to allow Count Bertrand to have the simple name 'Napoleon' inscribed on the tomb. He insisted that the inscription be 'Napoleon Bonaparte'. In exasperation the French gave way, knowing of course that the tomb needed no inscription. So in the end the stone was left bare. In 1860, when building the Washington Monument, the American Government requested a stone from Napoleon's tomb on St Helena, to be incorporated in the monument. This request was granted.

Back to Europe

After the funeral the French returned to Longwood, and hurriedly started to pack. Lady Lowe came to visit the house. She was appalled by the state of the place. Only now that the Emperor was gone did the French realise how awful their accommodation had been for the past five years. They packed and set out for Jamestown to face a new future in France. There was considerable difficulty finding a ship to take the French entourage. Eventually the captain of a cattle boat called *The Camel* decided to help out for an undisclosed sum. The ship was not very clean or comfortable, but the French were now so anxious to leave the island any boat would do. It was a most uncomfortable six-week voyage for all.

Chapter 7: Barry O'Meara in London

This stiff surgeon who maintained his cause
hath lost his place, but gained the world's applause.
Byron The Age of Bronze

In the meantime, what of Barry O'Meara, the Emperor's devoted Irish doctor? He had arrived in London six weeks after his departure from St Helena in September 1818. Within a few days he reported to the Admiralty. Initially he was well received, and is said to have had the valuable post of Surgeon to Greenwich Hospital offered to him. However, the mood changed as he continued his outspoken support of Napoleon and his denunciation of the conditions under which he was being kept. He described the situation on the island, stressing the poor climate and the damage it was doing to Napoleon's health. He pointed out that most of the favourable reports about the climate of St Helena came from those who had stayed in Jamestown, where the weather was Mediterranean, or, like Wellington, on the sheltered side (Wellington had in fact lodged in The Briars during his stay). On the exposed mountainside the climate was quite different. Mould grew on the damp walls. Rain leaked constantly through the roof during the long nine-month wet season. Large pink-eyed rats infested the walls and floorboards. These aggressive vermin infected food and water and destroyed the linen. O'Meara urged that Napoleon was sick, and should be returned to Europe—preferably England—for proper medical attention.

The reception committee listened in silence to the doctor's forceful report. The Chairman replied: 'Sir Hudson Lowe is of a different opinion. Every one of his reports stipulates that General Bonaparte might possibly be imagining that he was seriously ill.' Medically, of course, Sir Hudson's opinion was worthless since not only had he no medical qualification, but neither he nor any other doctor on the island (apart from O'Meara) had even seen Napoleon for many months. All he had was the old suspicion that O'Meara had been 'turned', and was acting as a propagandist for Napoleon's sly attempt to have his exile curtailed.

At this point O'Meara no doubt repeated his suspicion that Napoleon was not safe in the hands of Sir Hudson Lowe, and that broad hints had been dropped that O'Meara should help to 'get rid' of Napoleon. This accusation was, of course, impossible to prove, and would have required a ruthlessness far from Sir Hudson's character. It was also one that the Admiralty could not ignore.

O'Meara wrote a long letter supporting his claim, repeating the statement in a manner which, as the Admiralty noted, it was 'impossible to doubt the meaning this passage was intended to convey'. From their point of view the statement against his superior officer not only impugned Sir Hudson's character but, as they rather pompously put it, 'the honour of the nation'. If it was true, they argued, it should not 'have been reserved in your own head for two years, to be produced at last not (as it would appear) from a sense of public duty but in furtherance of your personal hostility against the Governor.' The Admiralty took a dim view of this, and informed him that they had 'directed that your name be erased from the list of naval surgeons'. O'Meara had now lost his pension, his place in the navy and his good name.

Because he had put the interests of his illustrious patient above everything O'Meara now, after nearly twelve years in the navy, was faced with the unappealing prospect of starting from scratch in London. (The ending of the Napoleonic wars a few years before had thrown many ex-naval and military doctors into the medical marketplaces in Dublin and London—O'Meara's years on St Helena meant that he was a few years behind that group.) He sent a 38-page letter to the Admiralty explaining his awkward position on the island. 'I was in charge of a sick man who happened to be the country's greatest enemy. My position as an officer demanded that I serve my country. My profession expected me to give my patient the best medical attention possible—this was a task I had carried out to the best of my ability.'

Selling everything he possessed, he rented rooms on the ground floor of a tall imposing building on Edgeware Road. His lack of local contacts meant that his best strategy was to develop the dental skills he had learned as an apprentice surgeon in Dublin and had no doubt honed on board ship. By way of advertising, he hung Napoleon's wisdom tooth in the window and opened up as a dentist. Business was slow. His notoriety as a supporter of Napoleon, and some of the hard things that had been written about him in the press no doubt did not help.

His treatment by the British naval authorities, in unilaterally removing his means of livelihood without the semblance of a trial, no doubt hardened his opinion of the British establishment, and he evidently took an active part with other radicals in supporting the struggle of Queen Caroline against her husband George IV. Caroline had been offered a bribe of £50,000 a year to stay out of England, but had refused this. So the government dredged up an 18th-century precedent and initiated a Bill of Pains and Penalties to deprive her of her privileges as Queen and incidentally to dissolve the marriage. The debate on this bill amounted to a trial in the House of Lords of the question as to whether Caroline had committed adultery with her handsome courtier Bartolemmeo Pergami. In the clubs the wags, remembering that the King as Prince of Wales had undergone a form of marriage with his former mistress, told each other that she certainly *had* committed adultery— with the husband of Mrs Fitzherbert!

For weeks, witness after witness retailed more or less squalid tittle-tattle about stained sheets and private doors and unexpected intimacies. One of the Italian witnesses achieved a temporary fame by his constant reply '*non mi ricordo*' which became a catchphrase indicating something one did not choose to remember. For most of the witnesses there was considerable doubt as to whether the King's agents had bribed them. Barry O'Meara was deeply involved in the Queen's cause. We catch a glimpse of him in Thomas Moore's diaries from Paris in September 1820: 'O'Meara, the celebrated surgeon of Napoleon is here,' Moore writes, 'upon the Queen's business—forwarding witnesses etc.' In the end, although no one had any doubt that Caroline had been at the very least indiscreet, the Bill was passed with such a small majority that with great relief all round it was dropped. The Queen herself died three months after Napoleon. (When the King was informed that his 'greatest enemy was dead', he said, 'Is she, by God?' He was somewhat crestfallen to be informed 'No, Sire—Napoleon.')

To keep himself occupied O'Meara invented a tooth powder, which sold quite well. He also decided to edit his lengthy diary, which he had meticulously written up night after night for two and a half years. There were 18 volumes in all, each one containing over 100 pages of tightly written script. He had quite a lot of editing to do.

Although the weight of English public opinion was against Napoleon, and broadly in favour of the government's policy, there was a small but well-connected and vocal group that believed that the government's actions in imprisoning Napoleon were illegal, and that the conditions under which he was being held were oppressive. At the same time, the

enormous public interest in anything to do with Napoleon was difficult to interpret. The display of his famous campaign carriage in Bul-
lock's Museum, Piccadilly, soon after Waterloo, brought tens of thousands to view it. Was this to be interpreted as support, or was it no
more than interest in an old enemy about whom people had heard so
much? Conscious of this ambiguity, the government sponsored a pamphlet supporting its position by a literary hack called Theodore Hook—
*Transactions that have taken place at St Helena, subsequent to the ap-
pointment of Sir Hudson Lowe.*

The publication infuriated O'Meara, who described it as 'a vehicle
of slander, calumny and misrepresentation'. He interrupted his work in
editing his longer narrative of the events on the island, and in a very
short time had published his 200-page point by point riposte, called, in
the elaborate mode of the time, *An Exposition of some of the Transactions
that have taken place at St Helena since the appointment of Sir Hudson
Lowe.* This sold remarkably well, with a second edition coming a few
months later.

The success of this publication encouraged him to continue with
the mammoth task of editing his diary. He moved into a more comfortable apartment. He bought a small library of French novels and histori-
cal works, which he knew would be of interest to Napoleon. These
books were carefully packed in wooden crates and shipped to St Helena.
Barry had them delivered to the shopkeeper Mr Solomons, with instructions that two or three novels should be sent up to Longwood with
the shopping every day. Unfortunately, Sir Hudson Lowe discovered
the plot. The entire collection was confiscated. Napoleon would never
hear of O'Meara's generous gift. On their side, the government put out
rumours that O'Meara was attempting to arrange a rescue, to be fi-
nanced by Madame Mère (Napoleon's mother) in Rome.

Since his return O'Meara, in common with other returnees from St
Helena such as Las Cases, the Polish officer Piontkowski, General
Gourgaud and Madame de Montholon, had been a welcome dinner
guest at Holland House. Here, Charles James Fox's nephew and his
wife Lady Holland were the centre of the British Napoleonist movement. With Irish tact, O'Meara had presented Lady Holland soon after
his return with a lock of Napoleon's hair, neatly tied in a silver wire.
Equally enthusiastic, Lord Holland helped O'Meara prepare his claims
that Hudson Lowe had at best treated Napoleon's health as a matter of
indifference. At its most extreme, this amounted to accusing Sir Hud-

son of actively hastening Napoleon's death. This aspect of O'Meara's diary continued to be the most frequently attacked, and certainly in the cold light of London some of the more paranoid fears of the entourage at Longwood (as for instance that the wine was being poisoned) did seem far fetched. On the other hand there was no doubt that the ministers would have been glad to have been relieved of the responsibility (and expense) of guarding Napoleon, and the issue was complicated by the fact that not even his most fervent admirer would deny that Napoleon was perfectly capable of acting or promulgating a lie to further his ends.

O'Meara became a frequent visitor to Holland House. The eighteen manuscript volumes were 'culled' down to four. In putting them into print, his editor further reduced them to two volumes. In May 1821 Napoleon died, and O'Meara now felt free to publish his diary of their memorable conversations. *Napoleon in Exile, or a Voice from St Helena*, with a dedication to Lady Holland, was published in July 1822. It was an immediate success, the crowds queuing to buy copies from the publisher, so it was said, blocking the street. The book quickly ran through several printings. It also was quickly translated into French. Suddenly O'Meara was a well-known London character, about whom everyone had an opinion. As the gossipy diarist Creevey put it, 'I wonder whether you will be anything like as much interested by O'Meara and Buonaparte as I have been and am still. I can think of nothing else . . . I am perfectly satisfied Buonaparte said everything O'Meara puts into his mouth. Whether *that* is true is another thing . . .'

Soon enough the government side began to hit back, largely with personal attacks on O'Meara and his way of handling the ambiguous position in which he had found himself. A very aggressive review of *A Voice from St Helena* was published in the *Quarterly Review* in March 1823, and another in *Blackwood's*. The *Quarterly's* review was written by J. W. Croker, a man much hated in literary circles for his unfair attacks on Keats and other young poets. As secretary of the Admiralty, Croker had drafted the letter that informed O'Meara that he had been erased from the list of naval surgeons.

The weather-vane Creevey recorded how his own opinions, which had initially been positive, began to shift. 'I am curious to see O'Meara's defence. How he is to exculpate himself from the many charges of double dealing baffles my poor imagination.' Others were less ambivalent: Daniel O'Connell met O'Meara in Dublin, as he wrote to his wife

(July 1823): 'We dined with him at Lyons. He is a plain, unaffected young man, greatly attached to the memory of the unfortunate great man.'

The stress O'Meara was under at this time was revealed by a court case. *The Times,* Britain's most influential paper, was extremely anti Napoleon and his supporters. One article in particular reflecting adversely on his *Voice from St Helena* infuriated O'Meara. Thus it was in Knightsbridge, one afternoon, that O'Meara suddenly crossed the road and accosted a tall, burly, well-dressed man. Pinning the surprised man against the wall O'Meara was about to give him a good thrashing—when he realised that this startled Mr Walters was not the owner of *The Times.* With the greatest embarrassment O'Meara released his grip on the unfortunate man and offered his profuse apologies.

On Thursday 22 July 1822 O'Meara appeared at Marylebone Court in front of magistrate Sir John Rawlingsome. Mr Walters was about to be sworn in when O'Meara's solicitor (Mr Charles Philips) stepped forward stating that 'he attended for the defendant who had asked him to express his sorrow for the unprovoked attack he had committed on Mr Walters—and also to state should the matter be adjusted, that he was most willing to make an apology. He also begged leave to observe that the breach of the peace committed on Mr Walter was entirely by mistake.'

Mr Walters then addressed the Magistrate saying that all he wanted was a public apology. 'The Magistrate then said that if Mr Walters felt himself satisfied with an apology and did not wish to proceed he would certainly not press the case, but it must certainly appear that Mr O'Meara intended to commit a breach of the peace, and to prevent a repetition of such an outrage he could not allow the defendant to depart without calling on him to find sureties to keep the peace.'

O'Meara was then bound over in his own recognisance of £500, and a promise to keep the peace towards all the King's subjects.

Sir Hudson Lowe returns to England

In the meantime, Sir Hudson Lowe had returned to England. He and his family had sailed for home in July 1821, not long after Napoleon's death. He felt he had done his job well. If he had been harsh on a few occasions he consoled himself that he was only doing his job. His return to London proved to be a disappointment. O'Meara and others had raised significant questions about the way in which St Helena had been governed, and although there was a façade of official solidarity, there was no doubt considerable embarrassment too. The Foreign Office gave him the less than glowing 'satisfi' report. At a levée, George IV merely shook his hand and gave him a nod without saying a word. He went to Holland House in an attempt to revive the welcome he had received before he went out to St Helena. He could not gain admission. The door was firmly shut in his face.

The publication of *A Voice from St Helena* with its strong attacks on the regime on the island excited public controversy, and Sir Hudson sought legal redress for what he perceived as libels. He spent a considerable amount of time collecting more or less reluctant testimonies from all his previous subordinates on the island. He even forced William Balcombe into agreeing to sign an affidavit, something Balcombe did with the greatest reluctance. (Balcombe, who was never one of the world's great managers, as we have seen, had done badly in England. He had been writing to Lowe for three years hoping to return to St Helena. Lowe had refused on each occasion. Now that he had agreed to support Hudson Lowe against O'Meara, he became gainfully employed. He was appointed to the important post of Colonial Treasurer of New South Wales. Balcombe immediately set off for Australia with all his family. Sadly, the elder daughter, Jane, died during the voyage and was buried at sea.)

Unfortunately, Lowe spent much too long on the preparation of his case, and when it was finally brought it was struck out for being late— technically 'lost in point of time'. Then he was urged to publish his own account of matters with backing documents. Instead he decided to pester the government for some official vindication, which it was reluctant to give.

In October 1823, in a bizarre incident, Lowe was attacked by a young man just outside his home in Paddington. He was hit with a small riding whip. The assailant was the young Emanuel de Las Cases, attempting to revenge a supposed insult to his father. He had been stalking the Governor for some days—seizing his chance that morning.

Lowe turned to pursue his attacker, but was baulked by a bystander. So he turned and entered his carriage. Las Cases, who was now in his mid-twenties, ran after the carriage and threw his card through the open window—it was flung out instantly. Later, on his return, Sir Hudson found more cards had been found on the ground. Sir Hudson took the view that this was no more than a treacherous attack on him in the course of his public duties, and informed the Government and the legal authorities of the matter. A warrant was issued for the arrest of Las Cases, but he could not be found.

In October 1825 Sir Hudson was made commander of forces in Ceylon, finally returning to England in 1831. By this time he was in straitened circumstances, having to sell his magnificent library with its Napoleonic memorabilia. He died in 1844, so poor that the government organised a small pension for his surviving daughter.

O'Meara's marriage

O'Meara became a most accomplished after-dinner speaker. One who came in two minds about him said that he 'left the meeting enchanted by Dr O'Meara's delivery and likeable personality. His speeches rang true. Napoleon was a genius.'

It was at one of these dinners that Barry first met the Lady Theodosia Leigh *née* Boughton. She had been first married while still in her teens. Four years and two children into her first marriage in 1777 to Captain John Donellan, her husband was sensationally hanged for the murder by poison of her brother Sir Theodosius Boughton. Donellan's defence was a flat denial backed by an attempt to cast suspicion on the victim's mother, his mother-in-law. Since the young man had died before coming of age, the outcome left Theodosia independently wealthy.

Some years later the young widow met the amusing but overweight Lord Leigh. He had money, land and social standing. Their marriage, which lasted until 1818, was childless. O'Meara's after-dinner speeches and his amusing anecdotes fascinated Lady Leigh, and in 1823 they married.

O'Meara could devote himself to his radical political interests. A man of open heart and generous disposition, his political opinions were strong, and he continued to support liberal causes. He spent his time, as one obituary put it, 'in the enjoyment of the society of choice spirits. He had a very large circle of acquaintance in the various clubs of the West End.' Daniel O'Connell recorded enjoying 'a most splendid entertainment' at O'Meara's in January 1824, 'including some beautiful champagne. I stayed there till near one in the morning listening to some fine singing and conversing.' Records survive of O'Meara's involvement on the committee of the Westminster Reform Club; he was proposed as a member by O'Connell. Among the other members was the famous Alderman Wood, Queen Caroline's great supporter. Less famous at this time was Benjamin Disraeli who, the committee noted, was in arrears with his subscription. O'Meara was also, with Daniel O'Connell and others, on the first committee of the New Reform Club, founded in 1836 (later known simply as the Reform). However, the good life was beginning, so the obituary declared, to take its toll, as he was growing corpulent.

O'Meara's death

It was at a political meeting of O'Connell's that O'Meara caught the chill that prematurely ended his life. Although he had been in 'exuberant health' before this, he woke with a fever, and then erysipelas. He took to his bed. He became quite ill and even delirious, supposing himself on occasion to be still in Longwood. Despite the best medical attention, his condition rapidly deteriorated. The illness progressed into bronchial pneumonia. As the obituary in the medical journal *The Medico-Chirurgical Review* put it, 'delirium set in early and continued to the last. The powers of life ebbed—pulse got daily weaker—and the patient sank in the tenth day of the disease.' On 12 June 1836 Barry Edward O'Meara died at his home, 16 Cambridge Terrace, Edgeware Road, London.

The contents of his house were put up for auction in July. As the *Annual Register* recorded, 'in the Edgeware Road on 18th and 19th of July a sale of Barry Edward O'Meara's effects took place. There was considerable competition among the purchasers for various articles, which had been the property of Napoleon. For example:

A few lines of the Emperor's writing was sold for 11 guineas

A lock of the Emperor's hair sold for £2 11 shillings

His wisdom tooth (*extracted by O'Meara*) sold for 7 guineas

Some articles of plate formally the property of Napoleon were sold for about 6 times their intrinsic value.'

In his will he left virtually everything to his nephew Barry and niece Harriet, then living at no 72 Dame Street, Dublin (now the site of the Olympia Theatre). They were his sister Charlotte's children—unexpectedly, there is no mention of his son Dennis. He asked that his funeral expenses be moderate, but somewhat belying this he requested that the following be put on his tomb: 'I take this opportunity of declaring that, with the exception of some unintentional errors in *Napoleon in Exile*, the book is a faithful narrative of the treatment inflicted upon that great man Napoleon, by Sir Hudson Lowe and his subordinates. I

St Mary's Paddington, where Barry O'Meara is buried

have even suppressed some facts which, although true, might have been considered to have been exaggerated and not credited.'

On 13 June 1836 the following leader appeared in *The Courier:* 'The island of St Helena has given to Mr O'Meara a place in history and when time shall have permitted all personal feelings to subside, history

Terence Barry O'Meara, Barry O'Meara's oldest living relative

will do him justice. She will record him as a man of the most rigid integrity capable of any sacrifice in the support of principle and with a practical chivalry defying power and welcoming privation in the maintenance of his proud consistency. His was not the mere theory of patriotism but he avowed he felt and proved his sincerity by suffering in its defence. Power might have elevated, and wealth might have enriched, could he have stooped to attain a dishonourable silence. But he disdained the compromise, and the gloomy rock of Napoleon's imprisonment has borrowed one gleam from the virtue of its historian. To those who could not be misled by the partisanship of politics, it may be satisfactory to hear that with his dying breath he authenticated the details communicated in his work. He left in his will an inscription to that effect to be recorded on his tomb, thus *Napoleon in Exile* will be henceforth a voice speaking from the grave. A more warm-hearted or a more sincere friend than O'Meara never lived.'

His surgical instruments were all sold for 2 guineas. They were eventually donated (1910) to the Royal College of Physicians, Kildare Street, Dublin where to this day they are on display in a special glass cabinet.

The O'Mearas

Most of O'Meara's relatives appear to have done well. His only child Dennis became a farmer in Tipperary. Dennis had one daughter, she was called Kathleen. She moved to Paris at an early age and remained there for the rest of her life. She became a writer, publishing several novels, typically on the theme of conversion to Catholicism—no doubt reflecting her own experience—and was the Paris correspondent for the *Tablet* and other Catholic publications. She died from breast cancer aged forty-nine. She had no children.

O'Meara's nieces and nephews appear to have been remarkably successful in their chosen careers including Divines of the Church, explorers, and engineers and, of course, the army.

Some years ago I was fortunate enough to meet Barry O'Meara's oldest living relative. This delightful man lived in the beautiful little village of Copworth, Sussex. He was quite proud of his name, Terence Barry O'Meara. Yes, he had fought in the Second World War as an engineer. 'I was fortunate enough to get out at Dunkirk. I went missing for a few weeks; however, with help from the French underground I was eventually able to make my way back to England. It was assumed by all that I had been killed.

'I knew that my family would be told that I had been killed. We did not have mobile phones in those days, you know,' he said with a quiet smile. It was typical O'Meara.

Chapter 8: Napoleon returns to France

For nearly twenty years after his death the cult of Napoleon was officially discouraged in France. Although poems were published, for years mention of his name in the theatre was forbidden. Nonetheless, the lacklustre nature of the monarchies of Louis XVIII and Charles X meant that patriots could not prevent themselves looking back, nostalgically, to the time of glory. Workers became increasingly Bonapartist, hoping above all, so the police thought, for revenge for Waterloo.

In the so-called 'July Revolution' of 1830 Louis Philippe took over the throne from the Bourbon Charles X. Louis Philippe knew of the popular affection towards Napoleon, and decided to try and appease the population. Slowly, Napoleon's army officers were returned to their ranks, or appointed to political and legal posts throughout the country. The Arc de Triomphe was completed.

The Prime Minister Adolphe Thiers officially requested of the English that the Emperor's body be returned to France. Permission was granted. The Foreign Secretary, Lord Palmerston, wrote to the British Ambassador in Paris stating that 'he hoped that the promptness of his reply, would be considered as testimony to the eagerness of the British Government to extinguish any surviving remnants of the national animosities that had kept the two countries at arms during the life of the Emperor.'

Accordingly, the body was exhumed from its tomb in St Helena and brought solemnly back to France. The quality of preservation of the body after nearly twenty years, a common side-effect of arsenic, was remarked on. He was perfectly preserved. His hair and nails had grown considerably after death. He looked like a man aged thirty. His lips were slightly parted, showing white teeth—he appeared to be smiling.

At dawn on 14 December 1840 the hearse, pulled by sixteen black horses, carried the remains of the Emperor through the Arc de Triomphe, down the Champs Elysées to the Place de la Concorde, over the Seine to Les Invalides, the chapel of the military school, where Napoleon was to lie.

It was a freezing cold day, but that did not prevent an astonishing crowd, estimated at 600,000 people, from waiting to see the catafalque pass. Shafts of sunlight occasionally pierced the falling snow. An army of 80,000 men lined the route from the Arc de Triomphe to Les Invalides. Old soldiers had brought out their uniforms. They had brushed and polished their souvenirs for Napoleon's return to France. Cannons boomed and every church in Paris rang its bells.

The bent but dignified figure of a grey-haired old man followed the coffin. It was Count Bertrand, the constant and most trustworthy of all Napoleon's followers on St Helena. Around his ears rang shouts of *'Vive l'Empéreur!'* It was his greatest moment, his greatest reward.

Napoleon had come home.

Arsenic

Napoleon certainly died from carcinoma of the stomach which had spread into his liver. However, some one hundred and fifty years after his death it was found that during the last six years of his life on the island of St Helena the Emperor had abnormally high levels of arsenic in his system. This sensational discovery was made by Dr Sten

---

The arsenic in Napoleon's hair

Date	Arsenic concentration (PPM)*Source		Source
	High	*Low*	
14 Jan 1816	60.0	25.0	Commander John
	71.2	3.0	Reed
	62.0	33.0	
	23.0	15,0	
3 July 1817	4.9	1.5	Admiral Pulteney Malcolm
16 March 1818	26.0	1.8	Betsy Balcombe
6 May 1821 (day after death—head shaved)	51.0	3.7	Jean Noverraz
	23.0	4.4	
	20.0	2.83	

The normal amount in hair is 0.8 parts per milliion. Only the highest and lowest amounts are shown.

Source: Forshufvud, Hamilton Smith and Wassen 'Napoleon's illness (1816–1821) in the light of activation analysis of hairs from various dates' *Archiv fur Toxikologie* 20 (1964) pp 210–19.

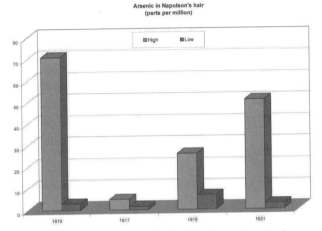

Arsenic in Napoleon's hair
(parts per million)

Analysis of the arsenic in Napoleon's hair makes it clear that he was ingesting much less arsenic when under Barry O'Meara's care between April 1816 and July 1818.

Forshufvud, a Swedish dentist with an interest in forensic pathology. He was convinced that Napoleon had all the signs and symptoms of arsenical poisoning. The discovery stimulated a rich flora of suggestions as to the source of the arsenic. Everything from the wallpaper to members of Napoleon's intimate group was proposed as the source. A favourite villain is Count Montholon; he presumably had the opportunity (though Longwood was always fully populated, as Appendix 1 makes clear), and his motives have been adduced as anything from jealousy at the attentions Napoleon was supposed to be paying to his wife, to a botched attempt to make Napoleon so sick that the great powers would permit a return to Europe.

Arsenic is stored in hair and nail. It has a half-life of two thousand years. Thus it can be detected many years after death. Dr Forshufvud decided to investigate, but firstly he had to find authentic samples of Napoleon's hair, a difficult task, and one which would occupy the greater part of the rest of his life. Hair grows at approximately five and a half inches per year—so if we know when the hair was cut then we can work out when the arsenic was taken. Fortunately, the date was written on each souvenir. On St Helena, Napoleon gave samples of his hair to his friends. Eventually, Dr Forshufvud found four people who had inherited four samples of genuine Napoleonic hair. They were all generous enough to donate a few strands of their precious souvenirs to Dr Forshufvud for examination.

The four samples were sent to the Harwell Institute under the care of Professor Hamilton Smith, a forensic pathologist who had devised a new method for detecting arsenic called 'activation analysis'. The hair was cut into many equal parts and then bombarded with thermal neutrons. This made every trace of arsenic radioactive. It is then a relatively simple matter to measure the amount of arsenic in each of the hair samples. The normal amount of arsenic in hair is approximately 0.8 parts per million (ppm). The level of arsenic in Napoleon's hair varied from double that, 1.5 ppm, to an astonishing 71·ppm.

In the past, arsenic was prescribed as a medical treatment for almost every known disease. It was given for everything from gout and ear infection to gonorrhoea. It is odourless, colourless, tasteless and mixes easily with other liquids. It was known as the silent death. Since it was readily available as rat poison, it was the favourite of Victorian poisoners. More sinisterly, because it is secreted in breast milk, it can be given to an unsuspecting wet nurse without causing her too much harm or discomfort, but in quantities lethal for the suckling infant.

Arsenic was widely available on the island. It was used in vast amounts by the local farmers to keep the hordes of starving black rats under control. The faithful *maître d'hôtel* Cipriani had no difficulty obtaining the poison from Mr Solomon's shop in Jamestown.

Napoleon was convinced that there was an 'inner force' within him—indeed within us all—which, when called upon, could prevent him from becoming ill or even poisoned. He told O'Meara that he could make himself feel better when he called upon this 'inner force'. He could make himself stay awake for many days without sleep and yet be fully clear-headed at the end of that time. If he were ill he would take to his bed for a few hours and make himself feel better. He was wrong, however, in assuming (like the Papal Borgias) that taking arsenic in minute amounts would protect him from arsenical poisoning.

It is this writer's belief that he was taking arsenic himself as a prophylactic from as early as 1805 (the earliest known sample of hair). He had a phobia about being poisoned. The amount taken varies strikingly. It is highest on his arrival at the island. The levels are lowest during 1817 and 1818. The values suddenly rise again after the forcible dismissal of Dr O'Meara from the island. We are told that Napoleon refused to take any medicine from anyone after O'Meara departed for

England. Yet in the last year of his life we now know that the Emperor had arsenic on no fewer than 21 occasions. It seems likely that in the absence of a doctor he trusted, Napoleon increased the amount he took.

This constitutes striking evidence that Napoleon liked and trusted his Irish doctor, perhaps far more than Barry O'Meara himself realised.

Sit finis libri sed non finis quaerendi.

Appendix 1: The residents at Longwood between 1815 and 1821

Antommarchi, Francesco, surgeon
Archambault, Achille, coachman
Archambault, Joseph, Achille's brother, groom

Bertrand, Arthur, son of Count and Countess Bertrand, born on St Helena
Bertrand, Count Henri, Grand Marshal
Bertrand, Henri, son of Count and Countess Bertrand
Bertrand, Countess Hortense, wife to Count Bertrand
Bertrand, Hortense, daughter of Count and Countess Bertrand
Bertrand, Napoleon, son of Count and Countess Bertrand
Bouges, Etienne, servant to the Bertrands
Broule, Josephine, maid to Madame Montholon, married to Noverraz
Buonavita, Antonio, priest

Chandelier, Jacques, cook
Cipriani, *maître d'hôtel*
Coursot, Jacques, butler

Dickson, Mrs, maternity nurse

Gentilini, Angelo, footman
Gentilini, Juliette, wife to Angelo
Goodson, Mrs, maternity nurse
Gourgaud, General Baron Gaspard de
Graafe, Adele and Guillaume, husband and wife, valet and femme de chambre to the Bertrands

Hall, Mary, governess to the Bertrand children, married to St Denis
Heyman, Bernard, servant to the Bertrands
Heyman, wife and daughter

Jeanette, cook

Kay, Mrs, maternity nurse

Laroche, cook
Las Cases, Marquis Emanuel de
Las Cases, Emanuel de, son of the Marquis
Le Page, Michel, cook
Lowden, Mrs, maternity nurse

Marchand, Louis, first valet
Montholon, Count Charles de
Montholon, Countess Albine de, wife to Count Montholon
Montholon, Napoleone, de, son of Count and Countess Montholon
Montholon, Tristan de, son of Count and Countess Montholon

NAPOLEON
Noverraz, Jean, third valet

O'Meara, Barry, surgeon

Pierron, butler
Piontkowski, Captain Charles

Quilton, Mrs, maternity nurse

Raven, Patrick, servant to the Montholons
Ridsdale, William, silver-cleaner
Rousseau, Theodore, lampiste

Santini, Jean, usher
St Denis (called Aly) Louis, second valet

Vesey, Esther, servant to the Montholons
Vignali, Ange, priest

Source: Arnold Chaplin *A St Helena's Who's Who* (London 1919)

Appendix 2: Civil and military establishment of St Helena

Military

Governor: Lieutenant-General Sir Hudson Lowe
Deputy Adjutant-General: Lieutenant-Colonel Sir Thomas Reade
Military Secretary: Lieutenant-Colonel Edward Wynyard
Aide-de-camp: Major Gideon Gorrequer
Inspector of Coasts and Volunteers: Lieutenant-Colonel Thomas Lyster
Deputy Inspector of Hospitals: Dr Alexander Baxter, succeeded in 1828 by
    Dr Thomas Shortt
General Officer Commanding the Troops: Brigadier-General Sir George
    Bingham, succeeded in 1820 by Brigadier-General John Pine-Coffin

Orderly officers at Longwood
10 December 1815 to 24 July 1817: Captain T. Poppleton
25 July 1817 to 16 July 1818: Captain Henry Blakeney
16 July 1818 to 25 July 1818: Lieutenant-Colonel Thomas Lyster
25 July 1818 to 5 September 1818: Captain Henry Blakeney
5 September 1818 to 9 February 1820: Captain George Nicholls
10 February 1820 to 26 April 1821: Captain Engelbert Lutyens
26 April 1821 to 6 May 1821: Captain William Crokat

Naval

Admirals commanding the St Helena station
15 October 1815 to 19 June 1816: Rear-Admiral Sir George Cockburn
17 June 1816 to 4 July 1817: Rear-Admiral Sir Pulteney Malcolm
20 June 1817 to 20 July 1820: Rear-Admiral Robert Plampin
14 July 1920 to 11 September 1821: Rear-Admiral Robert Lambert

Civil

Governor: Sir Hudson Lowe
Members of Council
Sir William Doveton
Robert Leech

Thomas Brooke
Thomas Greentree
Sir George Bingham

Commissioners

Arrived June 1816
Austrian: Barthelémy Baron de Sturmer (left 11 July 1818)
French: Claude Marquis de Montchenu (left 29 July 1821)
Russian: Alexandre Comte de Balmain (left 3 May 1820)

Source: Arnold Chaplin *A St Helena's Who's Who* (London 1919)

Appendix 3: Post-mortem and exhumation

Napoleon's post-mortem

Present at the examination were Dr Antommarchi (who carried out the post-mortem), and Drs Arnott, Shortt, Mitchell, Burton, Livingstone (for part only), Rutledge and Henry. There were also some non-medical people present such as Count Bertrand, Count Montholon, Marchand, St Denis and some British officers.

There were three post-mortem reports. The first one—signed by Dr Shortt with Drs Arnott, Burton, and Mitchell, was completely unacceptable to Hudson Lowe. It stipulated that the liver was enlarged and swollen. A second report omitted the remarks concerning the liver. This was accepted by Lowe, signed and despatched to London.

Dr Henry's report was written in Ireland some two years after the examination; it is not very accurate and a little too imaginative.

Dr Antommarchi's post-mortem report

Dr Antommarchi was a pathologist and an anatomist. He refused to sign the official report because it was inaccurate. He also refused to be influenced by Sir Hudson Lowe. The positive findings of his report were:

Left lung: the superior lobe contains some small tubercular cavities.

Mediastinal glands: enlarged and in a state of suppuration.

Heart: a little larger than his fist and containing more than the usual amount of fat.

Peritoneum: there was some clear peritoneal fluid present.

Spleen and liver: both had been enlarged and distended with blood. The liver affected by chronic hepatitis was clearly adherent to the diaphragm (adhesions of long-standing duration). The left lobe of the liver was firmly adherent tot the stomach. This lobe was thickened and swollen.

Stomach: appeared at first to be healthy, but on opening an ulcer was found approximately one inch from the pyloris. This ulcer was cancerous and had invaded the whole stomach. One finger could be put through this ulcer cancer. The glands on both the greater and lesser curvature of the stomach were enlarged.

Bladder: this contained some 'gravel'. There were also a few bladder calculae.

There were also numerous red patches on the bladder mucosae. *Kidneys:* there was a small deformity of the left kidney.

Dr Antommarchi wanted to open the skull and examine the brain, but Count Montholon felt that his great friend the Emperor had been mutilated enough, and insisted that the post-mortem end. The heart was therefore excised and put in a silver chalice containing alcohol. Next, the entire large and small bowel was excised and placed in another vessel. In order to make the billiard room a little more agreeable eau de cologne was now poured freely into the abdominal cavity. The body was then closed.

Exhumation

Almost twenty years after his burial the British government agreed to allow the return of the Emperor's body to France. Accordingly, on the morning of 6 October 1840 the body was exhumed.

Dr Gilliard was appointed to inspect the corpse. On opening the coffin, he said, 'we were absolutely startled, for Napoleon was perfectly preserved—he looked like a man aged 30. The face and figurer were instantly recognisable. In fact the body appeared as that of one that had only recently been interred.'

He went on to report:
1. The skull of ample volume.
2. The skin mummified hard and adherent in its upper part. Part of the eye-brows were retained.
3. Balls of the eyes entire but had lost some of their volume.
4. Nose was well preserved.
5. Face—soft well-preserved cheeks, full white in colour.
6. Lips thin and open, teeth were visible which were very white.
7. Chin was well preserved with a bluish appearance.
8. Hair—the hair had grown considerably after death.
9. Hands were perfect—pale long white fingers, the nails had grown approximately 1mm after death.
10. Legs—his leather boots had decomposed after 20 years, but his toes, easily visible on either side, were perfectly preserved.
11. The thorax was depressed—the coat had fallen in.
12. Genitalia –well preserved, visible underneath the cloth and of normal size.

Even during the time of two minutes allowed for the examination, Dr Gilliard noticed that the skin of the face had started to decompose, so the coffin was immediately closed and sealed.

Index of names

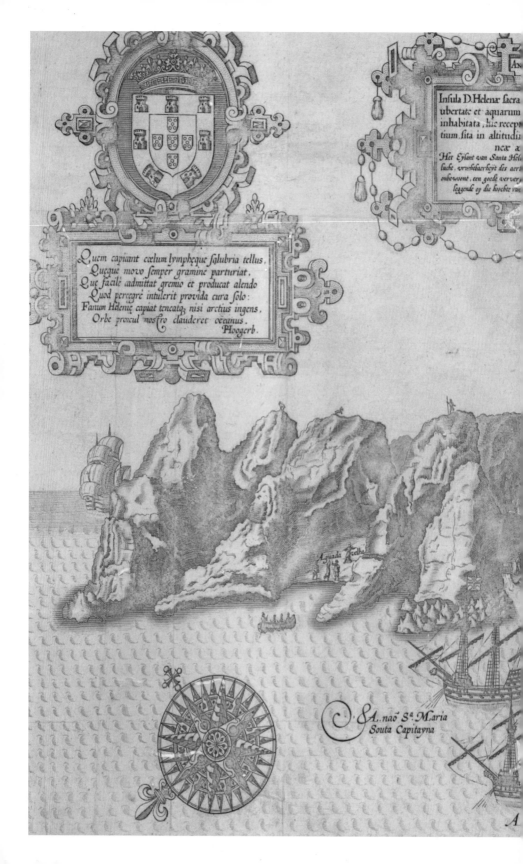

Insula D. Helenæ facra
ubertate et aquarum
inhabitata, hic recep...
tium, fita in altitudi...
neæ æ
Het Eylant van Santa Hele...
luche, vruchbaerheyt des aer...
onbewoont, een goede verver...
leggende of die hoechte van...

Quem capiant cœlum lympheque falubria tellus,
Queque novo femper gramine parturiat,
Que facile admittat gremio et producat alendo
Quod peregre intulerit provida cura folo:
Fanum Helenœ capiat teneatꝗ nisi arctius ingens,
Orbe procul noftro clauderet oceanus.
          Hoogerb.

Aguada Celha

A. naõ Sᵃ Maria
Souta Capitayna

A